London Topographical Record

London
Topographical
Record

VOL. XXXI

EDITED BY
ANN LOREILLE SAUNDERS, M.B.E., Ph.D., F.S.A.

Publication No. 176
London Topographical Society
2015

©

LONDON TOPOGRAPHICAL SOCIETY
3 Meadway Gate
London NW11 7LA
2015

ISBN
978-0-902087-63-7

PRODUCED IN GREAT BRITAIN BY
OUTSET SERVICES LIMITED

CONTENTS

EDITOR'S MESSAGE

The London Topographical Record which appears at five-yearly intervals is a collection of essays and illustrations which the authors and your Editor feel contribute something to our knowledge of London's past. You do not need to be a member to offer something though several highly successful careers have been built on a first essay in *The Record*. Each volume is individual; I hope that you will read and savour the essays in this one for 2015.

Having served as Honorary Editor for forty-one years, I am standing down from the task and handing over to Sheila O'Connell of the British Museum. She is the Curator of English water-colours, drawings and engravings in the Department of Prints and Drawings, and will be an inspiring Editor in the future.

I have enjoyed my years as Editor but feel that it is now the right time to stand down. I thank the membership for its support and our printer Graham Maney for all his hard work and imagination.

ANN SAUNDERS

NOTES ON CONTRIBUTORS

HENRY SUMMERSON completed a doctoral thesis on mid-thirteenth-century crime and law enforcement and began his career as the historian to the Carlisle Archaeological Unit. His two-volume history of the medieval city appeared in 1993. From that year until 2006 he worked for the *Oxford Dictionary of National Biography*. He is now research assistant to the Magna Carta AHRC project.

KERRY DOWNES studied at the Courtauld Institute. He is Emeritus Professor of History of Art in the University of Reading and an authority on Wren, Hawksmoor and Vanbrugh. He has also written books and papers on Rubens and Borromini.

CHRISTINE MERIE FOX received her BA in Humanities at Seattle University, and her MA and PhD at Royal Holloway, University of London, under the supervision of Professor Caroline M. Barron on 'The Royal Almshouse at Westminster c. 1500– c. 1600'.

DORIAN GERHOLD is a former House of Commons Clerk. He has written about road transport before the railways, Putney, Wandsworth, Westminster Hall, Chancery records, and other subjects. He is on the editorial boards of the *Journal of Transport History* and *Southern History*.

CLAIRE GAPPER is an architectural historian specializing in the decorative plasterwork of the sixteenth and seventeenth centuries. After completing her PhD thesis at the Courtauld Institute she has continued researching and publishing on the topic, lecturing and reporting to heritage and conservation bodies.

CLYVE JONES is an Honorary Fellow of the Institute of Historical Research in the University of London where he was until his retirement Reader in Modern History and Collection Development Librarian. He edited the journal *Parliamentary History* from 1986 to 2014, and has published extensively on the eighteenth-century House of Lords and the peerage.

ANN SAUNDERS read History at UCL, Gower Street; 2002 elected an Honorary Fellow thereof. 1951–55 cleaned and reorganized Lambeth Palace Library after wartime bombing, Deputy Librarian to Dr C. R. Dodwell. 1955–57 temporary assistant in British Library. 1955–63 Archivist at St Marylebone Public Library. Had children. 1967–2008 Editor to Costume Society. 1974–2015 Hon. Editor of London Topographical Society. She has written more than a dozen books on London.

DEREK KEENE is Professor and Honorary Fellow at the Institute of Historical Research, where he was the founding director of the Centre for Metropolitan History. He has published on the history of London and other towns and other parts of the world between the early Middle Ages and the nineteenth century. He advises a number of academic and other bodies in Britain and elsewhere on urban history and the historic environment.

TRACEY LOGAN is BBC Science reporter, several of whose documentaries have won prizes. She is currently studying for a Masters at the Institute for Historical Research.

SHEILA O'CONNELL is curator of British prints before 1900 at the British Museum. In 2015 the exhibition *Bonaparte and the British: Prints and Propaganda in the Age of Napoleon* that she organized with Tim Clayton will be on show at the British Museum from 5 February to 16 August. Previous exhibitions include: *Britain Meets the World 1714–1830* (Forbidden City, Beijing, 2007), *London 1753* (BM, 2003), *The Popular Print in England* (BM, 1999).

ROGER BOWDLER is the Director for Designation at Historic England (formerly English Heritage), where he has worked since 1989. He is a trustee of the Mausolea and Monuments Trust, and has lectured extensively on churchyards and cemeteries.

I.   SEEN THROUGH THE EYES OF THE LAW:
JUDICIAL RECORDS AS EVIDENCE FOR LONDON'S
PHYSICAL ENVIRONMENT, 1272–1327[1]

By HENRY SUMMERSON

THE purpose of this article is to draw attention to the value of records of litigation, disorder and crime as evidence for the physical environment of London, its buildings, streets and waterways, and for the ways in which they were used, during the reigns of Edward I and Edward II. Such records of this kind as are readily available — the 1244 and 1276 London eyres,[2] for instance, and the thirteenth- and fourteenth-century city coroners' rolls[3] — have been exploited, but many others have been neglected or ignored. This applies particularly to the crown pleas roll of the 1321 London eyre (TNA, JUST 1/547A), which sheds invaluable light upon every sort of activity in the city in the forty-five years which preceded it, and which provides the basis for this essay. The issue of reliability is too large for a close examination here,[4] but comparisons between the eyre roll and accounts of the same events in other sources suggest that on points of detail the former is usually trustworthy, and since the presentation and analysis of detail is the essential purpose of this paper, a measure of confidence in the accuracy of its principal source seems permissible.

Legal records usually focus on the doings of individual people in particular places, but sometimes they illuminate whole neighbourhoods. An example is the proof of age of Geoffrey de Say, taken in king's bench in January 1303 and recording memories of Geoffrey's baptism at St Dunstan's in the East, Tower ward, late in August 1281.[5] The witnesses, all men of property, did not attend the ceremony, but they claimed to have been aware of it; 'informed by the word of the parish', in the words of Edmund de Cumbe, who lived in Thames Street in the house next to Geoffrey's birthplace. Geoffrey Hurel, another near neighbour, remembered the event in terms of his leasing arrangements — just before Geoffrey was born he had taken the other next-door house for a term of seven years, before moving to another nearby residence. Two other witnesses recorded that in 1282 they had just come to London and begun their apprenticeships; they had been living close to St Dunstan's then, and were still in the neighbourhood twenty-one years later. Two more neighbours lived close enough to Geoffrey's birthplace to be able to define their spatial relationship to it in numerical terms — Walter le Mouner had been living fourteen houses away, Robert le Treyere only twelve. Robert was living in the parish of St Mary at Hill, so Geoffrey's birthplace must have been close to the boundary between the two parishes. Neighbourhood transcended parish boundaries, and other witnesses lived in the nearby parishes of St Botolph, Billingsgate, All Hallows Barking and St Mary Abchurch; St Mary's was the home of Stephen le Jovene, whose wife became the wet-nurse for Geoffrey, after his mother Elizabeth had failed to command the services of the woman who was then suckling the newborn son of Robert le Treyere. William Pikeman, who lived in St Botolph's, had just built a house in Marte Lane, north-east of St Dunstan's, and was walking to it when he observed the christening party, and saw one of the godfathers giving the infant Geoffrey a silver cup full of pennies. John of Mocking, another inhabitant of St Mary at Hill, offered a more dramatic but no less localized recollection, when he dated the baptism by reference to the breaking of London Bridge, on 30 January 1282; the bridge was barely 200 yards from the church, while the parish extended to the river. Men of substance the witnesses may have been — one of them, Peter Blakeney, died in 1311 as sheriff of London[6] — but their viewpoint in these proceedings was a circumscribed one.

London has often been described as a city of villages. Presentments at the 1321 eyre were made by individual wards rather than by representatives of the whole city, as had happened in 1244 and 1276, emphasizing the localism of the capital. This can be seen very clearly in the numerous presentments of purprestures — encroachments — and nuisances, which were considerably fuller and more numerous than those made at earlier eyres. They have much to say about watercourses, for instance those at the north end of the city — Walbrook and its tributaries. Thus the bridge giving access to Moorfields over Walbrook at the west end of All Hallows in the Wall was said to have broken down around 1317. Described as made of stone and wood, it had been used by men with horses and carts, implying a structure of some size.[7] About two years earlier the abbot of Ramsey and the prior of Holy Trinity Aldgate replaced the wooden bridge at the White Cross in Cripplegate ward, where it crossed a watercourse flowing from Smithfield towards the Barbican, with a stone one, its predecessor having broken down almost every year; but they clearly miscalculated the height of the arch, since it was too narrow for the stream beneath, which as a result was flooding the neighbourhood.[8] Flooding was indeed a constant problem. When a narrow watercourse in Tower ward called 'Lurtebourne', which drew off water from Aldgate and the area of St Katherine Coleman, on Fenchurch Street, was blocked up c. 1311, the overspill was described as swamping houses, inundating the adjacent ground, and constituting a nuisance to all who wished to pass there.[9]

The encroachments of buildings, or parts of buildings, on the city streets were more numerous. Some originated in concerns over security. In 1321 the Aldgate jury presented that around 1307 a palisade one hundred feet long and twelve feet broad had been put up between the postern of the Tower and the 'Wayhous' at Aldgate itself; it transpired that Goscelin le Seriaunt, a sheriff's officer, had constructed it with the consent of the mayor and aldermen, 'because many malefactors were wont to lurk in that place at night and to do many evil deeds to many people there ...'.[10] In other cases individuals saw to their own protection, for instance Simon Parys, a former sheriff and chamberlain, who put gates at the end of Popkirtle Lane, running south off Cheapside; in 1321 the justices told him to keep it open during the day, but licensed its closure after dark 'for fear of malefactors'.[11] Palisades were a common form of obstruction, others included porches, pentices, cellar doors, and jetties, which might be accompanied by solars (upper-floor rooms). These last offended when they were built too low, hindering the free passage of horsemen and carts in the streets; since they were expected to clear the street by at least nine feet, the solar built by the prior of Newark in Farringdon ward must have been low indeed to have been four feet too near the ground.[12] On another occasion the offending feature was a walkway, which Joan Breanzon, the owner of tenements on both sides of 'Latheslane' in Queenhithe ward (unidentified, but leading down to the river), had put up to connect her properties; in 1321 its new owner obtained permission to rebuild it higher.[13]

Stalls were frequently presented as encroachments, particularly in Cripplegate and Candlewick Street wards. Commonly described as made of boards, they could differ considerably in size, with those in Cripplegate being markedly narrower than those of Candlewick Street, where the largest was reportedly nineteen feet long and ten feet wide.[14] Some may have been essentially boards on trestles, but others were substantial structures. One such was the subject of a lawsuit in May 1293, in which the mercer Richard Hauteyn alleged that on 16 February the twenty defendants had broken into the stall which he leased on Soper's Lane (a short distance west of Langbourn, linking Cordwainer Street and Cheap wards) and taken or destroyed goods worth £40. Its owner, Rose of Coventry, replied that, under the terms of his lease, Richard was permitted to have only chests and cupboards in the stall, that he had contravened his lease by constructing what she described as 'tabernacles' in it, and that she had therefore demolished them, as she was entitled to do. Two other merchants (one of them also a mercer) testified that they were present when this happened, standing in particular places (*in certis locis*) in the stall 'to show their wares and sell them', and with nothing besides chests and cupboards to keep their goods in. Richard's lease (and no doubt the leases of all the other occupants) required him to maintain the roofs and gutters, suggesting a long building with doors and windows at the front, under a watertight roof, and perhaps with only light partitions inside. The word 'tabernacle' is more often found in an ecclesiastical context, meaning a canopied niche to hold a sacred image. Here it probably meant an unusually elaborate kind of shelving, constructed by Richard to display wares which included hangings, boots, kerchiefs and muslin cloths.[15]

Richard Hauteyn's stall was apparently made of wood. Preparations for building an entire house of wood were outlined in the lawsuit which John Dymmok, an usher of the exchequer, brought against John of Horne in the exchequer of pleas in 1314. Dymmok claimed that Horne had agreed to provide him with the timber needed to construct a house 48 feet long and 34 feet wide. It was to come from the Weald in Surrey, and Dymmok alleged that he had sent carts to collect it, together with carpenters to cut it up, but that Horne had failed to supply it. It transpired that Horne had in fact delivered some of the wood, but much remained to be handed over. Details of this residue suggest that the house was to be on three floors, connected by six sets of stairs each of twelve feet, and with shutters for windows of three different lengths — seven, four and three feet, with the longest presumably at ground level. Boards for the doors were to be eight feet long. Beams, struts, joists and uprights were to provide the basic structure for the house (the spaces within the timber frame were doubtless to be filled with plaster or wattle-and-daub), while wall-plates would support the framework of a gabled roof resting upon 6,000 laths and covered by tiles — 16,000 tile-pins were required to secure these. Two planks 52 feet long were to carry external gutters. Inside, there were to be plank floors resting on cross-beams, and at least one internal partition. Dymmok won his case and was awarded £5 damages, along with five marks (£3 6s. 8d.) for the wood which Horne failed to supply.[16] Unfortunately, neither party said where this house was to be built, though it may be significant that in 1319 a Henry Dymmok and a John Horn were listed among the taxpayers of Queenhithe ward.[17]

Some houses were impressively large, for instance the house of Gilbert Seagrave in the close of St Paul's, as described in the inquest held in 1306 into the death of John Reymund, killed there by John Belgrave. Reymund as household steward had refused to provide provender for the horse of Belgrave, who therefore went to complain to Seagrave, who had gone to bed. Seagrave sent for his chamberlain, and through him ordered that the provender be made available. Reymund went sulking downstairs and sat on a bench in the hall, where he met Belgrave again, ordered him out of the house, and finally attacked him with a knife. Belgrave fled for the gate, but when he reached it found it locked, and a furious brawl followed, ending when Belgrave struck Reymund a fatal blow.[18] Clearly, this was a courtyard house of the kind described by John Schofield, where a streetside gateway gave access to a courtyard with a hall on its other side.[19] It would have been an appropriate residence for a man like Seagrave, who became precentor of St Paul's around this time and bishop of London in 1313.[20]

A number of cases shed light on the premises inhabited by people of 'the middling sort' — shopkeepers, minor officials and the like, who usually owned the houses they lived in. Their layout, on two or three levels, with a shop at ground level, perhaps with a stall in front,[21] and with a solar above and a cellar below, is basically familiar. In 1279 Giles of Stansted, an inhabitant of Billingsgate ward, was asleep in bed when awoken by the sound of his household brawling in the cellar; going down to administer discipline, he was struck dead by one of his servants.[22] Going the other way, when Clemencia Pencyn quarrelled with her husband John in their house in St Mary Staining Lane, Aldersgate ward, in 1322, and left the house in a rage, John was said to have locked the front door and then gone up to his solar, where he shut the door and went to sleep in the bed. When Clemencia returned and found herself locked out of the house, she made an uproar to which one of the neighbours responded by hacking down the door with an axe and rushing upstairs, where John slew him in self-defence.[23]

*   *   *

Some more precise descriptions of London interiors are provided by appeals of felony, where the formalities required considerable, and exact, detail. Late in 1297, Alice, the widow of Hugh le Taillur, accused three men of robbing her late husband's house in the suburban parish of St Botolph Without Billingsgate, and described how around sunset on 20 August they had used axes to break down its entrance, a gate made of oak boards 12 feet high and 10 feet broad, on the north side of the street. This gave them access to a large open space, perhaps with buildings on three sides, for a 22-yard walk brought them to an west-facing door, also made of oak, and also 10 feet high, though only 5 feet wide. This too, they broke down, to enter a room which appears to have doubled as a bedchamber and a store-room (it was referred to as Alice's *chef chambre*), since along with a bed it contained a large oak chest, the target for their raid, which contained Alice's valuables — £20 in cash, silver plate and spoons, armour, lengths of cloth, including some cloth of gold, a mazer bowl, two silver seals, a gold and silver cross, and a charter for a Wiltshire manor. The cross was said to be for the chapel which presumably formed another part of the complex.[24]

Appeals of rape can also contain valuable information, though usually about less elaborate dwellings. Master John of Windsor, convicted of raping Ydonea, the daughter of Geoffrey le Chesemonger, in May 1286, was said by her to have dragged her off Old Fish Street into a house opposite St Mary Magdalen, up a wooden stair on its south side and into a stone solar roofed with tiles.[25] Matilda, daughter of Michael of Chiswick, in 1295 accused John de Vilers, a Frenchman whose sick son she was babysitting, of dragging her into a deep cellar in the house he was renting, also in Old Fish Street, described as made of stone and lime and with an adjoining hall to the south, and assaulting her on a bed made of wheat straw.[26] She did not say if the floor was tiled or made of stone. In at least one case, this time of murder, an earthen floor may be assumed. In 1314, William Salisbury, a cobbler, his wife and son killed William le Messager in his bed in a house in Billingsgate, and buried his body in a hole in the floor, where it was subsequently discovered in a state of advanced decay (*semiputridum*) by a workman digging in the house, presumably preparing it for a new occupant.[27]

In each of these cases the house in question seems to have been occupied by a single household — William le Messager was probably a lodger with the Salisburys. But court records also shed light on another sort of domestic organization, namely the tenement block, the house with a single street entrance subdivided within into lodgings, each with its own internal door. Inevitably, these varied in quality and size. The infamous Malcolm Musard was said to have pursued two of his many enemies to London's Farringdon ward in 1310 or 1311. Obtaining access to the house in which they were staying, he was alleged to have hidden himself in a suite (*camera*) and then when night fell he went upstairs to kill one man, came down again to kill the other, both in different suites, slew his second victim's servant in the hall, and fled with a large sum of money.[28] The house in Bassishaw which John Bacwell broke into some five years later seems to have been similarly organized, since it had a keeper whom John stabbed to death when he refused to hand over the keys to the rooms.[29]

There were other forms of shared accommodation, for instance the places where a master and his employee slept in the same room. It was in such surroundings that the taverner Simon of Winchester came to a gruesome end — his servant Roger, with whom he shared a room in Cheap ward, beheaded Simon with a knife as he slept, afterwards hiding head and body in separate places around the house.[30] At least they did not have to share a bed, something probably common among the very poor. Nicholas Uweyn of Northampton and Geoffrey of Oxford, both skinners, and on the evidence of their toponyms both strangers to London, were doing so in Dowgate ward in 1309/10 when they quarrelled, whereupon Nicholas got out of bed, reached for his sword, and ran Geoffrey through with it.[31] Described as having no chattels, he probably owned nothing but the clothes he wore and anything — like his sword — which he could carry with him. The houses such people occupied, whatever their layout, must often have been very rickety. Felicia de Creye, who was hanged with her daughter in 1306 for harbouring thieves, had two houses in Cripplegate ward, perhaps just outside the city walls since she owed rent to the vicar of St Giles. After her execution one of these was removed bodily by the sheriff's clerk, who left the other in a state described as 'decrepit and empty', so decrepit that it fell down, whereupon poor people carried off the timber.[32]

Poor people may sometimes have been glad to get out of their homes. The record of John of Nedging's suicide in Castle Baynard ward is made even more depressing by the information that John was alone in a dark room when he hanged himself.[33] Perhaps he had the shutters closed at the time.

In daylight hours they would usually be open, thereby presenting quite literally windows of opportunity to enterprising criminals who used hooks to fish out whatever they could latch onto inside. One such was William Hardyng of Southwick, hanged in 1319 after being arrested with 'an iron hook for extracting clothes and other things through windows and openings in Billingsgate and elsewhere in London'.[34] People did not necessarily go out into the streets, however, there might be gardens behind, large ones in the case of wealthy citizens. That of Simon Corp, probably outside the walls in Cripplegate ward, contained a fishpond (a servant of one of his neighbours drowned herself in it),[35] and he also grew fruit, employing a gardener who was killed in 1316 by a man who broke in to steal apples.[36] Some gardens contained wells, into which people might fall,[37] providing an inducement to those within range of it to obtain water from the Great Conduit in Cheap. A case from 1289 describes two men arriving there together, each with a little bucket (*tinellum*), and then quarrelling as to who should fill his vessel first — the issue was settled when one used his crock to strike the other dead.[38] An alternative source of water was the River Thames. In the mid-1270s the alderman of Castle Baynard ward was said to have obstructed a lane down to the river 'by which people used to go to draw water with buckets'.[39]

People might work in their houses, or in buildings attached to them. In 1312/13, Agnes, daughter of John Knight, was drowned when she fell into a vat of black dye in Castle Baynard ward,[40] while in 1306 one John Muf came to a violent end in Tower ward when he quarrelled fatally with three men whom he found packing wool in an upper-floor room.[41] In 1318 Thomas Prentyz was found to have killed William Scot in a brawl that began when William took Thomas at a disadvantage, first insulting and then attacking him as he stood in a barrel 5½ feet deep preparing hides for currying.[42] The record describes Thomas as a tawyer, but here he was clearly acting as a tanner, in breach of the regulations.

A different sort of occupation, not least in its being restricted in terms of gender, was prostitution, whose working environment features in a number of cases of violence and disorder. Its being subject to control by the city authorities explains the information supplied by the mayor's court rolls about prostitutes occupying a house right outside Holy Trinity, Aldgate, in 1305, and the attack on houses in Cok Lane, likewise inhabited by prostitutes, which the beadle of Farringdon Extra ward mounted in 1300; on the latter occasion eleven doors and five windows were removed, implying a substantial establishment.[43] Some prostitutes lived by themselves, however, and maintained their own establishments. One such, unfortunately unnamed, was recorded in a lawsuit from 1314, when two men from the ship *La Valaunce*, recently arrived in port, were said to have visited her in a solar in the cemetery of St Lawrence Jewry, just south of the Guildhall, and to have amused themselves by taking her cat and throwing it up to the beams of the house. The woman, furious at seeing her pet thus airborne, raised the hue and cry and the usual free-for-all ensued, ended only by the arrival of the mayor's officer.[44] But overall it seems to have been far more common for men to take the women they picked up to places of their choosing, like the tenement lodging in Broad Street ward occupied by John of Nottingham, an exchequer employee, where in November 1323 he was seized by the watch as he lay naked in bed with an unidentified woman. John claimed that the men arresting him had smashed their way into the house, but the jurors described how the watch had found the main door open, and a maid with the keys who admitted them to John's suite.[45]

Those less well accommodated might resort to public conveniences, like the one in London wall in Cripplegate ward to which Stephen le Spicer and William Ballard led a common woman in 1284, and in which Stephen killed William after a quarrel as to which 'should know her first in sin', in the modest words of the eyre roll.[46] It may have been the one in Cripplegate in which Walter Moryz was accused of killing a man and a woman in 1286 (no verdict was given); it was described as having been provided by Henry le Waleys, no doubt as part of his great campaign of civic improvement between 1281 and 1284.[47] If it was also identical with one referred to in a case from 1291, in which the Cripplegate jurors described John of Abingdon becoming involved in a fatal quarrel as he came from a latrine down Philips Lane, then it was probably somewhere near St Alphege's church.[48] It seems likely that there was another one in the wall further east, in Bassishaw ward,[49] and one near the Tower, next to one of the mills built at the entrance to the new moat which Edward I had had dug there — the heads of two thieves who had escaped from the Tower in 1282, only to be caught and killed by the garrison, were flung into it.[50]

Inevitably, people eased themselves in other places as well. In the case of Robert Barndon this was outside his own shop in Aldgate ward — he was urinating there when in 1313/14 he was taken by surprise by an old enemy, who stabbed him while his mind was on other things.[51] But William Brewere, making his way through Bassishaw ward in 1303, obviously could not wait till he got home, for he spotted a hole in the door of Robert le Brewer and proceeded to relieve himself through it; one Ralph Wyger, who was presumably on the receiving end of the unexpected flow, promptly came out and struck William dead.[52] Unsurprisingly, the London streets were commonly in a revolting state. In 1321, the Billingsgate jurors underlined the point when they described how fetid water and blood from the Scalding House, where pigs and geese were butchered, were being poured into Rother Lane (later Pudding Lane), while four women of East Cheap selling tripe were said to be throwing 'putrid blood and the vilest filth' into the street — they were told that in future they should throw it into the Thames at low tide.[53]

Court records contain frequent references to the Thames, and also to the ditches round the outer walls of the city. Houndsditch — a sizeable watercourse, where a groom drowned *per profunditatem aque* in 1309/10 while watering his master's horse[54] — could be put to semi-industrial uses; in 1313, Richard Soudour was described as using it to soak hides in, that is, washing them before they could be tanned or tawed.[55] And both Houndsditch and the ditches on the east of the city were also used for sadder purposes, as places where women could dispose of unwanted babies. A beggar named Nicola of Cardiff was said to have gone privily to the ditch outside Aldgate on 18 October 1315 with a three-month-old child named Alice, and there to have drowned her while pretending to wash her.[56]

The Thames, which was inevitably exploited to the same bleak end,[57] is a recurrent presence in the court rolls, also appearing as the scene of suicides and accidental deaths, and of the movement of people and goods. The story of the death of John of Kingston shows a river boatman at work. By his name a Surrey man, but obviously plying on both side of the river, on 20 July 1291 John agreed to take Richard le Mazun from Billingsgate to Gravesend (a long way to row). But the tide was running against them, and John refused to set out until he had the current behind him. Exasperated at the delay, Richard struck John, and made to hit him again, causing John, in his efforts to avoid the blow, to fall overboard and drown.[58] In another case it was the wind that obstructed movement. In 1314/15 a Flemish ship laden with tiles — presumably floor tiles — had docked by the watergate of the Tower, where its crew expected to sell their cargo. But a quarrel broke out among them in which a man was killed and his body thrown overboard. The survivors could not escape by water because the wind was against them, so they fled by land, through St Katherine's hospital, while the ship and its contents were commandeered by the constable of the Tower.[59]

The church was as pervasive a presence in London as the river, with numerous buildings needing to be maintained. At Michaelmas 1310 the treasurer of the realm, responding to an order from Edward II, instructed the mayor to send twenty-four masons to Scotland. The mayor ordered the sheriff Simon Corp to take appropriate action, whereupon Simon press-ganged ten masons from the Greyfriars and fourteen from St Paul's, only to be thwarted by forcible resistance from the household of the precentor, Gilbert Seagrave[60] — the building of the cathedral's 'new work' was still two years from completion, while the construction of the great Minorite church on Newgate Street was probably not finished until the 1350s. Before 1321 building work had also been in progress at the Austin friary on Broad Street, just inside Bishopsgate, where walls 150 feet long at the friary's north end, and 200 feet long on Broad Street itself, were built, in around 1306 and 1315 respectively, obviously enclosing the house. The latter wall was allowed to stand, but the former, which had blocked a ditch carrying water into Walbrook and caused flooding in the street, was to be demolished.[61]

Something about the internal layout of a major ecclesiastical complex can be learnt from the records of a sensational crime committed in 1305, one also briefly recorded in two chronicles. In around that year Sir Eustace de Hacche, a west country landowner of some consequence in Edward I's government, deposited £300 in the Carmelite friary, in Castle Baynard ward, south of Fleet Street. The temptation was too much for William Portehors, one of the friars, for in order to rob his own house he reportedly concealed no fewer than eleven men in his chamber, clearly a spacious one — again, suite would probably be a better word. He was then said to have gone round the chambers of the other friars, summoning each in turn to come to speak with the prior. As they did so, they were seized, bound and put in William's chamber. One, named Geoffrey of Stratton, cried out and was immediately killed, all the others were secured, after which the conspirators broke into the treasury and robbed it. The friary was rebuilt in the mid-fourteenth century, but this brief account shows that it was a large establishment fifty years earlier, with separate accommodation for its inmates.[62]

Church precincts were often the scene of brawls, like the one in which Thomas Maye was said to have killed James le Kyng in 1301, at the end of a free-for-all during which James was said to have chased Thomas three times round St Mary's, Fenchurch Street.[63] Their quarrel had erupted when Thomas tried to prevent James from taking apples from a poor man selling them outside his house — one of the many aperçus of the London streets which the legal records provide. Narrowed by stalls and every other sort of construction, they were also crowded with people, and liable to be further congested by animals, as shown by a case from 1309/10, telling how one Richard Prat was riding through Farringdon ward towards Newgate, leading two other horses with him, when he encountered two other men bringing a flock of sheep in the opposite direction. The sheep were scattered, and the usual deadly fracas resulted.[64] Cheapside was doubtless thronged all the time. So was the equally central but much less fashionable area of Cornhill, where in breach of the regulations the sale of 'old clothes, shoes and other wares' was continuing after nightfall, among what the 1321 roll describes as the 'great multitudes of people' who had gathered to buy what often turned out to be stolen goods. The justices ordered that all trading must stop when the hour of vespers struck in the church of St Thomas of Acon.[65]

Judicial records afford glimpses of a wide variety of other occupations and activities, lawful and unlawful, in the streets and houses of medieval London. For instance, they attest the danger of being caught up in archery practice. Cecilia de Burne was killed in 1281 when she walked into an arrow which Walter of Malling had fired at a target he had set up in Broad Street,[66] though Walter's recklessness pales next to that of John le Fourbour of Cornhill, described in the mayor's court in 1305 as practising with his stone-bow by shooting at churches and houses (the authorities made him promise to desist).[67] They offer vignettes of life in the city's hostelries, of three men eating and drinking in an alehouse in East Cheap, where one of them paid his share of the bill by pawning his purse for 3d.,[68] or of two Italians sitting long over their wine in a tavern in Coleman Street ward, until they quarrelled with the landlord.[69] They show Londoners falling out over their sports, like that of 'penystone', seemingly a throwing game, in which William Bat killed his fellow dyer James of Newport in Queenhithe ward in 1314/15,[70] over board games (on one occasion specifically chess),[71] and even after singing.[72] They even record how on 25 August 1305 Roger of Southcote, a maker of paternosters, sued two men for trespass in the mayor's court, complaining that they had wrongfully arrested him when he was in the road north of St Michael le Querne, looking at William Wallace's head.[73] The Scottish leader had been executed at Tyburn just two days previously, and his head was doubtless being taken through the city to London Bridge. The incident says something about how and where a fourteenth-century Londoner might choose to spend his time. It also furnishes a reminder that the city where Wallace's head was put on show was not just an agglomeration of villages, but was chosen for this particular display because it was also the capital of the realm.

1. This article originated in a paper read to the Medieval and Early Modern London seminar at the Institute of Historical Research on 27 May 2010, and benefited from comments and suggestions made on that occasion. I am also grateful to Dr Anne Bowtell, Professor Paul Brand and Dr Clive Burgess for advice and information on individual points. For a map of London showing its wards, see A. R. Myers, *London in the Age of Chaucer* (Norman, Okla., 1972), pp. 6–7. Unless otherwise stated, all unpublished documents cited are in The National Archives, Kew, while all printed books were published in London.

2. H. M. Chew and M. Weinbaum (eds.), *The London Eyre of 1244*, London Record Society, 6 (1970); M. Weinbaum (ed.), *The London Eyre of 1276*, London Record Society, 12 (1976).

3. R. R. Sharpe (ed.), *Calendar of Coroners' Rolls of the City of London, A.D. 1300–1378*, (London, 1913).

4. I hope to discuss this issue, with specific reference to the 1321 London crown pleas, in a future publication.

5. KB 27/171, mm. 35, 35d.

6. C. M. Barron, *London in the Later Middle Ages: Government and People, 1200–1500* (Oxford, 2004), p. 325.

7. JUST 1/547A, m. 29d.

8. JUST 1/547A, m. 4d.

9. JUST 1/547A, m. 51d.

10. JUST 1/547A, m. 56d.

11. JUST 1/547A, m. 41d.

12. JUST 1/547A, m. 18.

13. JUST 1/547A, m. 21d.

14. JUST 1/547A, mm. 32 (Cripplegate), 45 (Candlewick Street).
15. JUST 1/1292, mm. 16, 16d. I am grateful to Dr Clive Burgess for advice concerning the tabernacles.
16. E 13/36, m. 43.
17. E. Ekwall, *Two Early London Subsidy Rolls* (Lund, 1951), pp. 332–8.
18. C 260/17, no. 13.
19. J. Schofield, *Medieval London Houses* (Yale, 2003), pp. 35–51.
20. Philippa Hoskin, 'Seagrave , Gilbert (*b*. before 1258, *d*. 1316)', *Oxford Dictionary of National Biography* (Oxford University Press, 2004), http://www.oxforddnb.com/view/article/25036 (accessed 26 June 2014).
21. JUST 1/547A, m. 8d offers an example.
22. JUST 1/547A, m. 18d.
23. JUST 3/42/1, m. 9.
24. CP 40/121, mm. 131, 131d; British Library, London, MS Stowe 386, fos. 153ᵛ–155ʳ. I owe my knowledge, and transcripts, of these documents to the kindness of Professor Paul Brand.
25. JUST 1/1256, m. 64.
26. KB 27/146, m. 19.
27. JUST 2/94A, m. 1. This record can be more easily read in a nineteenth-century transcript made by R. R. Sharpe, which forms part of London Metropolitan Archives, CLC/511/MS00126, pp. 47–8. See also JUST 1/547A, m. 18d.
28. JUST 1/547A, m. 11. For Musard's career of crime, see R. H. Hilton, *A Medieval Society: The West Midlands at the End of the Thirteenth Century* (1966), pp. 255–8.
29. JUST 1/547A, m. 28.
30. JUST 1/547A, m. 41d.
31. JUST 1/547A, m. 25; similar killings are recorded at mm. 21, 38 and 44d.
32. JUST 1/547A, m. 33.
33. JUST 1/547A, m. 18.
34. JUST 3/41/1, m. 24.
35. JUST 1/547A, m. 30d.
36. JUST 2/94A m. 9; London Metropolitan Archives, CLC/511/MS00126, pp. 102–3; JUST 1/547A m. 31.
37. E.g. JUST 1/547A mm. 7, 8d, 9, 42, 57; Sharpe, *Calendar of Coroners Rolls*, pp. 94, 100–1.
38. JUST 1/547A, m. 40.
39. SC 5/LONDON/TOWER, m. 19. I am grateful to Dr Anne Bowtell for drawing my attention to this document.
40. JUST 1/547A, m. 17d.
41. JUST 1/547A, m. 50.
42. JUST 3/41/1, m. 16d; JUST 1/547A, m. 27d.
43. A. H. Thomas (ed.), *Calendar of Early Mayor's Court Rolls, 1298–1307* (Cambridge, 1924), pp. 211, 218–19.
44. E 13/37, m. 7d.
45. E 13/46, m. 9d.
46. JUST 1/547A, m. 29d.
47. JUST 1/1267, m. 20. For Waleys, see G. A. William, *Medieval London: from commune to capital*, University of London historical studies 11 (1963), pp. 85, 252–3.
48. JUST 1/547A, m. 29d.
49. JUST 1/547A, m. 28.
50. JUST 1/547A, m. 14.
51. JUST 1/547A, m. 56.
52. JUST 1/547A, m. 28.
53. JUST 1/547A, m. 20.

54. JUST 1/547A, m. 3d.
55. JUST 1/547A, m. 66.
56. JUST 2/94A, m. 1; London Metropolitan Archives, CLC/511/MS00126, pp. 50–1; JUST 1/547A, m. 51. Other examples are JUST 1/547A, mm. 3, 57.
57. JUST 1/547A, m. 49.
58. JUST 1/547A, m. 19; JUST 3/87, m. 14d.
59. JUST 1/547A, mm. 50d, 63.
60. E 13/34, m. 1.
61. JUST 1/547A, m. 34.
62. JUST 1/547A, m. 9d; R. B. Pugh (ed.), *Calendar of London Trailbaston Trials under Commissions of 1305 and 1306* (1975), nos. 279, 285, 341; W. Stubbs (ed.), *Chronicles of the Reigns of Edward I and Edward II*, 2 vols. (Rolls Series, 1882–3), I, p. 144; H. R. Luard (ed.), *Flores historiarum*, 3 vols. (Rolls Series, 1890), III, p. 128.
63. JUST 1/547A, m. 25; Sharpe, *Calendar of Coroners Rolls*, pp. 14–15; KB 27/168, m. 26d.
64. JUST 1/547A, m. 10d.
65. JUST 1/547A, m. 35d.
66. JUST 1/547A, m. 33d.
67. Thomas, *Calendar of Early Mayor's Court Rolls*, p. 205.
68. JUST 2/94A, m. 1d; London Metropolitan Archives, CLC/511/MS00126, pp. 116–17.
69. JUST 1/ 547A, m. 29.
70. JUST 1/547A, m. 21.
71. JUST 1/547A, mm. 18, 20d, 26d.
72. JUST 1/547A, m. 12.
73. Thomas, *Calendar of Early Mayor's Court Rolls*, p. 220.

Fig. 1.   St Vedast, steeple (1709–12).

II. WREN, HAWKSMOOR AND THE ROMAN BAROQUE IN LONDON

By KERRY DOWNES

[Wren's] own works, ranging from the simple Renaissance classicism of Pembroke College Chapel to the Borrominesque spire of St Vedast's church, epitomize the whole history of English architecture during the fifty years after the Restoration.[1]

COLVIN's arresting one-sentence epitomization of Sir Christopher Wren's architecture adopts, consciously or not, a time-frame conceived by Geoffrey Webb 'as if English architecture had passed through all the stages from Brunelleschi to Cortona in a single generation'.[2] In the same edition Colvin wrote of 'the complex forms of the [Queen Anne] churches, whether in internal planning or in external embellishment ... as eloquent as anything by Borromini, the Italian architect with whom Nicholas Hawksmoor most obviously invites comparison'.[3] This paper will examine the comparison, first in respect of specific motifs used by either Hawksmoor or Wren, and secondly in respect of character. The first point to be made is that Wren's first-hand experience of Roman Baroque was limited to a few minutes' view of Gianlorenzo Bernini's design for the Louvre in 1665; Hawksmoor's knowledge was solely through prints, which before 1700 were rather few in number and relevance.

St Vedast's Steeple

In the light of Colvin's sentence, the obvious place to begin is St Vedast, which is certainly unique among Wren's big steeples (Fig. 1) and whose play in successive storeys of convex and concave walls indeed reminds anyone who has seen both buildings to compare it with the belfry of San Carlino alle Quattro Fontane in Rome (Fig. 2). In 1957, Nikolaus Pevsner called St Vedast 'the most Baroque of all Wren's steeples — in the sense of the Italian Baroque of Borromini'.[4] In the same year Margaret Whinney saw 'a Baroque pattern' in St Vedast.[5] Ten years later, in an Italian congress paper, Pevsner did not mention St Vedast at all.[6] Sir John Summerson, at least as early as the fourth edition of his monumental *Architecture in Britain 1530–1830* (1963),[7] described St Vedast as 'one of those Wren designs which owes its inspiration to Borromini'. Which others, one may ask. He compared it with 'the concave façade and convex balustrade' of Borromini's clock tower at the north end of the Roman Oratory House (Fig. 3), but went on to find in

Fig. 2.   Rome, S. Carlino alle Quattro   Fig. 3.   Rome, Oratory House,
   Fontane. Etching by Falda, detail.   clock tower by Borromini.

Wren's steeple 'a sobriety and elegance remote from Borromini'. The
summary of his Roman example is neither accurate nor clear, and there is
still a hint, in the tail, of the traditional view of Borromini as a crazy
maverick. Summerson's last editions (1983/93) convey a more careful
impression, with the addition of a suggestion of Hawksmoor's involvement,
for which there is no evidence. It became generally known in the late 1970s
that the late accounts for the post-Fire City churches survived in the
Guildhall Library, forcing the redating of the steeples in particular after 1700;
thus the traditional date of 1694–7 applied only to St Vedast's tower, the
steeple being added in 1709–12.[8] Hawksmoor's association with the City
Churches office ended in 1699, and other hands, in particular those of
William Dickinson, took over his work while he continued to help Wren at
St Paul's and elsewhere. In 1969, the present writer tentatively suggested
Hawksmoor's hand in the three-dimensional strapwork and other
geometrical features of the steeple of St James Garlickhythe (Fig. 4), but in

reality they are more foreign to him than to Wren — or, for that matter, to Borromini.[9]

Although it is illustrated in Pevsner's *Outline*, none of these writers made the perhaps obvious comparison with San Carlino's little street-corner belfry, which in plan is a square with concave sides. Giovanni Battista Falda's urban prospect of the church (Fig. 2) is undated, but the volume containing it is presumed to have been published in 1665, so it is possible that some returning traveller brought a copy which Wren saw. However, the connection is not very helpful, first because all that Falda manages to convey is that in this case there is no convex form to contrast with the concavities. And, secondly, as a matter of historical accuracy, Borromini's original belfry of 1658–9 was on a triangular plan and was replaced in 1670, after his death, by the present one, designed by his nephew and successor Bernardo Borromini Castelli, who also designed and built the upper half of the church front.

Borromini was not a habitual designer of towers or steeples, although he built a beautiful and fantastic belfry for Sant'Andrea delle Fratte and was the original designer of the twin towers of Sant' Agnese in the Piazza Navona — for which, see below. His alternative project to Bernini's ill-starred bell-towers for St Peter's is not relevant since it was rejected. Bernini had been commissioned by Pope Urban VIII in 1637 to build towers at the corners of the façade; when the first one was built up to two storeys, it was found that the original foundations would not take the weight; the tower was demolished in 1646 and the columns recycled. Israel Silvestre's print (detail, Fig. 5) shows the state at the beginning of that year.

Fig. 4. St James Garlickhythe, steeple, detail (1714–17).

Fig. 5. Israel Silvestre. Rome, St Peter's, *c.* 1646, detail.

St Paul's and Rome

It was made very clear to Wren in 1673–4 that his Great Model for the
cathedral was an unacceptable reminder of Michelangelo's centrally planned
St Peter's; he therefore 'turn'd his Thoughts', as his son tells us,[10] 'to a
Cathedral-form', that is, a Latin cross with a long nave which, for all its
clothing in modern Classical rather than antiquarian Gothic dress, should
symbolize the tradition and continuity of the English church rather than the
Roman. And so long as that symbolism was evident Wren must have felt free
to follow 'true Latin' and Continental precedents. Here, too, in our time the
name of Borromini has been dropped into the discussion of details: the west
towers, the niches of the ground storey beneath them, the interior walling of
the aisles, and the north and south porticoes. Most of these instances were
first put into print in the record of a photographic exhibition organized by
the Warburg Institute in 1941 and subsequently published in book form;
§§46–47 concern the cathedral.[11] Taking them in order, several of
Hawksmoor's drawings survive for the development of the west towers,
which in the 'autograph' prints of 1702 by Simon Gribelin still recall
Bramante's little Tempietto at San Pietro in Montorio, formed by a ring of
columns around a cylinder with a hemispherical cap (Fig. 6). But the sequence
ends before the crucial addition of the angular masses projecting on the
diagonals which, rising as far as the lead-covered and now bell-like caps,
transform the towers as if by magic into both fellows of the church steeples
and contrasting companions to the sheer and massive solid geometry of the
dome. The drawings show only the beginning of the whole process, but they
tell enough for us to perceive a logic, an organic quality, in the growth of an
idea from simple to complex, from Renaissance to Baroque.

It is also important to recognize that this organic quality exists both in
the design that meets the eye and in the ingenuity that secures a stable
structure — the affordance of both *venustas* (delight) and *firmitas*
(firmness), two of the three elements of architecture named by the ancient
Roman architect Vitruvius and never improved upon.[12] And the same is true
of all Wren's big steeples, starting with St Mary-le-Bow, a paragon
completed in 1680 and a presage of what, given money and longevity, he
would produce later (Fig. 7). Ultimately, these steeples derive their form from
Leone Battista Alberti's recipe for adapting the upright Gothic (and earlier)
tower form to the balance of horizontal and vertical implicit in the Classical
Orders, piling one little temple on another in pagoda fashion; Figure 8 is
from the first illustrated edition of Alberti's *De Re Aedificatoria*, published
(in Italian translation) in 1550 by Cosimo Bartoli. Alberti began the
accumulation at ground level, Wren at the top of a plain square tower, and
his designs are far more refined than either Bartoli's specimen or Early
Modern bell-towers in the Netherlands or France.

Fig. 6. St Paul's, Design for bell-tower, *c.* 1702. Engraving by Gribelin, detail.

Fig. 7. St Mary-le-Bow, steeple (1676–80).

Returning to St Paul's, the Warburg exhibition juxtaposed the west towers (Fig. 9) with one of the twin towers of Sant'Agnese, ascribed to 'Borromini and followers' and known to Wren 'possibly through Falda's popular *Nuovo Teatro delle fabriche di Roma,* 1665'; perhaps not in the copy the compilers used for another item, since their illustration is a photograph (compare Fig. 10). The detailed building history of Sant' Agnese is a sorry tale, and subsequent research has shown that the lower stage of the towers follows Borromini's design, with a cylinder tightly enclosed in what is basically a cubic block. But he was sacked, and the upper stage and cap were designed quite differently by Carlo Rainaldi, with curved projections on the diagonals, a change that satisfies neither logic nor the eye, and makes little sense with the lower stage. The resemblance to St Paul's is quite superficial.

The second item is below, at the base of Wren's towers (Fig. 11) where, partly for structural reasons, he designed smaller windows than those lighting

Fig. 8.
Cosimo Bartoli,
Albertian tower
design, Florence,
1550.

the aisles. Two windows at right angles are adequate to light the stairwell on the south and a small room on the north. What is as important, looking at the whole, is that their small size matches that of their neighbours on the west front, while on the long sides they are a long way from the big aisle windows (see Fig. 16). So, in order to please the eye and fill the space, he set them in niches, whose sides and heads he divided into panels, according to the exhibition text 'a device used by Bernini', constructing false perspective 'in order to produce the effect of a large-scale window'. The comparison is with the top-floor windows on the piazza side of the Palazzo Barberini in Rome, as shown in Ferrerio's *Palazzi di Roma* of 1655 (Fig. 12). The details of that front had been decided before the death of Carlo Maderno, the palace's first architect, who was interested in false perspective arches and passages and built them elsewhere. At this stage Bernini had not succeeded Maderno, and the drawings were made under the latter's direction by Borromini. But on the spot the illusion only half works, and requires the beholder's willing suspension of disbelief: at most, it is

far left
Fig. 9.
St Paul's,
north-west
tower.

left
Fig. 10.
Rome, Sant'
Agnese, south
tower.

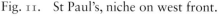

Fig. 11.   St Paul's, niche on west front.

Fig. 12.   Rome, Palazzo Barberini.
Perspective window (Ferrerio, 1655, detail).

more a conceit than a deception. There is also a critical difference between the two windows: Borromini's architraves and panels do converge to a vanishing point, whereas Wren's architraves are horizontal, like all the divisions below them. This may be most obvious from the top of a bus, but the eye is not deceived even at street level. There is nothing Baroque here, and any illusion lies not in the building but in the photograph library.

Niches were on Wren's mind from the start of construction in 1675, and large niches inside the aisle walls already appear in the Warrant Design, which he rejected that year as soon as it was approved in Whitehall. These huge cavities hollowed out of the aisle walls (Fig. 13) were at the time a novel and perhaps unique way of saving masonry and increasing interior space in a basilican building. The niche, like the arch, is a device for using the law of gravity against itself, by concentrating the mass and weight of a wall in piers between the niches or arches. At St Paul's this led to truly massive piers — which also have to carry cross-arches and saucer-domes

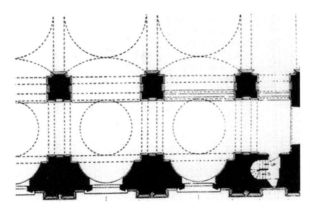

Fig. 13.   St Paul's, plan of
south choir aisle.

and provide abutment for the central aisle structure as well as for each by
its neighbours. Wren liked good lighting in his public buildings, and he used
the thinnest areas of the outer walls to admit copious daylight to the aisles
by the large windows. Structure or visual effect — chicken or egg — the
sequence of the thought process cannot be determined. The Gothic cathedral
builders had done something analogous with tracery windows in the upper
half of what was a much lighter wall system. Renaissance and later churches
in Italy, France and other Catholic countries often had no aisle windows at
all since, as the aisles were in effect more often than not sequences of little
votive chapels, the outer walls were largely occupied by painted altarpieces.
We know from Wren's son that the St Paul's aisles were not intended for
processions;[13] their functions were normal circulation, illumination,
increased space and grandeur, and a more stable construction.

   The nave niches have hexagonal coffering in their upper parts, a pattern
common to many crafts from ancient times. Those in the choir aisles, built
earlier, have quadrilateral coffers set diagonally (Fig. 14) and those in the
transepts are wedge-shaped with radial and concentric partitions. Pevsner
in Rome in 1967,[14] seeking to flesh out a jejune topic, derived the choir
pattern from the four apses in Borromini's San Carlino, ignoring the crucial
difference that in the latter the pattern runs vertically and horizontally, not
at 45°. However, we have a source for Wren that is not only accurate but
unquestionable, since he must have been familiar with Philibert de l'Orme's
book[15] and seen there his small but monumental chapel in the chateau of
Anet (Fig. 15). As Anet is about 80 km from Paris, it is possible that he saw
the original, although it is not mentioned in his letter home.

   Finally, there are the side porticoes of the cathedral, for which the
suggested source (via Falda) is the portico added by Pietro da Cortona to
Santa Maria della Pace in Rome. It is not a very good match, for the plan
of Cortona's structure is a broad half-oval and the columns are spaced in
pairs. Completing an earlier church, he was able with the help of some

Fig. 14. St Paul's, view of choir in 1706, detail showing aisle niche.

Fig. 15. Philibert de l'Orme. Chapel at Anet, section detail, woodcut.

demolitions to make a very small symmetrical piazza in front of it, for which a conventional rectangular arcade or colonnade would have been too large. The piazza was needed because the church had become fashionable among the aristocracy, who arrived and departed in their private carriages. The coupled columns, of which Cortona certainly knew an earlier example, afforded three wide openings for full-skirted ladies (Fig. 17).

Characters and Aspirations

Wren started from quite different premisses. As a Latin-cross church, St Paul's naturally required subsidiary transept entrances, and indeed the earlier Great Model has them. The long and partly asymmetrical sides of the cathedral, to which Wren was committed, needed a central feature both to indicate and invite entry and to provide a focal point for the eye in an otherwise rather repetitive articulation (Fig. 16), and that may indeed have been his starting point: if one thinks away the portico, the building is impoverished. He once wrote that 'the Middle is the Place of Greatest Dignity, and first arrests the Eye; and rather projecting forward in the Middle, than hollow'.[16] The fact that no other prototype has been found is not an argument for Cortona's building to be one, for Wren may actually have invented the form on the basis of these and other considerations.

Fig. 16.   St Paul's from the south.

Fig. 17. Rome, Santa
Maria della Pace. Etching
by Falda, detail.

To a modern eye, the semi-circular portico is most easily described as half
a garden temple, a common ornament in Georgian landscape gardens, often
with a statue sheltering in the centre. However, this was a modern, not
antique, form; there are some circular Roman temples, but while the outside
peristyle makes a statement about the nature and purpose of the building
and the high status of the location, there is always a *cella* in the middle,
dark and closed except to the priest or priestess of the honoured divinity.
The first stage of Bow steeple (Fig. 7) is similar in form; it was not beyond
the ability of Wren the intuitive geometer and pragmatic logician to conceive
both the visual and the structural evolution of this attractive new feature
from Antique forms intended for other purposes.

Colvin suggested that Hawksmoor most obviously invited comparison
with Borromini, and he was not the last person to find this idea attractive.
Both were attacked by hostile critics in their own lifetimes and had to defend

themselves and their art as best they could; both gained new popularity and admiration during the latter half of the twentieth century, yet in recent years both have been presented on British television as exciting but quite mad. Both were, in fact, remarkably sane but did not suffer fools gladly. Both knew the so-called rules of architecture and both knew when to break them and when not. Both were more interested in shapes than styles. Both mastered graphite as a medium for architectural drawing at once precise and expressive. Both were appreciated in their own day, even by some critics of their style, for their professional knowledge and expert practical advice. But while a particular feature or detail in the work of one may remind us of the other, we would never confuse them.[17] But what do these assimilations really mean? Surely that both were, as many architects are and all ought to be, true disciples of Vitruvius who based their work on *commodity*, *firmness* and *delight*. The same goes for Wren. In all three, the allegiance to Vitruvius is quite evident from their own words in letters, narratives, reports or memoranda. The most frivolous and ephemeral of buildings must stand up and stand firm — even stage scenery. Even a Greek temple, which only the anointed would enter, must fit its function with solidity and convenience, and only the imprudent embark on a building enterprise without at least the faith that it can be paid for. Beauty in architecture is subjective, and principles and tastes change. Some buildings take more time and more intense and intuitive looking to understand and appreciate, but it is a sad one that pleases nobody's eye. It is the function of the critic and the historian to foster understanding.

1. Howard Colvin, *Biographical Dictionary of British Architects*, 2nd edn. (1978), p. 920.
2. Introduction to Sir John Vanbrugh, *Complete Works*, IV, *The Letters* (1928), p. xxxiv. The present writer has used a similar phrase, at least once in print.
3. In the Hawksmoor entry, 2nd edn. (1978), p. 402.
4. Nikolaus Pevsner, *The Buildings of England, City of London* (1957), p. 162. Pevsner's paperback, *Outline of European Architecture* (1946), was the first English book to bring Borromini's work to the notice of a mass readership.
5. Margaret Whinney and Oliver Millar, *English Art 1615–1725* (1957), p. 161.
6. 'Borromini e l'Inghilterra', in *Studi sul Borromini, Atti del Convegno … Roma*, I (1967), pp. 383–90. For this paper, see further below.
7. John Summerson, *Architecture in Britain 1530–1830*, Pelican History of Art, 9th edn. (1993), p. 200. It is difficult these days to find early editions of this much-revised work, but this is not a paper on Summerson.
8. And first dry-built in the mason's yard. The redating was first noted, I believe, in Gerald Cobb's revision of his little pamphlet published by the Corporation of London, *London City Churches, a Brief Guide*, 4th edn. (1979), p. 47.
9. Kerry Downes, *Hawksmoor (The World of Art)* (1969), p. 60, and again in *idem*, *The Architecture of Wren* (1982), n. 244. But looking again at the four structures illustrated on pp. 60–1, all designed within about a decade, St James now seems entirely the odd one out.

10. Christopher Wren, *Parentalia* (1750), p. 282.
11. Fritz Saxl and Rudolf Wittkower, *British Art and the Mediterranean* (1948), no pagination.
12. The third is *utilitas* (commodity). The translation is that of Sir Henry Wotton, *The Elements of Architecture* (1624), p. 1: the three conditions of well building, also known as the Vitruvian Tripos.
13. Wren, op. cit., p. 281.
14. See n. 4.
15. Philibert de l'Orme, *Architecture*, 2nd edn. (1648), p. 254.
16. Wren, op. cit., p. 352.
17. But what has the present writer had to say in the past about Borromini and England? Nothing very substantial, and more often than not either to indicate something in common or by way of analogy. In the course of sixty years one is entitled to change — or clarify — one's mind.

III. HENRY VII'S ALMSHOUSE AT WESTMINSTER

By CHRISTINE MERIE FOX

Introduction

THE almshouse of Henry VII (Fig. 1) was built in conjunction with his new Lady Chapel at Westminster Abbey in the first half of the sixteenth century. The role of the almshouse was to help support his chantry in the Abbey while providing care to ex-Crown officials who had served the King and Abbey loyally. Henry VII's Lady Chapel has been studied extensively, but the almshouse has been omitted from most of these studies. Sir Howard Colvin oversaw and wrote most of the definitive history of English royal buildings in *A History of the King's Works* in six volumes covering the period from the early Middle Ages to the nineteenth century.[1] In volume three, Colvin devotes an entire section to the buildings of Henry VII, specifically the chapel of King's College Cambridge, Richmond Friary, the Savoy Hospital, and Henry's memorial at Westminster Abbey comprising the chapel and almshouse. Colvin's analysis of the almshouse focuses on the building, not on the site or its subsequent history. Nevertheless, there are numerous sources held at Westminster Abbey Muniments (WAM) which shed light on the complicated but important history of Henry VII's almshouse for the Tudors and their successors.

Fig. 1.   Watercolour of Henry VII's almshouse by Dr Claire Anne Martin.

TABLE 1

Important dates for Henry VII's almshouse at Westminster Abbey

1498	Plans begin for memorial.
1500	Abbot Fascet dies and Abbot Islip appointed with oversight of the memorial. Building begins on almshouse.
1504	Almshouse complete. Indentures complete.
1532	Abbot John Islip dies.
1539/40	Westminster Abbey dissolved.
1540	Keeper of the Gatehouse acquires small house in the eastern section of almshouse complex.
1546/7	Richard Cecil gives eastern portion of almshouse to David Vincent, who then sells it to Nicholas Brigham.
1546/7	David Vincent grants the Keeper of the Gatehouse access to the larger of the three almsmen's gardens.
1547	David Vincent pays for a conduit to be made to provide water to the almshouse complex.
1547	Brigham and Cecil build a dividing wall between the western and eastern sections of the almshouse site.
1558	Queen Elizabeth grants Sir Thomas Perry the almshouse after Brigham dies.
1560	Thomas Hunnis is granted the eastern portion of the almshouse once Perry dies by right of his marriage to Margaret Warner, widow of Nicholas Brigham.
1560	Almsmen petition Queen Elizabeth for their garden located on the eastern section of the old almshouse site. These petitions continue up to 1604.
1604	Almsmen regain eastern portion of the almshouse site minus the garden.
1654	Almsmen petition Dean and Chapter of Westminster for rights over their ancient garden which is being used by the Keeper of the Gatehouse for his own private garden.
1691	Almsmen regain rights over the garden and rent it out to the Keeper of the Gatehouse.
1778/9	Demolition of the almshouse to expand Tothill Street.

The Building of the Almshouse 1500–4

As early as the 1490s, Henry VII began to plan his memorial. His original plan focused on Windsor, where the Chapel of St George stands today, and was intended to house the shrine of Henry VI, once he was canonized, and also the tomb of Henry VII.[2] Throughout Henry VII's reign he tried to associate himself with his great-great-uncle Henry VI (1421–71), not only to help promote his pious concerns but also to legitimize his claim to the throne. The site of Henry VII's memorial to Henry VI at Windsor was

disputed both by the monks of Chertsey Abbey, where Henry VI's body had
originally been buried before being transferred by Richard III to Windsor
in 1484, and by the monks of Westminster Abbey. After much dispute, the
plans for the memorial at Windsor fell through. Westminster Abbey had
been the first choice of Henry VI and had long been the burial place for
English kings, so it seemed appropriate for Henry VII to transfer his energies
to Westminster, leaving Windsor in the hands of others.[3]

The building of Henry VII's memorial at Westminster Abbey began *c.*
1500. The Abbot, John Islip, oversaw all building works on the chapel and
almshouse and worked closely with Henry's contractors Thomas Lovell and
Richard Guildford. The original almshouse site stood on the north-western
perimeter of the Abbey precinct. Although the almshouse does not exist
today, its location would have been just inside of the north entrance into
Dean's Yard (see Fig. 2).

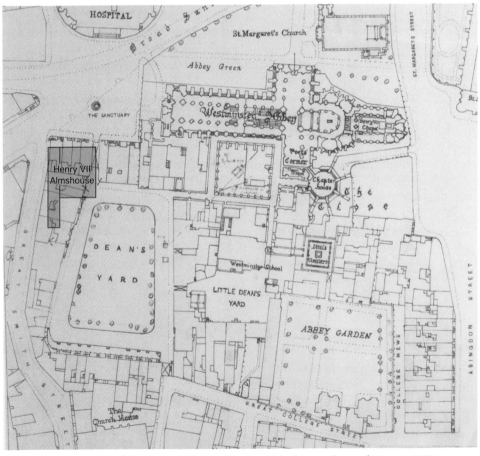

Fig. 2.   1905 OS map of Westminster with the outline of Henry VII's
sixteenth-century almshouse.

The original site contained four main buildings and three gardens. The almsmen's living accommodations stood on the most western border of the almshouse site, abutting Black's Ditch, whilst the remaining buildings (chapel, priest's house, almswomen's accommodation, hall, and other auxiliary buildings) stood on the eastern border of the almshouse site, separated by a large garden. By about 1504 the building of the almshouse complex had been completed at the cost of £564.[4]

Henry VII's almshouse overlooked the Abbey's almonry complex which, at the time Henry VII was founding his almshouse, had suffered forty years of mismanagement, so the King chose not to rebuild and refound the almonry but to build a new almshouse, and he set out careful instructions for its oversight and funding.[5] The almspeople who inhabited Henry VII's almshouse were different from those who lived and received care in the almonry. They were a chosen 'deserving' few who were selected from members of the Tudor court, who had served the Crown and Abbey loyally, but could no longer maintain that service and had no family to help them

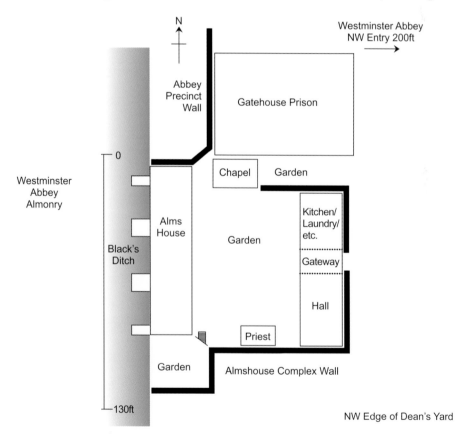

Fig. 3.   Sketch map of the almshouse site, c. 1504–47.[6]

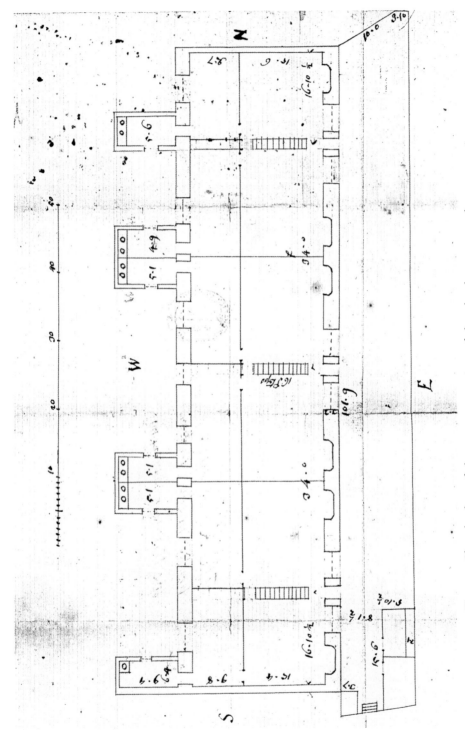

Fig. 4.   Sketch plan of the western section of the almshouse complex, *c.* 1719/20.
© *Dean and Chapter of Westminster.*[16]

in their old age. In return for their living accommodation and keep, the almsmen were expected to attend services around the tomb of Henry VII (and Elizabeth) and pray for their dead benefactor.

The Site and Buildings of the Almshouse

The approximate site of the almshouse buildings has been known, but by looking at legal disputes and complaints dating from the late sixteenth century up to the eighteenth century it is possible to recreate the size and layout of the almshouse area in the first half of the sixteenth century[7] (see Fig. 3).

According to these sources, the most easterly boundary of the almshouse site measured about 80 ft long, whilst the most southern was said to be over 86 ft long.[8] The western perimeter was anywhere from 95 to 120 ft long, whilst the most northern perimeter wall was said to have been about 65 ft long, but does not include the almsmen's chapel or the grounds lying on the western side of this building[9] (see Fig. 3).

The almshouse building itself stood on the most western perimeter and measured 120 ft long, including its garden, 26 ft wide between the walls, and 18 ft high to the eaves.[10] Later sketch surveys show the almshouse building on the western border measuring just over 100 ft long, making the garden abutting the south side of the house about 20 ft long[11] (see Fig. 4). The entire almshouse complex was surrounded by a very large wall. This wall was made of 90,000 bricks and cost £39 2s. 6d. to build.[12] Tudor bricks were variable in size.[13] Mortar often made up the difference in size between bricks, but in general they were slightly smaller than a modern-day brick which measures 8.5 × 4 × 2.5 in.[14] Bearing this in mind, if one assumes the thickness of the wall to have been roughly 3½ bricks thick, similar to the almshouse, then the surrounding wall could have stood about 10 ft high.[15]

The Almshouse

Although the western almshouse no longer exists, there survive two survey plans from the eighteenth century. The first of these plans was produced on 24 March 1719/20 and gives details of the length of the building, layout of the rooms, and the location of privies and chimneys[17] (see Fig. 4). This plan is invaluable for helping to understand the layout of the almshouse, but, unfortunately, it neglects to show the second storey. It would appear that the plan was initially drawn up by a surveyor commissioned by the Dean of Westminster, after several petitions from the almsmen had been sent to the Dean about the need for repairs. Although drawn up nearly 200 years after the original foundation, the sketch plan in Figure 4 can be considered a good indication of the almshouse in the later sixteenth century since, following Elizabeth I's renovations *c.* 1566, there are no major building works documented, but only minor repairs to individual almshouses.[18]

The second sketch plan of the almshouse was drawn sixty years after WAM 18410, and supposedly after the building had been torn down in 1778/9 to expand Tothill Street.[20] Figure 5 shows the almshouse from the east. It notes the almsmen living on both floors and that the area located directly in front of the house was their yard, which is not mentioned in the earlier plan (Fig. 4).These two eighteenth-century plans have made it possible to reconstruct the western almshouse floor plan using modern architectural programs (see Fig. 6).

Each apartment was approximately 25 ft long and was divided into two parts; the front room measured approximately 15 ft long and the back room measures just over 9 ft long. The apartment was divided by a thin interior wall with a small door. Each almshouse was fitted with a fireplace, windows in both the front and back rooms, and a private privy. Later documents confirm that the upper-storey almshouses were also fitted out with these amenities.[21]

The rooms had plastered walls, and the upper rooms had exposed ceiling beams which, by the seventeenth century, were in need of much repair and some had even fallen down.[22] By the mid-seventeenth century many of the almsmen complained to the Dean and Chapter of Westminster about the 'lofting' of their roofs and the stones which were falling down from them on to the lower floor.[23] Reports on several occasions called for replastering and tiling of the 'herth-paces', the mending of floors, and replacement of faulty tiles elsewhere in the almshouse.[24]

Fig. 5.   Sketch plan of the western section of the almshouse complex, *c.* 1779.
© *Dean and Chapter of Westminster.*[19]

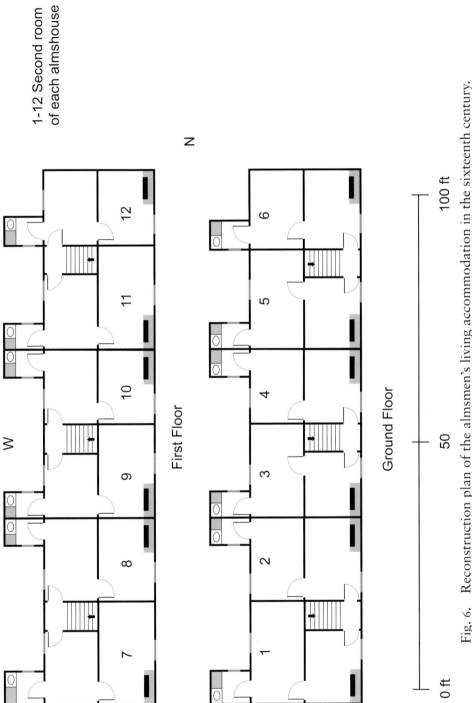

1-12 Second room of each almshouse

N

W

S

First Floor

Ground Floor

0 ft   50   100 ft

Fig. 6.   Reconstruction plan of the almsmen's living accommodation in the sixteenth century.

To the east of the almsmen's chambers fronting the almshouse was a large 'yard' area referred to in Figure 5 as a 'yard to the alms houses'. The yard measured a little over 101 ft 9 in. long and 10 ft wide.[25] At the time of its original construction, c. 1504, the almsmen would have been able walk out of their homes across their yard to their chapel or their garden located directly across from the almshouse in the eastern section, and thence to their common hall (see Fig. 3). The yard fronting the almsmen's accommodation had three steps at its southern end which led to the small almsmen's garden, located on the south of the almshouse. The fact that it was a solid surface and not just dirt is shown by a single boundary line marking out the specific area, and dimensions are then noted in Figure 4. It is not known whether this yard was covered to become a porch, but if so it would have greatly reduced the light to the lower-storey windows on the front of the almshouse.

The Kitchen and Hall

There is very little information regarding the layout of the eastern site. What is known is that the buildings on the eastern site appear to have been constructed primarily of wood, with brick foundations and chimneys. The main building in the eastern section of the almshouse complex was divided into two sections, the northern and the southern (see Fig. 3). According to the statutes for Henry VII's memorial, 'the King ... hathe caused to be purveyed and delyverd to the seid xiij poor men ... [a] commen hall and also their Botry, Pantry, Ewery, Kechyn, Larder and Laundry'.[26] In the northern section of this building stood the kitchen, buttery, larder, pantry and laundry on the ground floor, and directly above these rooms was the women's accommodation on the first floor (see Fig. 3).[27] The almsmen's common hall was located to the south of this building.[28] The total cost for carpentry for the hall and auxiliary buildings was £121 11s. 8d., and an additional £27 6s. 8d. was spent on the chimneys, ironwork, digging and the making of the almsmen's eastern garden, to a total of £148 18s. 4d.[29] An estimated 35,000 bricks were used which included the foundation work and chimneys. No dimensions are provided for these buildings; nevertheless, later Dissolution documents provide rough dimensions (80 ft to 100 ft long) of the most eastern perimeter of the almshouse complex, where they would have stood.[30] Later sources suggest that there was an arched gateway through the middle of the building, separating it into north and south sections and allowing access to one of the almsmen's gardens, and above this gateway Henry VII's arms were displayed.[31]

The Almsmen's Chapel

The building records also mention the almsmen's chapel which was located between the eastern and western side of the complex on the most northern perimeter [32] (see Fig. 3). The chapel was built of wood, but had a brick foundation similar to the almsmen's hall. The cost for carpentry and building the almsmen's chapel was £5, not including its foundation work, and it measured 20 ft long and 14 ft wide.[33] Very little else is known about this building. What we do know is derived mostly from the indentures which tell us about the services to be performed in the chapel and the bell which was to be rung throughout the day to summon the almsmen to prayer.[34] The purpose of this building was to provide a venue for the almsmen to perform their chantry services, and this may explain why, by 1552, it was neglected and noted to be falling down.[35]

The Almshouse Gardens

The almsmen had three gardens; one of which lay just south of the almsmen's accommodation, another was located in the north-eastern corner just outside the almshouse complex between the Gatehouse Prison and the eastern part of the almshouse, and the largest lay between the almshouse proper and the eastern buildings (hall and kitchen) (see Fig. 3). Originally, the entire area had belonged to the gatehouse of the Abbey, but, when Henry VII founded his memorial at Westminster Abbey, the land was allocated for the site of his almshouse complex.[36] A house that once belonged to the Abbey gatehouse became the almsmen's priest's house, and was located on the southern end of the eastern section of the almshouse complex [37] (see Fig. 3). After the Dissolution of the Abbey, the keeper of the gatehouse prison took back this house and continued to live there until the late seventeenth/early eighteenth century.[38]

There are no precise measurements for any of the gardens. The largest of the three gardens was said to have abutted the almsmen's chapel to the north, the almsmen's hall located on the east and the priest's house on the south, and measured about 80 ft from north to south and 20 ft from east to west [39] (see Fig. 3). The second garden lay on the south side of the almsmen's accommodations and was estimated to measure approximately 20 ft running north to south and 26 ft running east to west.[40] The third garden, located outside the almshouse site to the north abutting the gatehouse, was about 14 ft from north to south and about 45 ft running east to west.[41] This garden was a 'slip' of ground that backed onto the almsmen's chapel on its eastern side and the gatehouse on its northern boundary. Once the chapel had fallen down, the almsmen began using this slip of ground as a passageway to enter into the Abbey for prayers, much to the dislike of the gatehouse keeper and later tenants of the gatehouse prison property [42] (see Fig. 3).

The Almshouse Stable and Barn

Henry VII also built a stable and a barn for the almsmen. It has not been possible to locate these buildings.[43] What can be said is that they were made of wood with brick underpinning, similar to the chapel and almsmen's hall. The stable measured 24 ft long and 20 ft wide and cost £51 6s. 8d., whilst the barn measured 60 ft long and 26 ft wide and cost £23 13s. 4d.[44] These totals included the 'tymber', the 'sawyng', the workmanship, and smaller items such as hooks and latches for doors. The cost of the chimneys and underpinning of the chapel were included in these accounts. In total, these works cost £62 16s. 0d.[45]

The Almshouse Water Supply

The almshouse had a well which was later referred to as the watershed or just the shed.[46] The Abbey itself had a conduit which supplied its needs, and in December 1543/4 Guy Gascon, head sexton or sacrist of the Abbey, received £1 13s. 4d. for supervising building works, in which he hired Mr Grey, a plumber, to mend and replace the conduit head, bringing water to the surrounding residential houses, and to replace all the old pipes.[47] In 1547 David Vincent, formerly an officer of the Wardrobes and Beds, was paid £40 for making a conduit at Westminster for the use of the almsmen, and thus providing a good water supply to the converted home of Nicholas Brigham, administrator to the Crown, which was once the old almshouse hall and kitchen.[48]

Management of the Westminster Almshouse Site, 1532–1778

Once completed in 1504, the oversight of the almshouse and memorial became the responsibility of Abbot John Islip, and after his death, in 1532, this responsibility passed to his successor, Abbot William Boston, until the Dissolution of the Abbey in 1540.[49] During the Dissolution of Westminster Abbey, 1540–2, all its possessions were overseen by the Court of Augmentations, including the almshouse. Shortly after the Dissolution of the chantries, c. 1547, the almshouse, chapel, stable and barn, and all other buildings associated with the almshouse, were given or sold to the rising young courtier, Richard Cecil, father of Lord Burghley, who had a vested interest in Westminster and was a loyal servant to Henry VIII.[50] Richard Cecil then sold or granted several of the almshouse buildings to David Vincent, who was responsible for paying the rent to the Crown and evicted the three almswomen and priest from the almshouse.[51] David Vincent then transferred a portion of the lands to Nicholas Brigham, who, with the help of Richard Cecil, built a dividing wall that ran north to south and separated the almshouse site into two sections: the western section, which contained the almsmen's living accommodation and a small garden, and the eastern section, which had contained the almsmen's chapel, priest's house, the larger of their two gardens and their common hall, kitchen, larder, laundry, pantry, buttery and the almswomen's living accommodation which then became Brigham's personal dwelling[52] (see Fig. 7).

There is very little documentation for the almshouse site or buildings between 1553 and 1558.[54] The almsmen appear again, soon after Queen Elizabeth I came to the throne, when they filed a complaint to the Queen regarding their 'loss of all privileges and estate granted [to] them by Henry VII and taken away by David Vincent ... and then sold to Nicholas Brigham'.[55] The almsmen also complained that Nicholas Brigham 'converted ye same to a dwelling house for hym selfe and to his use and to take away ye armes standing and fixed over ye gate'.[56] This complaint does not appear

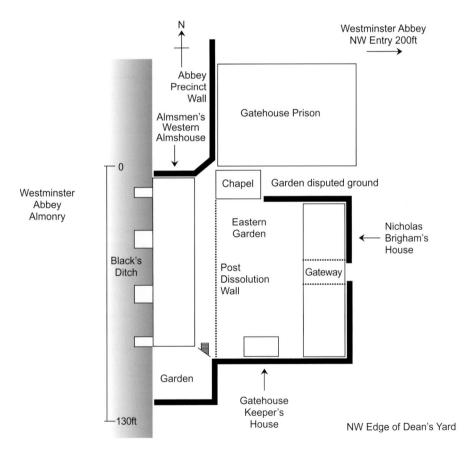

Fig. 7. Sketch map of the almshouse site, c. 1550.[53]

to have been effective because, after Nicholas Brigham died, Queen Elizabeth granted Sir Thomas Parry, the then treasurer of the household, the use of Brigham's premises, that is, the hall, chapel and garden.[57] Nevertheless, in 1559/60, Queen Elizabeth refounded the monastery as the Collegiate Church of Westminster. The almshouse was also refounded with new statutes and ordinances, and was afterwards known as the Queen's Almshouse.[58] This refoundation of the almshouse did not, however, include access to the buildings located on the eastern half of the original site which had once been granted to Brigham but were now in the possession of Parry. The lease agreements were complicated, and Sir Thomas Parry was still living in the house when he died in 1560. At that time, a gentleman by the name of William Hunnis, said to be of Her Majesty's Chapel, entered the premises, claiming them by right of his marriage to the widow of Nicholas Brigham, Margaret Warner, daughter of Richard Warner an Officer of the Exchequer. In February 1563, the almsmen petitioned Parliament regarding the oversight and ownership of the almshouse in a further attempt to recover their property.[59] According to their petition, the almsmen asked Parliament to evaluate the title of William Hunnis so that the 'petitioners [almsmen] may be re-established in the said almshouse'.[60] The outcome of the petition is not known, but the chapel, hall and kitchen (the original eastern portion of the almshouse grounds) were not restored to the Collegiate Church until 1604, and by this date these eastern buildings had been extensively rebuilt.[61] The almshouses remained in an increasingly decayed state until they were finally demolished in 1778.

In addition to giving Nicholas Brigham access to the eastern almshouse buildings, David Vincent also gave the Keeper of the Gatehouse Prison permission to use the garden located on the eastern portion of the almshouse site.[62] In 1547, the Keeper of the Gatehouse Prison began using it as his own personal garden because it fronted his private residence that had once been the almsmen's priest's house[63] (see Figs 3 and 7). After approximately twenty years of use as a personal garden, the formal ownership of the land had become obscured. This garden was cut off from the almsmen by the wall Richard Cecil and Nicolas Brigham had erected in the later 1540s.[64] It would appear that problems arose over the oversight of this garden when new houses and shops, which were erected near to the almsmen's western site, encroached upon the almsmen's other garden which abutted the house on the south.[65] When this began to happen, it would appear that the almsmen began to use or claim access to the garden located in the eastern section of their site.[66] Most of the eastern site no longer belonged to the almsmen, and it would have been quite difficult for them to get access to the garden unless they went through the centre gate in Brigham's house, or unless there was another entry into the area near to the dilapidated chapel, or a door in the dividing wall.[67]

Throughout the later sixteenth century, a handful of inquisitions were made into the property granted to the almsmen by Henry VII in order to resolve this garden dispute.[68] After consulting ancient deeds, the Gatehouse Keeper acknowledged that he had no formal title to the garden but claimed he had the right and use of the land because this had been the situation for many years. The dispute was renewed in 1654 when both the Gatehouse Keeper and the almsmen petitioned against one another for the rights and use of the land.[69] On 14 June 1655, John Pomeroy, solicitor to the Collegiate Church of Westminster, reopened the case after finding evidence in the Cathedral's records at the time, known as the 'Petty Bag'.[70] Arguments went back and forth for several more years with no real settlement and both parties continually petitioned the Dean and Chapter for a ruling on this matter. The Keeper of the Gatehouse Prison argued, first, that there was no formal deed specifying that the land belonged to the almsmen and, secondly, David Vincent and his predecessors had given the property to the Keeper of the Gatehouse for his use. The final settlement regarding the garden property did not come until the very end of the seventeenth century. By 1691 it would appear that the almsmen had regained control of the property and were then leasing it to the Keeper of the Gatehouse.[71] By 1699 the almsmen granted the Keeper of the Gatehouse Prison a forty-year lease of the land at an annual rent of £12.[72] Nevertheless, the Keeper was negligent in his payments and the almsmen had to petition the Dean and Chapter for the recovery of their rents.[73] A final recovery and agreement about payment was made in 1710, only sixty-eight years before the entire complex was redeveloped for the expansion of Tothill Street.[74]

Conclusion

The sixteenth century was a very difficult period for religious institutions, even for those that enjoyed royal favour. Westminster Abbey and Henry VII's almshouse posed a particular problem for the Crown because of their royal associations. The almshouse was, after all, the memorial for the first Tudor King, and yet its very purpose and function lay uneasily alongside the new Protestant ideas. However, its second function as a house for retired royal servants was still needed, and remained an important priority for the Crown.

By the end of the Elizabethan period, the almshouse, once surrounded by open spaces and fields to the south-west, would have been surrounded by ramshackle buildings, thrown up as quickly and cheaply as possible. The most significant building encroachment was on Black's Ditch on the western side of the house where the almshouse privies and windows were located.[75] Tall structures were being built which obstructed the almsmen's light, while the chimneys from these same residential and industrial buildings (one was a washhouse), filled the air with soot, obscuring and damaging the windows.[76] The almshouse enclosure that had once been a sanctuary for retired royal officials was now crowded and rundown. Nevertheless, people still petitioned the Dean of the College to be admitted as almsmen because the house provided security.[77]

Although intended to last in perpetuity, Henry VII's almshouse survived in its original form for less than forty years. After the Tudor dynasty, the maintenance of the almshouse became less of a priority to the Crown and the Dean and Chapter of Westminster. By 1779 when it was demolished, the state of the house can be summed up in one word: dilapidated. Its walls had fallen onto the banks of Black's Ditch and several of the rooms had been uninhabitable for years.[78] This dilapidation can be attributed to age and time, but it can also be attributed to the neglect and maladministration during the seventeenth and eighteenth centuries. Nevertheless, for nearly 300 years the almshouse had remained as a memorial to Henry VII's charitable intentions, and today the royal foundation continues to provide relief for royal and Abbey servants who can still be seen at special services wearing their red gowns.

1. H. M. Colvin and others (eds.), *The History of The King's Works 1485–1660*, vol. 3, pt. 1 (London, 1975), pp. 187–222.
2. When Henry VI body was interred at Chertsey Abbey, then removed in 1485 by Richard III and moved to Windsor. Colvin, *The History of the King's Works*, p. 210; Christopher Wilson, 'The Functional Design of Henry VII's Chapel: a Reconstruction', in *Westminster Abbey: The Lady Chapel of Henry VII*, ed. Tim Tatton-Brown and Richard Mortimer (Woodbridge, 2003), pp. 141–88 (p. 153).
3. Margaret Condon, 'God Save the King! Piety, propaganda and the perpetual memorial', *Westminster Abbey: The Lady Chapel of Henry VII*, ed. Tim Tatton-Brown and Richard Mortimer (Woodbridge, 2003), pp. 59–98 (pp. 60–63).
4. Westminster Abbey Muniments (WAM), 5398.
5. Neil Rushton, 'Monastic Charitable Provision in Later Medieval England c. 1260–1540' (unpublished PhD thesis, Cambridge, 2002), p. 147; and see Christine Merie Fox, 'The Royal Almshouse at Westminster c.1500–c.1600' (unpublished PhD thesis, Royal Holloway, University of London, 2013).
6. Figure 3 is a reconstruction of the almshouse site based upon information given in BL, Harley MS 1498, WAM, 5398, 18424A–C, 5368, 5347, 5320, 5328, 18174, 43722, 18317, 5326, 5325, 18379, 18396, 18398, 18395, 18406, 18399, 18404, 18408, 18410, 66003 (see Figs 4 and 5).
7. Barbara Harvey, *Living and Dying in England 1100–1540: The Monastic Experience* (Clarendon Press, 1993; repr. 2002), p. 214 fn. 3; Gervase Rosser, *Medieval Westminster 1200–1540* (Clarendon Press, 1989; repr. 2001), p. 297; Rushton, 'Monastic Charitable Provisions in Later Medieval England', pp. 79–160; L. E. Tanner, 'The Queen's Almsmen', in *Westminster Abbey Occasional Papers*, 23 (Westminster, 1969), pp. 9–10. For a detailed account of the land dispute, see Fox, 'The Royal Almshouse at Westminster', ch. 3, pp. 126–85 (p. 139 fn. 51).
8. WAM, 18424A–C, 18398.

9. Ibid. There are conflicting measurements given in the different sources regarding the length of the western perimeter. One source claims 95 ft, but appears to be inaccurate in its other measurements (WAM, 18424A–C), whilst the building records state that it measures 120 ft long (WAM, 5398) and finally an eighteenth-century survey shows the building measuring just over 100 ft long (WAM, 18410) (Fig. 4).

10. WAM, 5398.

11. See Figures 4 and 5; eighteenth-century sketch plans WAM, 18410, 66003.

12. WAM, 5398. This was a boundary wall which was built around the almshouse and not a part of the structure. Colvin, *The History of the King's Works*, p. 207.

13. John Schofield, *The Building of London* (New Haven, 1984), pp. 126–9.

14. John Schofield, *Medieval London Houses* (New Haven, 1994), p. 151.

15. WAM, 18424A–C, 5398, 5320, 18398, 18410.

16. WAM 18410.

17. WAM, 18410. A reproduction of the plan can be found in Colvin, *History of the King's Works*, p. 209, and in Rushton, 'Monastic Charitable Provision in Later Medieval England', p. 153.

18. See Fox, 'The Royal Almshouse at Westminster', ch. 3, pp. 126–85.

19. WAM 66003.

20. WAM, 65988–66002.

21. WAM, 18410; *Calendar of State Papers, Domestic Series, of the Reign of Elizabeth 1601–1603; with Addenda, 1547–1565* (CSP), no ed. (London, 1870), pp. 537–8.

22. WAM, 5340, 5347, 5328, 5319, 5283, 5289, 5290, 5345, 5314, 5363, 5332A–F, 42241, 5344, 5359, 5375, 5303, 5343, 37036, 5382.

23. Ibid.

24. WAM, 5345, 5332A–F, 5340, 5344, 5375, 5332, 5359, 5303, 5289, 5290, 5283, 18424A–C.

25. WAM, 18140.

26. BL, Harley MS 1498, fos. 75^{r-v}, also see *Calendar of Close Rolls Preserved in the Public Records Office, Henry VII 1500–1509*, 2 (London, 1963), p. 153.

27. WAM, 18424A–C, 18398, 5325.

28. Ibid.

29. WAM, 5398.

30. WAM, 18424A–C.

31. WAM, 5325, 18424A–C, 43500, 18406, 18177, 18174, 5320, 18398.

32. WAM, 43722, 18317, 18397, 5325.

33. WAM, 5398.

34. BL, Harley MS 1498, fos. 63^{r}, 70^{v}, 71^{v}.

35. WAM, 18177, 43500, 18406, 5325, 18174, 37036, 18397.

36. WAM, 18397.

37. WAM, 18174, 5320, 5368, 5326, 5328, 18177.

38. WAM, 5397, 18424A–C, 18395, 18406,18177, 18174,18317, 18397, 18396.

39. WAM, 34508D, 5398, 18140, 18397, 5325, 18177, 5340, 43722, 18424A–C, 18375, 5368.

40. WAM, 5398.

41. This measurement has been calculated based on the size of the chapel and the measurements given in later property disputes regarding the length of the dissolved almshouse site. WAM, 5398, 18424A–C.

42. WAM, 43500, 43722, 18424A–C, 18177, 18174, 5340, 18408–9.

43. WAM, 18424A–C (surrender of the almshouse *c.* 1547 lists all the buildings mentioned in WAM, 5398, but neglects to mention the barn and stable, referring to them as other 'curtaliages').

44. WAM, 5398.

45. WAM, 5398; Colvin, *The History of the King's Works*, p. 207.

46. WAM, 5340. There is no date on this document, but there is mention of a lease on the shed in 1620, so it can be assumed the shed was built before 1620: WAM, 43500 (shed lease). It is not clear within the lease where the shed stood, other than the fact that is was located in the almshouse yard, which suggests that it was one of the buildings that stood on the south-eastern corner of the almshouse yard.

47. The document itself reads 'pro supervisione operum'. WAM, 37043, fo. 10; 33603, fo. 4ᵛ. WAM, 37036, fo. 1; *Act Books*, C. S. Knighton ed., *Acts of the Dean and Chapter of Westminster 1543–1554*, vol. 1 (Woodbridge, 1997 and 1999), p. 13.

48. WAM, 5390. In 1691/2 a memorandum of lease from brethren of the almshouse of ground adjoining the almshouses states that there is water access in the almshouse yard; WAM, 35652.

49. Barbara Harvey, *The Obedientiaries of Westminster Abbey and their Financial Records, c.1275–1540* (Woodbridge, 2002), pp. 6, 9. Surrender of the Abbey, see TNA, E 322/260.

50. WAM, 5321, 5325, 5321, 18174, 18424A–C.

51. WAM, 18317, 18397.

52. WAM, 18397; Colvin, *The History of the King's Works*, p. 210.

53. Figure 7 is an adaptation of Figure 3; see details for sources in earlier footnote for Figure 3.

54. Land transaction of almshouse during Edwards reign: WAM, 5307, 54001, 37642B, 40093, 37709, 37713–14, 5305.

55. WAM, 5325.

56. Ibid.

57. WAM, 43500, 5325, 5397.

58. WAM, 5288, 5268, CJV/NFL1/423169.01; Tanner, 'The Queen's Almsmen', pp. 9–10.

59. *CSP*, pp. 537–38.

60. *CSP*, pp. 537–38.

61. WAM, 42095.

62. WAM, 18397.

63. The almsmen's priest's house had once belonged to the gatehouse, before Henry VII built his almshouse on the site.

64. WAM, 18397.

65. WAM, 5347.

66. WAM, 18177.

67. The eastern building is thought to have been divided into two sections; the hall on the south side, and on the north side the kitchen and another building with some sort of gate between them.

68. WAM, 5397, 18424A–C, 43722.

69. WAM, 18174, 18177, 43722.

70. WAM, 5397.

71. WAM, 35652.

72. WAM, 5326, 5368.

73. WAM, 18351.

74. WAM, 18375, 65988–66022, 66000–3.

75. WAM, 5340, 5347, 5320, 5346, 5358, 5283.

76. WAM, 5332F, 5347, 5340.

77. Unlike privately funded and company almshouses, Henry VII's almshouse was founded and supported by the Crown and Westminster Abbey.

78. WAM, 5363. The almshouse remained at least partially operational until 1779, when the building was demolished to make way for a widened entrance into Broad Sanctuary from Tothill Street. At that time there were only six almsmen living in the almshouse. WAM, 65988–66022, 66000–3.

IV.   NEW LIGHT ON RALPH TRESWELL

By DORIAN GERHOLD

RALPH TRESWELL is dear to London topographers for his detailed ground plans of London properties, mostly from 1610 to 1612.[1] It might be thought that there was little new to be said about him. However, one source which has not been exploited previously is legal proceedings, especially those of the Court of Chancery. Treswell gave evidence seven times between 1595 and 1611, and that evidence fills in several gaps in his story. The list of Treswell's maps published in 1987 can also be slightly enlarged, as shown in the Appendix.

One of the gaps is Treswell's date of birth, which John Schofield reasonably assigned to about 1540 on the basis of Treswell first being recorded at work in 1567/8.[2] Deponents in Chancery were required to state their age. The ages stated in six of Treswell's seven depositions are so consistent as to suggest that he knew exactly when he was born.[3] They place his date of birth firmly in 1542–3, between October 1542 and April 1543. He was therefore about 25 when first recorded working, 38 when his earliest surviving map was drawn, 68 to 70 when he drew most of his London plans and 74 when he died.

When giving evidence in 1610 about a Northamptonshire manor Sir Christopher Hatton had once considered purchasing, Treswell stated that he had known Hatton well, 'for he sayth he was his servant above the space of xx yeres'. He added that he knew Hatton's Northamptonshire manors 'because he was surveyor of Sr Cristofers lands'.[4] Hatton died in 1591, so Treswell had worked for him since 1571 or earlier. That was long before he drew his maps for Hatton, in 1580–7, and several years before anyone had drawn a scale map of an estate. Either Treswell had at first been employed in some capacity other than surveyor, perhaps in one or more of the roles of a painter-stainer, such as heraldic painting, or he had always worked as Hatton's surveyor but at first without drawing maps (possibly, he had both painted and surveyed). Either way, it was almost certainly in Hatton's employment, and with his encouragement, that Treswell learnt the skills of a surveyor. The maps make clear that Treswell was working as a surveyor not later than 1580. Being Hatton's 'servant' probably meant that Hatton had first call on his time, but evidently did not mean working exclusively for him. Although Treswell was still acting as Hatton's surveyor in 1591, several maps or plans of his for other landowners have survived from 1585–9: three London ones from 1585–6 (one for Christ's Hospital), and thirteen mostly rural ones from 1587–9, including five for St Bartholomew's Hospital, three for Augustine Steward, one for Winchester College and one for Thomas Palmer.

45

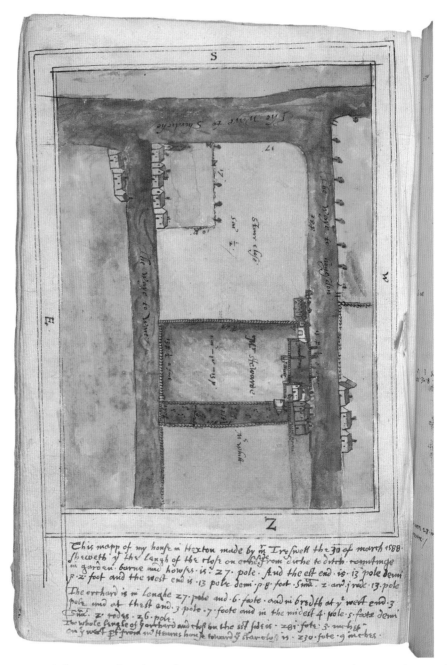

Fig. 1.   Ralph Treswell's plan of property in Hoxton, 30 March 1588. The roads
are Hoxton Street (west), Old Street (south) and Kingsland Road (east). See
Survey of London, vol. 8, *The Parish of St Leonard Shoreditch* (1922), pp. 47–53.
© *The British Library Board, Egerton 2599, fo. 31.*

The incident which gave rise to Treswell's evidence of 1610 occurred in 1591, when Hatton was considering purchasing Gages Manor in Wellingborough from Thomas Hurleston. Treswell was sent to examine the terrier and rental of the manor to determine the manor's 'goodness'. On the basis of Treswell's advice, Hatton abandoned the purchase, 'because he thought it a great deale to[o] deere'. This indicates an important point about surveyors in this period, which our own concentration on maps and surveys obscures: much of their work was giving oral advice on matters such as potential purchases and estate management, rather than just producing maps and surveys.

The depositions record some hitherto unknown work by Treswell, though in neither case has the map survived. Before 1601 he 'surveyed and made a plott' of houses, wharves and land at Wapping totalling almost eight acres for Bridewell Hospital.[5] In 1607 he stated that he had known Leadenhall for forty years, and 'hath surveyed and taken a plott of the whole place called Leaden Hall' — presumably for the City of London. He proceeded to give a detailed description of it.[6] Other previously unrecorded Treswell customers are Augustine Steward (1587–9), Winchester College (1588) and Robert Cecil (1602) (see Appendix). Another lost Treswell map is recorded in a catalogue of 1727 of the library of the Duke of Kingston at Holme-Pierrepont, Nottinghamshire, described as 'A plat of the conduit heads, earths and pipes on the west side of London, which convey water to the conduits about London, 1586'.[7] It was probably related to his plan of the area around St Michael le Querne, Cheapside, dated 1585, which is mainly concerned with the conduit and pipes there.[8] The library was destroyed by fire in 1745.

Treswell's last commission seems to have been surveys of the Sussex manors of the Earl of Dorset in 1615, of which apparently only a written survey of Imberhorne has survived.[9] On that occasion Treswell described Henry Lilly of London as his deputy, and Lilly's own maps are similar in style to Treswell's, for example in their borders and scales.[10] He may well have been the Henry Lilly who was a herald and a member of the Painter-Stainers' Company.[11] Treswell died in 1616–17.

Chancery records provide some new information about the two of Treswell's sons who were also surveyors. For Robert Treswell this is mainly an approximate date of birth — 1567–9.[12] Robert is the better recorded of the two because he held several offices — Bluemantle Pursuivant 1591–7, Somerset Herald 1597–1624 and Surveyor-General of Woods South of the Trent from 1610 until at least 1626. However, he drew fewer maps and plans, though these did include one London one of 1610 showing houses in Whitehall. He died not later than 1633.[13] As for Ralph Treswell junior, the ages he gave in depositions were much less consistent than his father's, but indicate that he was born in the period 1572–6.[14] Like his father, he described himself as free of the Painter-Stainers' Company. The first evidence of him surveying is his statement that in May 1596 he made a 'plott or survey in paper' of a farm in Chadwell, Essex, but his first surviving map is from 1603, covering part of Langley Marish, Buckinghamshire. When he drew a map of Dulwich Common in 1606 he described himself as Ralph Treswell the younger of Hosier Lane, London.[15] His greatest work was for the 9th Earl of Northumberland, for whom he drew magnificent maps of estates in Dorset, Middlesex, Somerset, Sussex and Yorkshire from 1608 to 1613. Indeed, these are the only work by him surviving from those years, apart from a map of Lawshall and Hanningfield in Suffolk for Sir Henry Lea in 1611, and they form the bulk of his surviving output of maps.[16] Subsequently, apart from written surveys, there is an undated map of two farms at Horley and Charlwood, Surrey, probably from 1620.[17] His maps are easily distinguished from his father's by means of the signature, which is not only different in style but also gives his name as 'Raphe' or 'Ralphe', rather than 'Radus' (for 'Radulphus'). Ralph junior was still living in London in January 1624, but by July 1624 he was describing himself as a gentleman of Blythburgh in Suffolk, and referred to himself as 'going out of London to dwell upon the premises' he had leased there.[18] Apparently his surveying activities, together perhaps with some inheritance from his father, had provided sufficient financial security to abandon surveying.

APPENDIX

Additions to Ralph Hyde's list of maps by Ralph Treswell senior

Place	Date	Dimensions (mm)	Location
Hailes, Glos	1587	710 × 1115	TNA, MF 1/59
Barking, Essex (2 fields)	1587	290 × 195 (page)	BL, Eg 2599, fo. 175
Hoxton, Middlesex	1588	290 × 187	BL, Eg 2599, fo. 31[19]
Merdon, Hants	1588	Unknown	Hants RO, COPY 390
Candover, Hants	1588	570 × 1135	Winchester Coll., 21443
Limehouse, Essex	1588	210 × 172	St Bartholomew's Hospital, HC/21/4[20]
Cransley, Northants	1589	315 × 620	Wilts RO, 1720/396
Hadham, Herts	1589	411 × 285	BL, Eg 2599, fo. 94
Brigstock	1602	930 × 1260	Hatfield House, CPM Supp. 40[21]
Esher*	1606	750 × 750	TNA, MPEE 1/213
Horsleydown, Southwark	1611	270 × 430	LMA, CLC/210/G/BBH/001/MS12918/002[22]

* Copy included in the Hyde list.

Note: A plan of land between Goswell Road and Brick Lane, London, is in the style of Treswell (St Bartholomew's Hospital, HC/22/12); so is a plan of land in Bermondsey in about 1601 (Hatfield House, CPM supp. 50). There are no grounds for attributing St Bartholomew's Hospital's plans of its London properties *c.* 1617 to Treswell (cf. Peter Whitfield, *London: A Life in Maps* (2006), p. 41, which also misattributes them to Christ's Hospital).

1. Published in John Schofield (ed.), *The London Surveys of Ralph Treswell*, LTS Publication No. 135 (1987) including Ralph Hyde's list of maps on pp. 5–8. I am grateful to Ralph Hyde for allowing me to inspect his file of papers about Treswell at LMA.
2. Schofield, *London Surveys*, p. 1.
3. 52 on 26 October 1595, 55 on 11 November 1597, 59 on 24 April 1601, 65 on 18 January 1608, 67 on 7 May 1610 and 68 on 30 April 1611; the exception was 54 on 9 November 1598 (TNA C 24/246, Fell v. Stone; TNA C 24/257, Hide v. Hare; TNA C 24/286, Tothill v. Mayor of London and Governors of Bridewell; TNA C 24/340, Mayor of London v. the Staple; TNA C 24/357, Ball v. Gage; TNA C 24/365, Richardson v. Savage; TNA C 24/265, Batthurst v. Heydon).
4. TNA C 24/357, Ball v. Gage.
5. TNA C 24/286, Tothill v. Mayor of London and Governors of Bridewell.
6. TNA C 24/340, Mayor of London v. the Staple.
7. Nigel Ramsay kindly supplied this reference, which is from *Catalogus Bibliothecae Kingstonianae* (n.p., n.d. [1727]).
8. Schofield, *London Surveys*, pp. 56–7.
9. British Library, Harley 4204, fo. 274; A2A entry for East Sussex Record Office, AMS5909/11.
10. See the example (the Week estate at Maidstone in 1619) in *Lords of All They Survey: Estate Maps at Guildhall Library* (Guildhall Library, 2004), p. 33.
11. Ibid., p. 32. However, Sarah Bendall, *Dictionary of Land Surveyors and Local Map-Makers of Great Britain and Ireland 1530–1850*, 2nd edn. (1997), vol. 2, p. 318, refers to Lilly as having been active from 1620 to 1663.
12. TNA, C 24/297, Crompton v. Scudamore; TNA, C 24/371, Holley v. Knowles.
13. Bendall, *Dictionary*, vol. 2, p. 518; TNA, E 134/2Chal/Mich17; TNA, MPB 1/12; LTS Publication No. 64 (1930).
14. TNA, C 24/351, Temple v. Tomlinson; TNA, C 24/446, Ogle v. Vaughan; TNA, C 24/497, Gotts v. Holman; TNA, C 24/505, Goldsmith v. Tryon; TNA, C 24/509, Holman v. Gotts; TNA, E 134/5Jasl/Hil26.
15. TNA, C 24/351, Temple v. Tomlinson; British Library, Add. 71149; TNA, MPB 1/18.
16. Catalogue references for Dorset RO, PE/HAZ/M1, Somerset RO, MAP\T\PH\cr/5, Somerset RO, MAP\DD\SAS C/923, West Sussex RO, PHA 3421, 3424, 3427, 3568, 3570, 3572, 3574, Suffolk RO (Ipswich), HA93; http://www.twickenham-museum.org.uk (for Syon, Middlesex).
17. LMA, SC/GL/PR/LA/VI/HOR/k1307574 (printed in *Lords of All They Survey*, p. 35).
18. TNA, C 24/497, Gotts v. Holman; TNA, C 24/505, Goldsmith v. Tryon; TNA, C 24/509, Holman v. Gotts.
19. Printed in *Survey of London*, vol. 8, *The Parish of St Leonard Shoreditch* (1922), pl. 2, but attributed to 'Troswell'.
20. See Judith Etherton, 'New Evidence – Ralph Treswell's Association with St Bartholomew's Hospital', *London Topographical Record*, XXVII (1995), pp. 103–17 (Limehouse plan printed on p. 112).
21. Included in *The Cecil Papers* (digital publication by ProQuest — available in British Library).
22. Two copies; the damaged one printed in Lena Cowen Orlin, *Locating Privacy in Tudor London* (2007), p. 124.

V.   FROM TIMBER TO PLASTER:
INIGO JONES'S CEILING DESIGNS AND LONDON
ARTISANS IN THE 1630s

By CLAIRE GAPPER

Introduction

INIGO JONES's approach to the design of ceilings was decisively influenced by his visit to Italy in 1613–14. As Surveyor to the King's Works from 1615 he was able to translate his new ideas into reality in the royal palaces, but until the mid-1630s he did not employ a plasterer to decorate his ceilings using lime plaster; the designs were all executed in timber or in paint on flat plaster. This situation only changed with his employment of Joseph Kinsman at Whitehall Palace in 1637–8, a plasterer who also worked at Ham House, Surrey, where his plasterwork survives. The relationship between the ceilings at the Queen's House and those at Ham House provides the clearest evidence for the transmission of the new court style to houses beyond the royal palaces. From this point, plaster was once more the material of choice for the creation of ceiling decoration, and it is the role of London artisans in interpreting this new fashion that this article will investigate.

Inigo Jones's Ceiling Designs

By 1615, Jacobean plasterwork was reaching new heights of extravagance, combining enriched ribs, low-relief decorative motifs, strapwork and pendants, as in the King's Great Chamber at Audley End. Jones's influence was not immediate and numerous ceilings in this full-blown Jacobean manner survive from the 1620s and 1630s, such as the long gallery at Blickling Hall (Norfolk, *c.* 1620), an amalgam of heraldry, emblematic vignettes and personifications, smothering a surface already ornamented with enriched ribs and strapwork.

Jones's designs, by contrast, were inspired firstly by the classical Roman models that he had seen for himself in Italy. The illustration of the Pantheon in his copy of Palladio was annotated by him during his stay in Rome, and the coffering of its dome was to influence several of his ceilings, including the barrel-vaulted nave of the Chapel Royal at St James's Palace (1623–7).[1]

The second Italian model Jones encountered was much more significant for his domestic interiors — namely, the deep beamed ceilings of Renaissance palaces and villas in Venice and Vicenza. This style of ceiling was much indebted to Palladio's attempts to reconstruct the compartmented ceilings of the ancient Roman house, illustrated in his *I Quattro Libri* of

1570.[2] Following this model, the ceiling was divided into simple geometric compartments by deep beams decorated with guilloche with large rosettes at the intersections, as in the Palazzo Barbaran, Vicenza (1570–5). Jones followed this model in his ceilings for the Banqueting House, Whitehall (1619–22),[3] the nave of Somerset House chapel (1630–5)[4] and the Queen's House at Greenwich (1635–40), where the hall, the Queen's Withdrawing Room and the Queen's Cabinet Room were all ceiled in this fashion.[5]

Plaster vs. Timber

Inigo Jones was well aware that the Romans had used lime plaster to create their coffering. Palladio himself had drawn attention to the Romans' use of stucco in the creation of coffered vaults. He labelled his illustration of the coffering of the Temple of Peace 'Compartimento di stucco fatto nei uolti', and described the 'compartimento di stucco lauorati molto diligentemente' in the Temple of the Sun and Moon.[6] And yet all the royal ceilings so far mentioned were constructed in timber, not plaster, by carpenters, joiners and carvers. The plasterers contributed nothing more than the layers of whitewash which concealed the carved wood.

After 1619, almost two decades were to elapse before decorative plasterwork was again recorded in the royal accounts. The eclipse of the plasterer's role within the King's Works was additionally highlighted when no successor to the Master Plasterer, Richard Talbott, was appointed following his death in 1627.[7]

Joseph Kinsman's Career as a Decorative Plasterer

However, many of Jones's timber ceilings were themselves painted white, including the Banqueting House (Rubens's paintings were not installed there until 1636) and the Chapel Royal, St James's; and this may well have encouraged the plasterers, in due course, to experiment with the new fashion in their own medium. The years 1637–40 witnessed a sudden outburst of activity on the part of Joseph Kinsman, who produced beamed ceilings enriched with plasterwork at the Goldsmiths' Hall (City of London), at Whitehall Palace and at Ham House. Only at Ham does any of Kinsman's work survive, and his ceilings and friezes there, together with the documentation referring to his work elsewhere, provide invaluable evidence for the emergence of the Jonesian style in plaster.

Joseph Kinsman is relatively well documented compared with most of his fellow plasterers. He was fortunate to have served his apprenticeship with one of the outstanding decorative plasterers of his time, Edward Stanyon, and Kinsman probably worked under his master at Blickling and Apethorpe Halls in the 1620s.[8] Having trained within the Jacobean tradition, Kinsman emerged as a freeman of the London Plasterers' Company just when the demand for such plasterwork was diminishing.[9] He must have decided that in order to make a successful career he needed to adopt the new Jonesian style and master a set of rather different techniques to achieve this.

Despite being the overall contractor, a plasterer was still dependent on woodworkers for the manufacture of the non-structural hollow timber beams and for the supply of moulds for repetitive items such as architectural mouldings. The major change in plastering technique arose from the need to create garlands of fruit and foliage in much higher relief than had been possible using moulds. Small armatures of wood or metal were embedded in each element, which could then be pressed into the still malleable surface of the lime plaster ceiling, resulting in much greater variety and more three-dimensional modelling of the surface. The observation of ceilings of this kind in royal buildings may have provided the crucial spur for a plasterer to adapt the newest court fashion to his own material.

Artisans from the City companies were constantly in demand at royal building sites, ensuring that the latest court styles were soon available to wealthy City dwellers as well as courtiers. Within the Royal Works, Inigo Jones assembled a group of younger craftsmen who could respond readily to his ideas. These included the masons Nicholas Stone (who worked at the Banqueting House and became royal Master Mason in 1632) and Edmund Kinsman.[10] Alongside the Sergeant Painter, Matthew Goodricke was frequently employed by Jones on decorative painting. Nicholas Stone was to prove particularly significant in the subsequent career of Joseph Kinsman. Kinsman's name first appears in the Royal Works' accounts for 1637–8 when he was 'making a Cornice of plaister in the new roome under the Qu[een's] closett' at Somerset House.[11] It did not take him long to graduate from cornices to ceilings.

Goldsmiths' Hall

Inigo Jones himself recommended Nicholas Stone to the Goldsmiths when they wanted to build a new Company Hall. In January 1637 Mr Stone presented his designs, and it was agreed that the ceiling of the hall should be 'of plaster Frett worke, according to his draught now shewed'.[12] That this 'draught' was for a beamed ceiling is made clear by two entries in the Company records. In the first place, Stone opposed the suggestion that his design should be shown to several plasterers to obtain competitive quotes, claiming that it would thereby 'bee Comon'. The rarity value of drawings based on court models was a professional asset that the committee accepted should be protected. They could rest assured that their new hall would outshine those of rival companies in its decoration. Secondly, when Joseph Kinsman contracted to plaster the ceilings in the great parlour and above the staircase with frets in November 1639, he was 'alsoe to doe all the Carpenters worke vpon the Ceelinge', which would only have been necessary if beamed ceilings were in question.

It is worth noting that Kinsman had no apprentices of his own until 1640. Plasterers frequently worked in small teams, but Kinsman seems to have gone solo in the 1630s. Perhaps he, too, felt that his newly gained expertise put him ahead of the competition, a situation to be exploited for as long as possible.

Whitehall, Queen's Old Bedchamber

In 1638–9, Kinsman was at Whitehall where Inigo Jones was masterminding the refurbishment of the Queen's lodgings and, for the first time, entrusting the ceiling decoration to a plasterer. For once, the clerk was inspired to enter an unusually detailed account of the plasterwork: 'a frett Ceelinge in the Queenes old Bedchamber wroughte with Ovalls and squares garnished with Garlandes Festoones and other enrichmentes'. To complete the makeover, Nicholas Stone carved a white marble chimneypiece to accompany Kinsman's ceiling.[13]

Ham House[14]

Three decorative ceilings created for the courtier, William Murray, in 1637 testify to Kinsman's outstanding skills. Although it is apparent that the Queen's House provided models for the overall layout and much of the detail, it is also clear from Kinsman's work at Ham that ceiling designs were continuing to evolve. Kinsman's technical mastery revealed the potential of plaster to satisfy the ardent follower of current court fashion more speedily (and cheaply) than timber.

At the Queen's House, Jones had introduced variations on the layout of the Banqueting House ceiling but, ever mindful of the requirement for 'decorum', he had modified the decoration to suit the more domestic context of the Queen's House. In the hall, for example, plain dentils were substituted for elaborate modillions in the mouldings within the panels. More fanciful was the fruit and foliage decoration, strung along the beams of the Queen's Withdrawing Room, which was to be incorporated into Kinsman's work at Ham.

Murray's new staircase at Ham provided an impressive approach to the state apartment. Classical bay garlands cast from moulds were not themselves a novelty, but here the hand-modelled relief of the leaves increased as the visitor ascended the stairs. Overhead, the layout of the ceiling matched almost exactly that of the hall in the Queen's House. At Greenwich the fields were to be filled with paintings, while at Ham more modest recessed circles and ovals were deemed sufficient. Identical guilloche covers the beams and four large rosettes at the intersections, with central projecting pine cones, complete the 'copycat' decoration (Fig. 1). The designer at Ham was, however, equally sensitive to the demands of 'decorum', and much simpler mouldings were applied to the sides of the beams there, omitting the dentils and enriched Vitruvian scroll that Jones had included at Greenwich.

Although Jones had followed Palladio's reconstruction of the four-column hall at the Banqueting House, making all the recessed panels of the ceiling of the same depth, he later annotated his copy of Palladio, remarking critically, 'In this designe the cornice of the sfondati [compartments] in the midell and on the sides is all of one hight which shuld nott be'.[15] As a result of this perceptive comment, the ceilings at the Queen's House were constructed differently, with the soffits of all the beams flush with one another, but the central panel more deeply recessed than the others. The ceilings at Ham all follow Jones's latest thinking on this topic in their construction.

Jones continued to follow Palladio in the hall at the Queen's House by treating the sides of the beams as the frieze of the three-part entablature, with only the architrave set below the beam. In the Queen's Withdrawing Room, however, both frieze and architrave are situated below the beams, to highlight the decorative relief of the frieze. Gordon Higgott pointed out that, at Ham, the latter solution was adopted for the staircase ceiling and a full set of cornice mouldings was applied to the sides of the beams, terminating in an egg-and-dart at the base. This treatment was less architecturally correct than that adopted at the Queen's House; but, viewed from below, the egg-and-dart provides a visually pleasing border to the various fields.

A similarly eclectic approach to Jones's models was followed in the Great Dining Room (now Hall Gallery). The deep beams are laid out in a rectilinear pattern with six small squares placed at the corners and in the middle of the long sides. These contain inset circles and octagons. The central oval is more deeply recessed than the other panels, but its curved beams are also superimposed over the central rectangle, adding to its depth in a way that is not found at the Queen's House. This oval is decorated with swags of fruit and flowers of the kind adorning the straight beams of the Queen's Withdrawing Room. In addition to the luscious artichokes, bunches of grapes, gourds, pomegranates and roses, Kinsman included the occasional caterpillar or worm wriggling among them. Leaves and insects project beyond the edge, as do the menacing claws of the fierce, hand-modelled lion masks, all adding to the height of the relief (Fig. 2). Mouldings of egg-and-dart, half-quatrefoil and waterleaf run along the sides of the beams, as at Greenwich, but in reversed order.

Fig. 1. Guilloche and rosettes on the ceiling beams of the hall at Queen's House (above) and the staircase at Ham House (below). *Richard Gapper*

Fig. 2.   Detail of the central oval of the ceiling of the dining chamber
at Ham House. *Richard Gapper*

Kinsman's 'freese' (actually a full entablature) in this room is the most
elaborate in the house. The Queen's Withdrawing Room seems to have
inspired the scrolling arabesques of the acanthus frieze and the fleur-de-lis
which punctuate it at the centre of each wall. A set of designs for friezes
incorporating these elements was published by another of Jones's close
associates, Edward Pearce the elder, in 1640, which makes him a possible
candidate as the designer of the Ham plasterwork.[16]

In the Withdrawing Room (now North Drawing Room) the blossoming
skills of the plasterer become fully apparent. All the beams here are bursting
with yet more luscious swags of fruit and flowers, held in calyxes with
ribbon bows, attached not to the usual rosettes but to charming,
hemispherical posies. The frieze maintains the floral theme and helps to
make this undoubtedly one of the most delightful and inventive schemes
inspired by Jones, which must have helped to convince patrons that plaster
was as acceptable a medium as timber. Patrons like William Murray, who
were close to the court circle that included Jones, must have been delighted
to be in a position to recreate the latest fashion in their own houses at a
greatly reduced cost.

Between the decorated beams, the white plaster surfaces of the ceilings at
Ham are strikingly plain, more akin to the small Cabinet Room at the

Queen's House than the colourful ceilings, filled with paintings on canvas, in the highest status rooms. This relative austerity is matched in another London suburban house built in the same decade where Jones's influence is also clearly apparent. Swakeleys (Middlesex) was built between 1629 and 1638 for Edmund Wright, a member of the Grocers' Company and Lord Mayor in 1640–1.[17] Despite the absence of documentary evidence, there seems no reason to date the ceiling of the great chamber any later than this. It is divided by deep beams, covered with the familiar guilloche, into five squares along the length of the room, flanked by rectangles of unequal size, with another square projecting into the central bay over the porch. The centre of the ceiling is marked by a circular beam, deeply recessed but otherwise plain. Bay garlands fill the two squares to either side. At each end, the square contains a recessed octagon with cherubs' heads in the four spandrels. The bay over the porch is the most highly decorated, with a beribboned floral garland in the centre and cherub heads in the corners, blowing vigorously with cheeks puffed (Fig. 3).

A somewhat discordant note is struck by the 'rosettes' at the intersections of the beams as they take the form of low-relief Tudor roses amidst these classical details. None of the execution is as fine as Kinsman's work at Ham. The garlands in particular are all rather solid in appearance and look as

Fig. 3.   Ceiling of the bay over the porch in the great chamber
at Swakeleys, Middlesex. *Richard Gapper*

though they have been cast from moulds rather than hand-modelled. The cherub heads, on the other hand, are in high relief and stand proud of the ceiling, as do the 'gusts' of wind issuing from the cherubs' mouths. It all creates the impression of a version of a Jonesian ceiling produced by a designer at some remove from direct experience of the Surveyor's work. Nevertheless, it provided the patron with a fashionable ceiling whose plainness would probably have met with Jones's approval.

An alternative treatment of the new style of plaster ceiling can be found at Cromwell House (Highgate), built for Richard Sprignell in 1637–8.[18] In this house we encounter Jacobean and Jonesian ceilings made at the same date under one roof. In the great chamber on the first floor the deep-beamed ceiling is based on the layout of the Banqueting House, with the central oval no more deeply recessed than the rectangles and squares surrounding it (Fig. 4). In addition to the familiar guilloche on the beam soffits, a varied assortment of classical mouldings is used to edge the panels, including egg-and-dart, waterleaf, overlapping threaded 'coins' and a band of single guilloche. At the centres of the two largest rectangles are garlands of bay, while a floral garland surrounds the Sprignell arms in the central oval. Large acanthus rosettes mark the intersections of the beams. No doubt all of this would have been perfectly acceptable to the Surveyor; but what would he have made of the strapwork that fills the remainder of the blank surfaces? It is entirely Jacobean in character, sprinkled with assorted cast motifs and accompanied by floral sprays. Does this represent the personal preference of the patron, or could it have been an attempt to reproduce in plaster a version of the painted arabesque that filled the spandrels in the hall ceiling of the Queen's House (Fig. 5)? In either case, one feels that Inigo Jones might have commented, as he did of the gateway to the Oxford Botanic Garden, that the ceiling had been designed 'lamly' by someone who did not understand the principles underlying classical architecture.[19]

A wholly Jacobean-style ceiling is to be found in the room adjacent to the great chamber, which can be linked to Blickling Hall and to Forty Hall (Enfield, 1629).[20] Edward Stanyon worked at both these houses before leaving his workshop to his son, Abraham, on his death in 1632. It is likely that this workshop was responsible for the plaster ceilings at Cromwell House, and it is possible that Joseph Kinsman was the route whereby Abraham Stanyon became familiar with the latest fashion. They had been apprentices together throughout the 1620s and maintained a professional relationship in their later careers. One of Kinsman's apprentices was 'turned over' to Abraham Stanyon before completing his term in 1641, and in 1654 it was agreed at the Royal Exchange that 'Capt. [Abraham] Stanion and Joseph Kinsman, plaisterers, should have £30 for whitening the Upper Pawn'.[21] Such links within the various building trades must have facilitated

Fig. 4. Measured drawing by Isaac Jones of part of the ceiling of
the great chamber at Cromwell House, Highgate.

Fig. 5.   Detail of the hall ceiling at the Queen's House showing the painted
arabesque filling one of the spandrels. *Richard Gapper*

the speedy acceptance of Jonesian designs, even if they were not always
entirely understood in the way the Surveyor would have hoped.

A final example from the 1630s will demonstrate what could happen to
such designs when executed at some distance from the capital. A major
remodelling was undertaken at Kirby Hall (Northants) by Nicholas Stone
between 1638 and 1640. The timbers of the roof of the long gallery have
been given a felling date of 1636 by dendrochronology, which indicates that
the barrel-vaulted gallery ceiling (of which only a small section remains)
was part of this refurbishment (Fig. 6).[22] The layout of the ceiling is
strikingly similar to a design by Inigo Jones for the coved ceiling of the Great
Stairs at Wilton House.[23] On both ceilings only the ribs were ornamented,
and at Kirby the clustered fruit and foliage of the Wilton drawing was not
repeated. Instead, an extremely narrow strip of ribbon-bound laurel runs
along the central rounded 'arris' of the ribs. More visually striking is the
decoration running along the sides of the ribs, which consists of small circles
filled with rosettes laid side-by-side to produce long chains. This is surely
an unsophisticated interpretation of classical guilloche, lacking the
continuous interlocking that characterizes the examples illustrated by Serlio
or Palladio. It would appear that the patron had acquired a fashionable
Jonesian design for his ceiling but was unable to find a local plasterer who

Fig. 6. The surviving fragment of the long gallery ceiling at
Kirby Hall, Northants. *Richard Gapper*

could interpret the unfamiliar classical vocabulary. Nicholas Stone may even
have provided the design himself but, if so, he cannot have remained on site
to supervise its execution.

Conclusion

The dependence of the King's Works on the London companies for its
workforce of skilled artisans ensured that the classically inspired interior
decoration masterminded by Inigo Jones in the royal palaces would soon
affect the taste of a wider clientele, whether in courtier houses or in the City.
It is clearly evident that the influence of Jones was permeating the design of
plaster ceilings in the late 1630s. London artisans such as Nicholas Stone,
Edward Pearce the elder and Joseph Kinsman were all in a position to act
as conduits for the new classicism promulgated by Jones — Stone and
Pearce through their designs for ceilings and Kinsman in his executed
plasterwork. What emerges very clearly from an examination of Kinsman's
work at Whitehall Palace, Ham House and Goldsmiths' Hall is the extent
to which the Queen's House served to kick-start this revolution in the design
of plaster ceilings.

Acknowledgement

I would like to thank Dr Gordon Higgott for the enormous help he has provided in our numerous discussions about Inigo Jones and ceilings; they underpin much of what I have written.

1. TNA, E 351/3260, St James's Palace, Task-work entries.
2. The most relevant illustrations are those in Book Two, pp. 26, 28 and 37.
3. TNA, E 351/3391.
4. This ceiling was lost during the demolition of Somerset House in the 1780s but is known from a drawing by Henry Flitcroft.
5. Illustrations of these ceilings can be found in G. Chettle, *The Queen's House, Greenwich*, Survey of London Monograph XIV (London, 1937).
6. Palladio, Book Four, pp. 11 and 36.
7. Possible reasons to account for Jones's reluctance to employ plasterers on decorative work are discussed in C. Gapper, 'The Impact of Inigo Jones on London Decorative Plasterwork', *Architectural History*, 44 (2001), pp. 82–7.
8. For a discussion of Stanyon's role at Blickling and Apethorpe, see C. Gapper, 'The Plaster Decoration of the State Apartment at Apethorpe Hall', *English Heritage Historical Review*, 3 (2008), pp. 86–101.
9. Guildhall Library, MS 6122/1, 23 April 1628.
10. It has proved impossible so far to establish a connection between Edmund and Joseph Kinsman, but the name was not a common one in London. Edmund was at least a generation older than Joseph, as he was working for the Skinners' Company in 1595 and could thus have been Joseph's father or uncle.
11. TNA, E 351/3271, Somerset House, Task-work: Joseph Kinsman.
12. Goldsmiths' Company, Wardens' Accounts and Court Minutes, Vol. 19, S, Part 2, pp. 474–5. For an account of the building, see J. Newman, 'Nicholas Stone's Goldsmiths' Hall: Design and Practice in the 1630s', *Architectural History*, 14 (1971), pp. 30–9.
13. TNA, E 351/3272, Whitehall, Task-work: Joseph Kinsman and Nicholas Stone.
14. For a detailed account of Kinsman's work at Ham, see Claire Gapper, 'Caroline Plasterwork at Ham: the 1630s and the 1670s', in Christopher Rowell (ed.), *Ham House. Four Hundred Years of Collecting and Patronage* (New Haven and London, 2013).
15. G. Higgott, 'Inigo Jones's Designs for the Queen's House in 1616', in M. Airs and G. Tyacke (eds.), *The Renaissance Villa in Britain 1500–1700* (Reading, 2007), pp. 140–66.
16. British Museum, Dept of Prints & Drawings: Etchings c5*. They are illustrated in S. Jervis, 'A Seventeenth-Century Book of Engraved Ornament', *Burlington Magazine*, 128 (December 1986), pp. 893–903.
17. W. Godfrey, *Swakeleys, Middlesex*, Survey of London Monograph XIII (1933).
18. P. Norman, *Cromwell House, Highgate*, Survey of London Monograph XII (1926). Although the house was badly damaged by fire in 1865, the ceilings were restored to their original appearance using the extensive fragments that survived.
19. Cited by John Newman in Nicholas Tyacke (ed.), *The History of the University of Oxford, Vol. IV, Seventeenth-Century Oxford* (Oxford, 1997), pp. 169–70.
20. For the argument assigning Forty Hall's plasterwork to Edward Stanyon, see www.clairegapper.info, ch. V.
21. A. Saunders (ed.), *The Royal Exchange*, LTS Publication No. 152 (1997), p. 97.
22. The dendrochronological evidence was reported to me by Dr Nicola Stacey of English Heritage.
23. J. Harris and A. A. Tait, *Catalogue of the Drawings by Inigo Jones, John Webb & Isaac de Caus at Worcester College Oxford* (Oxford, 1979), pp. 25–6 and pl. 40.

VI. LONDON ADDRESSES FOR EIGHTY-SIX MEMBERS OF PARLIAMENT FOR 1735

By CLYVE JONES

As I have written before in this journal, '[l]ists of London addresses for the political and parliamentary elite are quite rare before the publication of London directories', mainly in the late eighteenth century.[1] However, this was in reference to the addresses of peers and bishops, who were members of the House of Lords. This note is concerned with the addresses of a selected group of members of the House of Commons, which are usually rarer than those for members of the Upper House. Though the volumes of *The History of Parliament: The House of Commons* often give London addresses, they do not do it for all the MPs included in the volumes, and often such addresses as are given depend on correspondence[2] or official documents, and some volumes do not give any dates for when the addresses were being occupied. Indeed, the volumes for *The House of Commons, 1715–1754*[3] do not give any dates at all, and indeed give few London addresses, usually confining themselves to the country address of an MP.[4] Thus it is of particular interest that the list reproduced here gives the addresses of eighty-five MPs for the session of 1735.[5] It comes from the second deposit of the Marquess of Ailesbury's papers at the Wiltshire and Swindon History Centre (formerly the Wiltshire Record Office) at Chippenham. The list forms part of a collection of documents concerning a petition presented to the House of Commons in 1735 against the result of the general election of 1734 at Marlborough, a borough where the political interest was contested by the Seymour family, headed by the Earl of Hertford on behalf of his father, the aged 6th Duke of Somerset, and by the Bruce family, headed at the time by Lord Bruce, the Earl of Ailesbury's heir. (Bruce had been called to the House of Lords in his father's barony in 1711.) The Earl of Ailesbury was in exile, and had been since 1698, for his involvement in Jacobite intrigues. At the election in 1734, Bruce's candidates were elected, and in January 1735 the two losing Seymour candidates entered a petition in the House of Commons that some of the votes for the Bruce candidates were invalid.[6]

The documents concerning the petition to the Commons consist of eight separate lists of names of MPs which indicate different stages of the lobbying campaign (though their chronology is a matter of some speculation, except for one list dated 9 March). None the less, these lists form one of the best collections of such documentation concerning appeals again the return of an MP in the eighteenth century. Lord Bruce, who organized the opposition to the petition lobbied extensively among MPs

and constructed lists of those he approached or intended to approach for
support. The list reproduced here is the only one to survive in this section
of the Ailesbury papers which gives the addresses of the vast majority of the
MPs on the list.[7] (Lord Bruce at the time was living in 'Warwick Street near
Charing Cross'.[8] The house was left by Bruce in his will to his wife, who
took possession in 1747.)[9] The list gives ninety-six names, but eleven do not
have addresses, so we have eighty-five addresses given here (plus one other
from elsewhere in the archive). Sixty of the MPs are crossed out (they are
marked with a dagger in the list below), which probably indicates that they
are the ones who had been contacted. The list is arranged in a rough
alphabetical order of names. Though the list is undated, the names on the
back of the list of addresses of ten probable lobbyists to whom the list was
sent, including a 'Mr Hamilton', who was very probably George Hamilton
who lost his seat of Wells by petition on 25 March, may mean that the list
is after that date.[10]

A possibly later list in the collection, consisting of four sheets, gives
Bruce's considered results of his campaign of lobbying. This list, which
consists of around 500 names, divides MPs into five columns: 'Those of the
Court For me' (that is Whig MPs who supported Sir Robert Walpole's
ministry but who had deserted their ministerial allegiance to support Bruce,
as Walpole was supporting the Seymour petitioners); 'Against'; 'Absent'; and
'In the Opposition' (probably meaning those Whig opposition or 'patriot'
MPs, who in the later 1720s and early 1730s had deserted the ministry, and
the Tory MPs, who sometimes acted and voted together in the Commons);
a fifth column marked 'Q[uery]', placed next to the 'In the Opposition'
column probably meant that Bruce was unsure of some of the latter MPs
position on the question of the Marlborough petition.[11] Of the MPs on the
list with their addresses, five were 'of the Court For me', and fifty-four were
'In the opposition'. Thus the vast majority were thought to be supportive
of Bruce's cause, with only fifteen against. The rest were recorded as absent.

There were two divisions in the Marlborough petition case, both victories
for the ministry against Bruce, though the second one showed that Bruce's
side had held up its vote while the ministerial vote suffered a falling away
of support, and its majority fell from forty-five on 13 March to four by 27
March. However, though there are no division lists to show who supported
which side, the lobbying campaign by Bruce was successful in retaining its
supporter in sufficient numbers to persuade Walpole to give up the cause
without a decisive third division, despite putting up a vigorous fight and
letting it be known that he would not tolerate the return of MPs on the
Bruce family interest.[12]

The list which has the addresses gives no indication whether the houses
on the streets named were owned or rented by the MPs listed. (In some
cases, if rented, then sometimes only part of a house might be so rented.)

It is likely that some, if not most, were rented, possibly for the parliamentary session, which was of a variable length and the duration of which would have been unknown at the beginning of the session (thus possibly making renting more difficult, so some may have lived in lodgings). However, some peers owned houses or rented on a long lease, and some were owned with the intention of renting (possibly to MPs). One such peer was the Earl of Ilay, one of sixteen Scottish representative peers (that is, elected by the Scottish peerage at the beginning of each Parliament), who was the younger brother (and eventual successor) to the 2nd Duke of Argyle (who actually sat in the House of Lords first by virtue of his *English* peerage granted in 1705 as Earl of Greenwich and then by his *British*, or post-Union peerage, of 1719 as Duke of Greenwich). In 1738, Ilay wrote that 'I have been forced to repair the 2 great houses in Hanover Street & the House at Chelsea which otherwise would have been ruinous, & shall get Tenants as soon as I can'.[13]

It is unfortunate that this list of eighty-four addresses is too small a sample of the 534 MPs elected in 1734 to assess possible topographical groupings of MPs in the same or adjacent street who shared common characteristics, such as the same party or geographical origins.[14] For example, the most easily identified geographical group was the Scottish MPs, but Bruce's list has addresses for only three Scottish MPs: John Cockburn (Golden Square), Sir Richard Munro (St Martin's Street, off Leicester Fields, later Square) and John Murray (Stone Cutters Court, off Old Street). The financial position of Scottish MPs varied one from another, as indeed did that of the English MPs, but generally speaking Scottish MPs were much poorer than the English ones. This is reflected in the topographical location of the three such MPs listed by Bruce. It is a little strange, however, that Bruce only had three Scots on his list, considering his father the Earl of Ailesbury was also Earl of Elgin in the Scottish peerage, and considering how close Bruce was to some Scottish politicians over the various challenges by the Scots in 1735 to Walpole's ministry, especially the petition of the Scottish representative peers against the conduct of the election in 1734, but also including his own fight over the Marlborough election petition.[15]

Again, the small sample, and the fact that previous published work as cited[16] concerned the topography of addresses for peer and bishops as against MPs listed here, make a comparison of a movement of addresses over time difficult. However, the general trend of members of the upper part of society shifting their residences from the City to the West End is hinted at here, the most popular addresses being the Inns of Court (5), Golden Square and Pall Mall (4 each) and Grosvenor Square (6), a total for these four locations of 22 per cent of all addresses given in this 1735 list of MPs. The City has only three addresses listed, with the new West End having 54 (that is 64 per cent of the addresses listed).

Finally, it is of interest to speculate how this list of addresses may have been used. Did Bruce write to the MPs listed or did the persons he lists as lobbyists (including himself) visit the MPs personally? The latter is by far the most likely of these two options, as it would be the most effective of the two. The Earl of Chesterfield, a leading figure in the Whig opposition, had advised petitioners to 'attend and solicit your petition in town at the opening of Parliament, for solicitations *viva voce*, and of the persons themselves concerned, have much more weight than the remote applications by letter, or the intervention of friends'.[17] A personal visit allowed the lobbyist to enlighten and to argue with the person lobbied, and crucially to report back to Lord Bruce the response of those visited, enabling Bruce to compile lists of supporters, opponents and those not lobbied due to their absence.

Another lobbying campaign in 1735 was carried out by James Erskine (a former Scottish judge, Lord Grange[18]), a recently elected MP for Clackmannanshire, whose return as an MP had been petitioned against by the losing candidate. Erskine had solicited 'Day and Night and had two Chairman of my acquaintance who distributed 400 letters. He also had most of the Patriot Lords [the Whig peers who were in opposition to Walpole's Whig government] every Day at the Court of Requests', the second largest space in the palace of Westminster after Westminster Hall, which no longer functioned as a court, but was mainly used as a public space where members of the public met to exchange news and to lobby parliamentarians of both Houses. Such patriot lords would have been in a perfect position to waylay MPs and to lobby for Bruce. Despite the fact that Erskine used both methods of lobbying — by letter and personally in the palace of Westminster — his efforts were described, perhaps unfairly, by a fellow Scottish MP as 'indolency', yet Erskine's campaign was successful and he continued to sit in the Commons.[19] Erskine's use of 'two Chairmen' to distribute his letters is fascinating. These would have been the carriers of sedan chairs, employed because of their expert knowledge of addresses long before the existence of the modern 'knowledge' of taxi drivers or of the *London A–Z*. How often, may we ask, were these experts of London topography used for similar purposes? Quite often, one suspects, but only further such evidence in correspondence is likely to give the historian more than this tantalizing clue.[20]

TABLE 1

Distribution of addresses in 1735

Area	No. of MPs	% of total 1735[21]	% of total 1729[22]
A. The City and Environs[23]	3	3.5	5.9
B. Inns of Court	5	5.0	11.8
C. The Strand and Covent Garden	4	4.7	10.2
D. Bloomsbury and High Holborn	5	6.0	5.7
E. Soho and Leicester Fields	4	4.7	10.2
F. North of Piccadilly[24]	31	36.8	23.5
G. Mayfair and Marylebone	12	14.0	2.4
H. South of Piccadilly (St James's)	14	16.5	17.9
I. Whitehall	5	6.0	5.2
J. Westminster	3	3.5	5.5
K. Elsewhere	0	0	1.7
TOTAL	85	101.7	100

APPENDIX 1

Addresses of Eighty-Four Members of Parliament, 1735: A New Lobbying List Complied by Lord Bruce Concerning the Marlborough Election Petition.[25] All the names preceded by the dagger symbol were crossed out in the manuscript.

Source: Wiltshire and Swindon History Centre, Chippenham, Wiltshire: Ailesbury Papers, 3898/2.

(The political allegiance of the MPs is indicated in the footnotes by the following abbreviations: T = Tory; W = ministerial Whigs, WI = Whig independents,[26] WO = Whig opposition, or 'Patriots', i.e., those Whigs who opposed the Whig ministry of Sir Robert Walpole, and on occasion voted with the Tories.)

1735 List of the Members to be applied to in the Marlbor[ough] affair.[27]

Mr Munson[28]
Ld Orrery[29]
Oxford[30]
Kincardine[31]
Mr Hamilton[32]
Sr J. Kay[33]
Kerr[34]
D[uke of] Chandos[35]

Sr J. Isham[36]

†Mr Aislaby[37]	Brook Street
†Mr Ashe[38]	George Street
†Sir W. Baggot[39]	Grosv[enor] Street
Mr Banks[40]	Berry Street
†Mr Bayley[41]	New Bond Street
†Lord Barrymore[42]	Old Bond Street
†Mr B. Bathurst[43]	Dover Street
†Mr B. Bathurst[44]	Dover Street
†Sir John Barnard[45]	Mark Lane
Sir G. Beaumont[46]	Kings Street Cov[ent] Garden
Mr G. Berkeley[47]	
†Mr Blacket[48]	Golden Square
†Mr Boone[49]	New Bond Street
†Mr Bradshaw[50]	Norfolk Street
†Mr Bristow[51]	Coleman Street
†Sir J. Buckworth[52]	Brook Street
Sir R. Burgoigne[53]	
†Mr Carterat[54]	Alb[emarle] Street
Lord J. Cavendish[55]	Dover Street
†Mr Chetwynd[56]	
†Sir F. Child[57]	Lin[coln's] Inn Fields
†Mr Cholmondely[58]	James Street Westminster
†Mr Clarke[59]	Spring Garden
†Mr Cockburne[60]	Golden Square
†Mr Compton[61]	Tavistock Square
†Lord Cornbury[62]	Pall Mall
†Mr Cornwallis[63]	Grosv[enor] Street
Sir N. Curzon[64]	Brook Street[65]
Mr Dawkins[66]	Pall Mall
†Mr Delme[67]	Grosv[enor] Square
Mr Digby[68]	Clergis Street
Mr Dodington[69]	Pall Mall
Mr Drax[70]	Pall Mall

Mr A. Duncombe[71]	Soho Square
†Mr Evans[72]	Duke Street St James
†Mr Evelyn[73]	Charles Street Westm[inster]
†Mr Fazakerly[74]	Linc[oln's] Inn
†Mr Fenwick[75]	Lincoln's Inn
†Mr Finch[76]	Cavendish Square
†Mr Foley[77]	
Mr Forester[78]	Poland Street
†Mr Fortescue[79]	
Mr S. Fox[80]	Burlington Street
†Lord Gage[81]	Golden Square
†Mr Gough[82]	Golden Square
†Mr L. Gower[83]	Brook Street
†Mr Grenville[84]	Duke Street St James
†Mr Griffith[85]	Bernet Street St James
Mr Hanmer[86]	N[?ew] Bond Street
Mr Herbert[87]	George Street
Mr Hervey[88]	by Grosven[or] Square
†Mr Hooper [?][89]	Lincoln's Inn
†Mr Hore [?][90]	Conduit Street
†Sir Jo. Jekyll[91]	Chanc[ery] Lane
Mr Lambton[92]	Downing Street
†Mr Lechmere[93]	
Lord Middlesex[94]	Whitehall
†Mr Monson[95]	Grey's Inn
†Mr C. Montague[96]	
†Lord Montagu	Gro[svenor] Square
†Sir R. Munro[97]	St Mart[in's] Street
†Mr Murray[98]	Stone Cutters Court
†Sir M. Newton[99]	Burlington Street
Mr Noel[100]	Old Bond Street
Mr Noel[101]	New Bond Street
†The Speaker[102]	Leicester Square
†Mr Pigott[103]	Henrietta Street Cov[ent] Garden

Mr Pitt[104]	Arlington Street
†Mr Pleydell[105]	New Bond Street
†Mr Plumer[106]	Caven[dish] Square
†Mr Pollen[107]	Lincoln's Inn
†Mr Powis[108]	
†Mr Rolle[109]	Marlborough Street
†Sir J. Rustout[110]	Bloomsb[ury] Square
†Sir T. Sanderson[111]	
Mr Scawen[112]	St James's Square
Mr Selwyn }[113]	
Mr Selwyn }[114]	Cleveland Court
Mr Shepheard[115]	George Street
†Mr Shippen[116]	
Mr Spencer[117]	Hanover Square
Mr C. Stanhope[118]	Park Place
†Sir E. Stanley[119]	St James's Place
†Sir W. Stapleton[120]	Queen Street West[minster]
†Sir R. Sutton[121]	Gros[venor] Square
Mr Townshend[122]	Cleveland Court
Lord Tryconnel[123]	Arlington Street
†Mr Vane[124]	Gros[venor] Square
Mr V. Vernon[125]	Gros[venor] Square
Mr Vyner[126]	Conduit Street
Mr Waller[127]	Lincoln's Inn
Mr Edm[und] Waller[128]	Panton Square
†Lord Wallingford[129]	
†Sir W. Wentworth[130]	Clerges Street
†Mr Worsley[131]	Cavendish Square
†Mr Watkin William[132]	Downing Street
Mr York[133]	Norfolk Street

APPENDIX 2

Addresses Listed Topographically

Addresses	No. of MPs
A. *City and Environs*	
Coleman Street	1
Mark Lane	1
Stone Cutters Court	1
B. *Inns of Court*	
Grey's Inn	1
Lincoln's Inn	4
C. *The Strand and Covent Garden*	
Henrietta Street Covent Garden	1
King's Street Covent Garden	1
Norfolk Street	2
D. *Bloomsbury and High Holborn*	
Bloomsbury Square	1
Chancery Lane	1
Lincoln's Inn Fields	2
Tavistock Square	1
E. *Soho and Leicester Fields*	
Leicester Square	1
Marlborough Street	1
Soho Square	1
St Martin's Street	1
F. *North of Piccadilly*[134]	
Albemarle Street	1
Arlington Street	1
Brook Street	2
Cavendish Square	1
Burlington Street	2
Clarges Street	2
Conduit Street	2

Addresses	No. of MPs
Dover Street	3
George Street	2
Golden Square	4
New Bond Street	5
Old Bond Street	2
Poland Street	1
G. *Mayfair and Marylebone*	
Brook Street	1
Cavendish Square	1
Grosvenor Square	7
Grosvenor Street	2
Hanover Square	1
H. *South of Piccadilly (St James's)*	
Bernet St James's	1
Berry Street	1
Cleveland Court	2
Duke Street St James's	2
Pall Mall	4
Panton Square	1
Park Place	1
St James's Place	1
I. *Whitehall*	
Downing Street	2
George Street	1
Spring Gardens	1
Whitehall	1
J. *Westminster*	
Charles Street Westminster	1
Queen Street Westminster	1
K. *Elsewhere*	0

1. Clyve Jones, 'The London Topography of the Parliamentary Elite: Addresses for Peers and Bishops for 1706 and 1727–8', *London Topographical Record*, XXIX (2006), p. 43. In correspondence, the address of the sender at this time is usually no more than 'London'. A letter which gave the address as 'New Bond Street' (numbers of houses did not arrive until the late eighteenth century) is very unusual: National Library of Scotland, Saltoun papers, MS 16567, fo. 98: Alexander McMillan to Lord Milton, 3 March 1736.

2. An example is John Campbell, MP for Pembrokeshire 1727–47, who wrote to his young son Pryse that in future he should send all letters to his home address in Grosvenor Square: *The Correspondence of John Campbell MP with his Family, Henry Fox, Sir Robert Walpole and the Duke of Newcastle, 1734–1771*, ed. J. E. Davies, Parliamentary History Texts and Studies, 8 (Oxford, 2013), 13 March 1742. Sometimes MPs had their letters addressed to a nearby coffeehouse for collection by the MP; for example, National Library of Scotland, MS 115, fo. 63: ? to Alexander Abercomby, 'Glasgow Aprile 3d 1719':

   'To
   Captain Alexander Abercromby
   of Glasshaugh Member of
   parl[iamen]t. at old Mans Coffee
   house near Charing Cross
   London'.

   This system could cause problems if the recipient moved. For example, an anonymous correspondent wrote to Dr Colebatch, a fellow of Trinity College, Cambridge, that a letter had been 'left at the coffee house for me, I suppose by the gentleman you mention in it. I have removed to Westminster for the convenience of being near Parliament & so do not much frequent the Smyrna [probably the coffee house in Pall Mall, rather than the one in Cornhill] as I used, tho my letters are still directed thither': BL, Add. MS 22908, fo. 87: 11 December 1711. For the coffee houses mentioned here, see B. Lillywhite, *London Coffee Houses* (London, 1963), pp. 352, 420, 532.

3. Edited by Romney Sedgwick (2 vols, 1970) [hereafter cited as *HPC, 1715–54*].

4. This in contrast to the ongoing sections of *The History of Parliament: The House of Lords 1660–1715*, ed. Ruth Paley, where in some cases many addresses are given with dates: e.g., Lord Bruce, later 3rd Earl of Ailesbury, for whom nine addresses are given, seven of which are in London: Gerrard Street, by 1705–c. 1708; St James Square, c. 1708–c. 1710; Poland Street, c. 1710–14; Sackville Street, 1714–26; Warwick House, Warwick Street, 1726–47. See the unpublished biography of Bruce by Dr Charles Littleton, the copyright of which remains with The History of Parliament Trust.

5. It was found by Dr Charles Littleton of The History of Parliament section on the House of Lords, 1660–1832, and I would like to thank Dr Littleton for drawing it to my attention, and to thank the Wiltshire and Swindon History Centre [hereafter WSHS] for allowing me to publish the lobbying list.

6. For a study of the petitioning, see Clyve Jones, 'Lord Bruce and the Marlborough Election Petition in 1735: Aristocratic Lobbying of the House of Commons and a Blow against the Walpole Ministry', *Parliamentary History* (forthcoming).

7. It is also the only list not in Lord Bruce's hand, though the additional markings probably are in his hand. The original compiler of the list (possibly under Lord Bruce's direction) probably was one of the clerks of the House of Lords. The hand is a clerical one and it is known that such clerks compiled all sorts of lists (including lobbying lists) for members of the Lords to augment their income. See *History of Parliament. House of Commons 1660–1715*, ed. Eveline Cruickshanks, Stuart Handley and D. W. Hayton, 5 vols. (2002), [hereafter cited as *HPC 1660–1715*], I, pp. 23, 347.

8. WSHC, Ailesbury MSS, 9/34/17: Fra[ncis] Astry to Lord Bruce, 22 October 1733. This

letter clinches the address as the Warwick Street (a narrow lane) off Cockspur Street, and not the one in Soho north of Golden Square. In 1714, Bruce had lived in presumably rented accommodation in Poland Street and 'Piccadilly St James's London' before he purchased his house: WSHR, 1300/1437, 1422: S. Rolt to Bruce, 27 August 1714; John Fowler to Bruce, 5 October 1714.

9. *HPC 1660–1715*, II, p. 368.
10. For my reasoning for this date, see Jones, 'Lord Bruce and the Marlborough Election Petition'.
11. For details of my speculations concerning the dating and meaning of these lists, see Jones, 'Lord Bruce and the Marlborough Election Petition'.
12. Historical Manuscripts Commission, *Egmont Diary*, II, p. 167.
13. National Library of Scotland [hereafter cited as NLS], Saltoun Papers, MS 16572, fo. 90: to [Lord Milton], 23 May [1738]. For an example of the ownership of houses in London by Scottish peers, see Clyve Jones, 'The Financial Cost of being a Scottish Representative Peer in the Early Eighteenth Century: A Case Study of James Graham, the First Duke of Montrose' (forthcoming).
14. It has been known for some time, for example, that MPs from particular parts of England congregated in the same pubs or taverns while living in Westminster.
15. For details, see Jones, 'Lord Bruce and the Marlborough Election Petition'.
16. See note 1 above.
17. *The Letters of Philip Dormer Stanhope, 4th Earl of Chesterfield*, ed. Bonamy Dobree, 6 vols. (1932), II, pp. 287–90: Chesterfield to Lord Marchmont, 27 August 1734.
18. A Scottish legal title, held by Erskine as a lord of the court of session, which he had resigned when he stood for election to parliament.
19. NLS, Saltoun papers, MS 16564, fo. 158: Charles Campbell, MP for Argyllshire, to [Lord Milton, a judge of the court of session], 18 March 1736; *Journals of the House of Commons*, XXII, pp. 336–7, 418: 29 January, 17 March 1735; *HPC 1715–54*, I, p. 383.
20. The use of chairmen to deliver letters is comparable to the use by the Goldsmith's Company of messengers to warn shopkeepers of the loss of gold, silver and jewels, a service which was open to the public if they had similar losses. In the early 1740s, the fee for delivering a letter was 1s. See Judy Jowett, *The Warning Carriers: How Messengers of The Goldsmiths' Company Warned the Luxury Trades of Criminal Activities in Eighteenth-Century London, Silver Studies*, XVIII (2005), pp. 10, 13. (Thus Erskine's 400 letters would have cost £20 to deliver if the chairmen's fees were the same.)
21. The total on the new list is 96, but 12 of these were not given addresses, so the figures in this column are a percentage of the remaining 84.
22. For comparison, these figures have been taken from Clyve Jones, 'The First Printed "Directory" of British Politicians: A Note on the Residential Topography of Peers, Bishops and MPs in London in 1729', *London Topographical Record*, XXVIII (2001), p. 60, table 1. It should be remembered that here we are comparing figures for MPs from 1735 with figures for peers and bishop for 1729, so that no exact class comparison is being made.
23. Two MPs on the list, plus the extra one from elsewhere in the Ailesbury papers.
24. This area also includes the recent developments north of Oxford Street.
25. Where two or more streets of the same name existed, to avoid confusion, a location has been supplied where possible.
26. Those Whigs who only occasionally voted with the opposition (unlike the Whig opposition MPs who usually voted with the opposition). The identifications of these MPs (as well as Whig opposition MPs) have been taken from A. A. Hanham, 'Whig Opposition to Sir Robert Walpole in the House of Commons, 1727–1734' (University of Leicester , PhD thesis, 1992), pp. 401–17.

27. Lord Bruce's description of the list on the reverse side, followed by a list of five MPs and five peers, who, presumably, were involved in the lobbying of the MPs listed with their addresses below.

28. Probably Charles Monson, MP for Lincoln 1734–54 (W).

29. An Irish earl who sat in the Lords by right of his English peerage as 1st Lord Boyle of Marston.

30. Edward Harley, 2nd Earl of Oxford, was a friend of Lord Bruce; see Clyve Jones, 'Lord Bruce and the Marlborough Election Petition'.

31. A Scottish peer and distant relative of Bruce's. At Bruce's death in 1747, Kincardine's grandson succeeded to Bruce's Scottish title of the Earl of Elgin. He is probably listed as a lobbyist for the three Scottish MPs on Bruce's list, as was George Hamilton, MP, listed below.

32. Probably George Hamilton, the son of the 6th Earl of Abercorn (a Scottish peer), who had been elected an opposition Whig MP for Wells in the 1734 general election, but who was deprived of his seat by a petition carried on 25 March 1735 by a ministerial Whig majority in the Commons, the Prime Minister, Sir Robert Walpole, having actively intervened against him (*HPC 1715–54*, I, p. 318; II, pp. 100–1). Hamilton would have been very sympathetic to Bruce's case, as an opposition MP fighting the power of Walpole's ministry, and therefore a natural choice as a lobbyist for Bruce. Hamilton lost his seat three days before Bruce's triumph in defeating the petition against his candidates at Marlborough.

33. Sir John Kaye, 4th Baronet, MP for York 1734–43 (T).

34. Probably Earl Ker, eldest surviving son of 1st Duke of Roxburghe (one of the sixteen Scottish representative peers), who sat in the House of Lords by right of his British earldom created for his (deceased) elder brother (Earl Ker attended the House of Lords frequently in March 1735); or this could possibly be William Kerr (d. 1741), MP for Berwick-upon-Tweed until 1727, brother of 1st Duke of Roxburghe and a general in the army.

35. James Brydges (d. 1744), 1st Duke of Chandos.

36. Sir Justinian Isham, 5th Baronet, MP for Northamptonshire 1730–7 (T).

37. William Aislabie (c. 1690–1781), MP for Ripon 1721–81 (WO). The party allegiance of MPs comes from Hanham, 'Whig Opposition' (see above n. 26), and from *HPC 1715–54*, though this latter work is not entirely reliable. Also, occasionally the biographies are not clear as to the subject's party allegiance.

38. Edward Ashe (?1673–1748), MP for Heylesbury 1695–1747 (W).

39. Sir Walter Wagstaffe Bagot (1702–68), 2nd Baronet, MP for Newcastle-under-Lyme 1724–7, Staffordshire 1727–54, Oxford University 1762–8 (T).

40. Either John Banks (aft. 1691–1772), MP for Corfe Castle 1722–41 (T); or Jacob Banks (1704–38), MP for Christchurch 1726–7, Shaftesbury 1734–8 (T).

41. Nicholas Bayley (1709–82), MP for Anglesey 1734–41, 1747–61, 1770–4 (WO); elected with Tory support in 1734.

42. James Barry (1667–1748), 4th Earl of Barrymore [I], MP for Stockbridge 1710–13, 1714–15, Wigan 1715–27, 1734–47 (T). Irish peers were allowed to sit in the British House of Commons until the Anglo-Irish union of 1801.

43. Either Benjamin Bathurst (?1691–1767), MP for Cirencester 1713–27, Gloucester 1728–54, Monmouth 1754–67 (T); or the MP given in note 44.

44. Either the Hon. Benjamin Bathurst (1711–64), MP for Gloucestershire 1734–41, Cirencester 1754–61 (T); or the MP given in note 43.

45. Sir John Barnard (c. 1685–1764), MP for London 1722–61 (T).

46. Sir George Beaumont (?1664–1737), 4th Baronet, MP for Leicester 1702–37 (T).

47. Hon. George Berkeley (?1692–1746), MP for Dover 1720–34, Hedon 1734–41, 1742–6 (WO).

48. William Blackett (1707–77), Newcastle-upon-Tyne 1734–77 (T).
49. Daniel Boone (1710–70), MP for Lugershall 1734–41, Grampund 1741–7, Stockbridge 1747–54, Minehead 1754–61 (WO).
50. Ellerker Bradshaw (1660–1742), MP for Beverley 1727–9, 1734–41 (WI).
51. Either John Bristow (1701–68), MP for Bere Alston 1734–41, 1754–61, St Ives 1741–54, Arundel 1761–8 (W); or Robert Bristow (1688–1737), MP for Winchelsea 1708–37 (W).
52. Sir John Buckworth (1700–58), MP for Weobley 1734–41 (?WO).
53. Sir Roger Burgoyne (1710–78), 6th Baronet, MP for Bedfordshire 6 February 1735–47 (W; later WO).
54. There is no MP in 1735 with this name. However, the spellings of Carteret and Cartwright were interchangeable at this time (perhaps indicating that Cartwright was pronounces Carteret, or vice versa), so this probably is Thomas Cartwright (1671–1748), MP for Northamptonshire 1695–8, 1701–48 (T).
55. Lord James Cavendish (aft. 1673–1751), MP for Derby 1701–2, 1705–10, 1715–42 (WI).
56. William Richard Chetwynd (?1683–1770), MP for Stafford 1715–22, 1734–70, Plymouth 1723–7 (WO).
57. Sir Francis Child (c. 1684–1740), MP for London 1722–7, Middlesex 1727–40 (T).
58. Either Charles Chomondeley (1685–1756), MP for Cheshire 1710–15, 1722–56 (T); or Hon. James Cholmondeley (1708–75), MP for Bossiney 1731–4, Camelford 1734–41, Montgomery 1741–7 (W).
59. George Clerke (1661–1736), MP for Winchelsea 1702–5, East Looe 1705–8, Launceston 1711–13, Oxford University 1727–36 (T).
60. John Cockburn (c. 1679–1758), MP for Scotland 1707–8, Haddingtonshire 1708–41 (WO).
61. Hon. George Compton (1692–1758), MP for Tamworth 1727, Northampton 1727–54 (WO).
62. Henry Hyde (1710–53), Viscount Cornbury, MP for Oxford University 1732–51 (T). He was the heir of the Earl of Clarendon who used his father's courtesy title.
63. Either the Hon. John Cornwallis (1706–68), MP Eye 1727–47 (W); or the Hon. Stephen Cornwallis (1703–43), MP for Eye 1727–43 (W); they were brothers.
64. Sir Nathaniel Curzon, 4th Baronet, MP for Derbyshire 1727–54 (T).
65. This entry is from one of the other lists in the Bruce archive concerning the Marlborough election case (the one dated '9 March'); the only other list to have an address. There were three Brook Streets at the time: one in Holborn, one in north Wapping and one near Grosvenor Square in Mayfair. The latter is the most likely.
66. James Dawkin (?1696–1766), MP for New Woodstock 1734–47 (T).
67. Peter Delme (1710–70), MP for Ludgershall 1734–41, Southampton 1741–54 (WO).
68. Hon. Edward Digby (c. 1693–1746), MP for Warwickshire 1726–46 (T).
69. Either George Dodington (?1681–1754), MP for Weymouth and Melcombe Regis 1730–41, 1747–54 (W); or George Bubb Dodington (?1691–1762), MP for Winchelsea 1715–22, Bridgwater 1722–54, Weymouth and Melcombe Regis 1754–61 (W).
70. Henry Drax (?1693–1735), MP for Wareham 1718–22, 1734–48, 1751–5, Lyme Regis 1727–34 (WI).
71. Anthony Duncombe (c. 1695–1763), MP for Salisbury 1721–34, Downton 1734–47 (WI).
72. Richard Evans (d. 1762), MP for Queensborough 1729–54 (W).
73. John Evelyn (1706–67), MP for Helston 1727–41, 1747–67, Penryn 1741–7 (W), great-grandson of the famous diarist.
74. Nicholas Fazakerley (?1686–1767), MP for Preston (T).
75. Nicholas Fenwick (c. 1693–1752), MP for Newcastle-upon-Tyne 1727–47 (T).
76. One of five members of the Finch family: Hon. Edward (?1697–1771), MP for Cambridge University 1727–68, envoy to Sweden 1728–39 (so probably not available to support Bruce) (W); Hon. Henry (?1694–1761), MP for Malton 1724–61 (W); Hon. John (?1689–1740), MP for Maidstone 1722–40 (T); Hon. John (?1692–1763), MP for Higham

Ferrers 1724–41, Rutland 1741–7 (WO); William (1691–1766), MP for Cockermouth 1727–54, Bewdley 1755–61 (WO).

77. One of three members of the Foley family: Edward (1676–1747), MP for Droitwich 1701–11, 1732–41(T); Thomas ((?1670–1737), MP for Weobley 1691–1700, Hereford 1701–22, Stafford 1722–7, 1734–7 (T); Thomas (?1695–1749), MP for Hereford 1734–41, Herefordshire 1742–7 (T).

78. William Forester (1690–1758), MP for Wenlock (W).

79. Either Theophilus (c. 1707–46), MP for Barnstable 1727–41, Devon 1741–6 (WO); or William (1687–1749), MP for Newport Isle of Wight 1727–36 (W).

80. One of three members of the Fox family: George (c. 1690–1773), MP for Hindon 1734–41, York 1742–61 (T); Henry (1705–74), MP for Hindon 28 February 1735–41, Windsor 1741–61, Dunwich 1761–3 (W); Stephen (1704–76), MP for Shaftesbury 1726–34, 20 February 1735–41, Hindon 1734–28 February 1735 (W).

81. Thomas Gage (c. 1695–1754), cr. Viscount [I] 1720, MP for Minehead April–May 1717, Tewkesbury 1721–54 (WI).

82. Henry Gough (1681–1751), MP for Bramber 1734–51 (W).

83. Either Hon. Baptist Levenson Gower (?1703–82), MP for Newcastle-under-Lyme 1727–61 (T); or Hon. William (c. 1696–1756), MP for Staffordshire 1720–56 (T).

84. Richard Grenville (1711–79), MP for Buckingham 1734–41, 1747–52, Buckinghamshire 1741–7 (WO).

85. John Griffith (?1687–1739), MP for Caernarvonshire 1715–39 (W).

86. Thomas Hanmer (c. 1702–37), MP for Castle Rising 1734–7 (T?); or possibly Richard Hanmer (WI).

87. One of five Herbert MPs: Henry Arthur (c. 1703–72), MP for Bletchingley 1724–7, Ludlow 1727–43 (W); Richard (1704–54), MP for Ludlow 1727–41, 1743–54 (W); Hon. Robert Sawyer (1693–1769), MP for Wilton 1722–68 (W); Hon. Thomas (c. 1695–1739), MP for Newport 1726–39 (W); Hon. William (c. 1696–1757), MP for Wilton 1734–57 (W).

88. Hon. Thomas Hervey (1690–1773), MP for Bury St Edmunds 1733–47 (W).

89. Edward Hooper (?1701–95), MP for Christchurch 1734–48 (W).

90. Henry Hoare (1705–85), MP for Salisbury 1734–41 (T).

91. Sir Joseph Jekyll (c. 1662–1738), MP for Rye 1697–1713, Lymington 1713–22, Reigate 1722–38 (WI), Master of the Rolls 1717–38.

92. Henry Lambton (1697–1761), MP for Durham 1734–61 (W).

93. Edmund Lechmere (1710–1895), MP for Worcestershire 1734–47 (T).

94. Charles Sackville (1711–69), Earl of Middlesex, first son of 1st Duke of Dorset, MP for East Grinstead 1734–42, 1761–5, Sussex 1742–7, Old Sarum 1747–54 (W), succeeded as 2nd Duke of Dorset 1765. Lord Middlesex was his father's courtesy title.

95. Charles Monson (?1695–1764), MP for Lincoln 1734–54 (W).

96. Charles Montagu (aft. 1695–1750), MP for Westminster 1722–7, St Germans 1734–41, Camelford 1741–7, Northampton 1754–9 (W).

97. Sir Richard Munro (1684–1746), 6th Baronet, MP for Taun Burghs 1710–41 (W).

98. John Murray (d. 1753), MP for Linlithgow Burghs 1725–34, Selkirkshire 1734–53 (WO).

99. Michael Newton (c. 1695–1743), MP for Beverley 1722–7, Grantham 1727–43 (T/WO?).

100. Either Hon. James Noel (1711–52), MP for Rutland 1734–52 (T); Thomas Noel (c. 1704–88), MP for Rutland 1728–41, 1753–88 (WO); or William Noel (1695–1762), MP for Stamford 1722–47, West Looe 1747–57 (WO).

101. See note 100 above.

102. Arthur Onslow (1692–1768), MP for Guildford 1720–7, Surrey 1727–61 (W), Speaker of the House of Commons 1728–61.

103. Robert Pigott (1664–1746), MP for Huntingdonshire 1713–22, 1730–41 (WI).

104. Either John Pitt (?1706–87), MP for Wareham 1734–47, 1761–8, Dorchester 1751–61

(T); Thomas Pitt (c. 1705–61), MP for Okehampton 1727–54, Old Sarum 1754–61 (WI); or William Pitt the Elder (1708–78), MP for Old Sarum 18 February 1735–47, and later four other constituencies to 1766 (WO).

105. Edmund Morton Pleydell (?1693–1754), MP for Dorchester 1722–3, Dorset 1727–47 (T).

106. One of three brothers: Richard Plumer (c. 1689–1750), MP for Lichfield 1722–34; St Mawes 1734–41, Aldeburgh 1741–7, Weymouth and Melcombe Regis 1747–51 (WO); Walter Plumer (?1682–1746), MP for Aldeburgh 1719–27, Appleby 1730–41 ((W); or William Plumer (?1686–1767), MP for Yarmouth, Isle of Wight 1721–2, Hertfordshire 1734–41, 1755–61 (W).

107. John Pollen (?1702–75), MP for Andover 1734–54 (W).

108. Richard Powys (c. 1707–43), MP for Orford 1734–41 (T).

109. Henry Rolle (1708–50), MP for Devon 1730–43, Barnstable 1741–8 (T).

110. Sir John Rushout (1685–2775), 4th Baronet, MP for Malmesbury 1713–22, Evesham 1722–68 (WO).

111. Hon. Sir Thomas Saunderson (c. 1691–1752) (born Thomas Lumley, son of the 1st Earl of Scarbrough, in 1723 he changed his name to Saunderson on inheriting the estates of his cousin 1st Earl of Castleton [I], KB 1725, MP for Arundel 1722–7, Lincolnshire 1727–40 (WO).

112. Thomas Scawen (d. 1774), MP for Surrey 1727–41 (WO).

113. John Selwyn (1688–1751), MP for Truro 1715–21, Whitchurch 1727–34, Gloucester 1734–51 (W).

114. John Selwynn (c. 1709–51), son of the above, MP for Whitchurch 1734–51 (W).

115. Samuel Shepheard (d.1748), MP for Malmesbury 1701, Cambridge 1708–22, 1747–8, Cambridgeshire 1724–47 (WO) or James Shepherd (WI).

116. William Shippen (1673–43), MP for Bramber 1707–9, 1710–13, Saltash 1713–15, Newton 1715–43 (T).

117. Hon. John Spencer (1708–46), MP for New Woodstock 1732–46 (W).

118. Either Charles Stanhope (1673–1760), MP for Milborne Port 1717–22, Aldborough 1722–34, Harwich 1734–41 (W); or Hon. Charles Stanhope (1708–36), MP for Derby 1720–36 (WO).

119. Sir Edward Stanley (1689–1776), 5th Baronet, MP for Lancashire 1727–36 (WO).

120. Sir William Stapleton (?1698–1740), 4th Baronet, MP for Oxfordshire 1727–40 (T).

121. There is no MP called E. Sutton at this time, so the 'E' may be a mistake for an 'R', in which case it would have been Sir Robert Sutton (?1671–1746), MP for Nottinghamshire 1722–32, Great Grimsby 1734–41 (W).

122. Hon. Thomas Townshend (1701–80), MP for Winchelsea 1722–7, Cambridge University 1727–74 (W).

123. Sir John Brownlow (1690–1754), 5th Baronet, cr. Viscount Tyrconnel [I] in 1718, MP for Grantham 1713–15, 1722–41, Lincolnshire 1715–22 (W/WO).

124. Hon. Henry Vane (c. 1705–58), MP for Launceston 1726–7, St Mawes 1727–41, Ripon 1741–7, Durham Co. 1747–53 (WO).

125. George Venables Vernon (1710–80), MP for Lichfield 1731–47, Derby 1754–62 (T).

126. Robert Vyner (c. 1685–1777), MP for Great Grimsby 1710–13, Lincolnshire 1724–61 (WO).

127. Harry Waller (c. 1720–72), MP for Chipping Wycombe 1726–47 (WO).

128. Edmund Waller (c. 1699–1771), MP for Great Marlow 1722–41, Chipping Wycombe 1741–54 (WO); brother of the above.

129. William Knollys (1694–1740), Viscount Wallingford, MP for Banbury 1733–40 (W?); son of the titular Earl of Banbury (who failed on several occasions to claim the title), he had incorrectly assumed his father's courtesy title.

130. Sir William Wentworth (1686–1763), 4th Baronet, MP for Malton 1731–41 (WI).

131. James Worsley (?1671–1756), MP for Newtown, Isle of Wight 1695–1701, 1705–22, 1727–9, 1734–41 (T).
132. Watkins Williams Wynn (?1693–1749), MP for Denbighshire 1716–41, 1742–9, Montgomeryshire 1741–2 (T); he had assumed the name Wynn in 1719 upon inheriting estates from a distant kinsman.
133. John Yorke (1685–1757), MP for Richmond 1710–13, 1717–27, 1728–57 (WI).
134. Including north of Oxford Street.

VII. ARCHES OF TRIUMPH: JAMES VI AND I'S (UNFORTUNATE) CEREMONIAL ENTRY INTO THE CITY OF LONDON, 1604

By ANN SAUNDERS

Q UEEN ELIZABETH died on the morning of 24 March 1603; she was succeeded by her nephew, James, King of Scotland; his mother Mary, Queen of Scots, had been beheaded on 18 February 1587. James was now James VI and I, ruler of two domains; preparations were made as quickly as possible for the long journey south and the court set out on 4 April, leaving his Queen, Anna of Denmark, to follow with their eldest son Henry and four-year-old Elizabeth; their second son Charles, being delicate, remained in Dunfermline in the care of the Lord President, Lord Fyvie and his wife.

James travelled slowly, to allow time for Elizabeth's funeral to take place on 28 April. His appearance in the capital aroused the greatest excitement and crowds followed him wherever he went. Unfortunately, his temperament was very different from that of his great predecessor — however tired she was, Elizabeth had always smiled on the cheering crowds; James, after the first few occasions, did not — his way was to make it all too obvious that he preferred to be followed with silent respect. He was crowned on 25 July 1603 in Westminster Abbey, but with little ceremony since he went directly from St James's Palace to the abbey without the expected formal royal procession through the city, where there was an outbreak of plague.

Preparations for such a procession had been under way since April, when five triumphal arches began to be prepared. Nevertheless, work on all five arches continued until 24 August and that on 'Londinium' (Fig. 4) into October. Plans then appear to have changed and sites for seven arches were laid out, the two additional ones perhaps being those built and paid for by the Italians (Fig. 7) and the Dutchmen or 'Belgians' (Fig. 9), while the citizens paid for the other five by means of a levy on all the livery companies. Both groups of strangers would have wished to express their loyalty and assure their continued presence in the city. All seven were ready for King James's entry into and passage through the city on 15 March 1604. The prefabricated structures, between 40 and 70 feet high, were presumably set up shortly before the appointed day and dismantled soon afterwards (Fig. 19). In his descriptions of the designs Harrison referred to the structures as Arches, Devices and Pegmes, the last term denoting frameworks or stages of a type used in theatrical displays or pageants, such as this Entertainment, as the event came commonly to be described.

On leaving the Tower between eleven and twelve o'clock on 15 March King James first encountered 300 children from Christ's Hospital placed on a scaffold constructed in the churchyard of All Hallows Barking near the Tower (see Fig. 19). The king's entry proper took place at 'Londinium', the first of the seven arches and set up in Fenchurch Street, where he was welcomed by a striking representation of the city, the music of the City Waits and joyous speeches, emphasising the occasion as a formal royal entry or *joyeuse entrée* (Fig. 4). Next was the arch erected by the Italians in Gracechurch Street (Fig. 7). The third arch was that of the Dutchmen in Cornhill, appropriately near the Royal Exchange (Fig. 10). The fourth, celebrating the unity of the two kingdoms, was at the east end of Cheapside (Fig. 11). At the Great Cross, halfway along Cheapside, where James's succession had been proclaimed, the City Recorder, Aldermen, City Chamberlain, Town Clerk, and Common Council met the king and presented him with three gold cups. The Fifth arch, celebrating peace and prosperity, was at the west end of the street (Fig. 13). King James then progressed via Newgate to the Sixth arch, erected in Fleet Street (Fig. 15). He left the City at the Seventh, close to Temple Bar (Fig. 17).

The postponement proved disastrous. Instead of the fine weather as might have reasonably been expected in the previous July, the middle of March proved bitterly cold and wet. James did not react as the late Queen would have done whatever the weather; the new monarch, loathing the pressure of the crowds, turned irritable, refusing to listen to the flowery speeches in his honour and pressing on as fast as he could to the end. The ordeal on 15 March still lasted five hours and both King and Londoners were cold, wet and disgruntled.

The playwrights Thomas Dekker, Ben Jonson and Thomas Middleton were responsible for the thematic content and the songs and speeches of this royal entertainment. The City entrusted the architectural design and the execution of five arches to Stephen Harrison, joiner, who supervised a workforce of more than 250 craftsmen. Harrison's role in relation to the Italian and Dutch arches is less clear. Both communities of strangers paid for their arches. The Italians also designed theirs but probably entrusted its construction to Harrison, while the Dutch appear to have entrusted both design and construction to him. Jonson published an account of this Entertainment on 19 March 1604 and Dekker another one shortly afterwards, with another edition in the same year. About that time Harrison conceived the idea of publishing, as a 'perpetuall monument', a book of his designs with accompanying texts; the latter were largely derived from Jonson's and Dekker's works but with valuable architectural and other descriptions of his own. William Kip was working on the engravings by 2 April and in May the City decided to reward Harrison for the book, which was to be kept by the City Chamberlain. Publication was probably on 16 June 1604, the date of Harrison's dedication to the Lord Mayor.

Harrison, evidently a talented and learned designer, is known only from this publication, where he styles himself 'Joyner and Architect', and for work as a joiner at Syon house in 1604–5. The seven arches are presented as architectural designs rather than illustrations and represent the most extensive use of arches in English civic pageantry up to that date. For the most part of 'Flemish mannerist' character, with the Italian arch being the most purely classical, they identify Harrison as a pioneer in the use of classicist principles of modular proportions and musical harmonies. This presumably reflects his collaboration with the dramatists, especially Jonson who worked with Harrison well before he began his better-known association with Inigo Jones. Harrison's designs for the arches have been claimed as an important step towards Jones's design for the Whitehall Banqueting House of 1619.

I have provided no more than brief descriptions of the arches, but you may read Stephen Harrison's own account of his remarkable achievement, which includes some material from Dekker and Jonson.

Additional Notes on the figures

Fig 1. The note at the bottom, 'Are to be sould at the white horse in Popes head Alley, by John Sudbury and George Humble', is an addition to the original plate of 1604 (modern style) and indicates that this impression was made c.1613. The original edition was sold from Harrison's house in Lime Street 'at the signe of the snayle' (see Fig. 19).

Fig. 2. The dedication is dated 16 June 1604, probably the date of publication.

Fig. 3. The arms are those of King James and the City of London.

Fig. 4. The arch occupied the full width of the street and leaned against the east end of the church of St Gabriel. Music was played from the galleries over the two arches of the gate. The dominant message is in the upper central panel, where the Monarchy of Britain is supported by Divine Wisdom and six of the female virtues of the city.

Fig. 6. The speeches were delivered as if by figures on the arch representing the Genius of the City and the Thames.

Fig. 7. The arch occupied the full width of the street and was probably close to the junction of Lombard Street, a locality where the Italians traditionally congregated. The pure classicism of the design presumably reflected its 'invention' by the Italians. Representative Italians are visible within two small galleries under the arch. Their speech was delivered in Latin.

Fig. 9.   The arch of the Dutchmen or 'Belgians' occupied the full width of
           Cornhill, near the Royal Exchange. Their speech, translated in Fig.
           10, was given by a boy in Latin. Dominant themes are the unity of
           the Seventeen Provinces, the importance of true religion and the
           protection that the English monarch had afforded to the Protestant
           refugees, along with husbandry and fishing.

Fig. 11.   'New Arabia Felix' was erected 'above' the Great Conduit at the
           east end of Cheapside. Dekker's account indicates that it was
           situated a short distance to the west of the Conduit at the end of
           Soper Lane. The arch celebrated the arrival of James by imagining
           the whole island of Britain as a new Arabia Felix, in Classical times
           the most fertile, fragrant and prosperous of the three parts of
           Arabia. The four speakers spoke from the balustraded stage at the
           top of the main structure.

Fig. 13.   The 'Garden of Plentie', which backed on to the Little Conduit at
           the west end of Cheapside, was in the form of a summer arbour
           and celebrated fertility, peace, plenty, the sciences and the arts.

Fig 15.   The 'New World', erected 'above' the conduit in Fleet Street and
           occupying the full width of the street. The conduit stood in Fleet
           Street at the south end of Shoe Lane and the arch was probably
           situated a short distance to the west of it. The arch celebrates the
           globe; the four elements; justice, virtue and fortune; envy; the four
           virtues; and the four kingdoms over which James claimed to rule.

Fig. 17.   A Temple of Janus, the god of gates, close to the gate at Temple
           Bar, where King James left the city shortly before 5 pm. The
           decoration of the arch emphasised peace and liberty. Genius
           (representing the City) and a Flamin (high priest) delivered
           speeches. One of the themes of the Entertainment as a whole
           concerned the wisdom of the ruler. The proximity of this Temple
           to the Round Church within the Temple precinct nearby was
           almost certainly an allusion to Solomon and to English laws. Ben
           Jonson provides a copy of the speech which King James made 'in
           the Strand' in response to these last presentations.

Fig. 19.   Harrison explains that, in publishing the drawings of these now
           dismantled 'great Triumphal bodies', he aims to preserve them as
           'perpetuall monuments'. He also provides further details of the
           'Entertainment' and its timing, organisation, and financing.

Fig. 20.   The inscription appears to read: 'John Sanderson oneth this book
           lost [?] 2. 6.d', but the latter part is obscure. The same hand may have
           been responsible for identifications (now partly cut away) on several
           of the designs in the set belonging to the Society of Antiquaries.

Bibliographical Note

Copies of *The Arch's of Trivmph* survive in several libraries in England and the United States, but many of them are incomplete and with the folios, which were unnumbered in the original edition, out of order. They usually survive as sets of trimmed folios, measuring about 16 inches by 12 inches, mounted and bound by later collectors. There are two versions of the title page, one for the 1604 edition (ESCT S122021) and another with an addition which dates it to *c.*1613 (ESCT S92869). So far as it is possible to tell (given that collectors have been more interested in the designs than the text) the later edition comprised the title page and the designs, but not the text. The designs reproduced here are from the mounted set in BM, Prints and Drawings, 166.d.1*, where the title page is of *c.*1613 and the designs are out of order. The texts are reproduced from the mounted set at the Society of Antiquaries of London, Harley Collection vol. 5, fols 1–17 (shelfmark 196h), where the title page is that of 1604 and the designs and texts are out of order (but not in the same order as in the BM copy). The images are presented in their original order (where designs appeared on versos and texts on the facing rectos, with the 'Odes' of Fig. 3 on a verso), as indicated by internal evidence (including the printer's sigla) and by reference to the well-ordered mounted set from the collection of Thomas Grenville, which includes the 1604 title page (BL, G.10866). The set of reproductions presented here omits the blank pages.

Good accounts of Harrison and his publication (including an edition of 1662), along with additional bibliography, are to be found in the article on him by Eileen Harris in *Oxford Dictionary of National Biography,* Oxford University Press, 2004 [http://o-www.oxforddnb.com.catalogue.ulrls.lon.ac.uk/view/article/12445, accessed 27 Feb 2015] and in her *British architectural books and writers, 1556–1785* (Cambridge, 1990), pp. 229–31. G. Parry, *The Golden Age Restor'd: the Culture of the Stuart Court* (Manchester, 1981), pp. 2–24 and D. M. Bergeron, 'King James's Civic Pageant and Parliamentary Speech in March 1604', *Albion* 34 (2002), pp. 213–31 describe the entertainment and analyse its political and symbolic meanings. The relevant works of Dekker and Jonson are:

T. Dekker, *The Magnificent Entertainment: giuen to King Iames, Queene Anne his wife, and Henry Frederick the Prince, vpon the day of his Maiesties tryumphant passage from the Tower through his honourable citie and chamber of London, being the 15. of March. 1603. As well by the English as by the strangers: with the speeches and songes, deliuered in the seuerall pageants* (London, 1604: two impressions)

B. Jon[son], *His Part of King James his Royall and Magnificent Entertainement through his Honorable Cittie of London Thurseday The 15. of March 1603 [O.S.]. So much as was presented in the first and last of their Triumphall Arch's. With his speach made to the last Presentation in the Strand ... Also, a brief panegyre of his Majesties first and well auspicated entrance to his high Court of Parliament on Monday, the 19. of the same Moneth. With other additions* (London, 1604).

Table

Incidence of figures and blank folios in the seventeen unnumbered folios of the text published in 1604.

recto	verso	recto	verso	recto	verso
Fig. 1	blank	blank	Fig. 9	blank	Fig. 15
Fig. 2	Fig. 3	Fig. 10	blank	Fig. 16	blank
blank	Fig. 4	blank	Fig. 11	blank	Fig. 17
Fig. 5	Fig. 6	Fig. 12	blank	Fig. 18	blank
blank	Fig. 7	blank	Fig. 13	Fig. 19	blank
Fig. 8	blank	Fig. 14	blank		

Acknowledgements

The author is most grateful to Derek Keene for his major contribution towards the development of this work.

The London Topographical Society is grateful to the British Museum Department of Prints and Drawings and to the Society of Antiquaries of London for providing photographs of the following images in their collections and granting permission to publish them:

British Museum, Prints and Drawings, 166.d1*, fols 1 (Fig. 1), 2 (Fig. 17), 3 (Fig. 9), 4 (Fig. 7), 5 (Fig. 11), 6 (Fig. 4), 7 (Fig. 15), 8 (Fig. 13).

Society of Antiquaries, Harley Collection, vol. 5 (shelfmark 196h), fols 2 (Fig. 19), 2ᵛ (Fig. 20), 3 (Fig 2), 3ᵛ (Fig. 3), 4 (Fig. 18), 6 (Fig. 14), 7 (13), 8 (Fig. 16), 10 (Fig. 10), 12 (Fig. 12), 14 (Fig. 5), 14ᵛ (Fig. 6), 16 (Fig. 8).

Particular help was given by Adrian James, Assistant Librarian at the Society of Antiquaries of London.

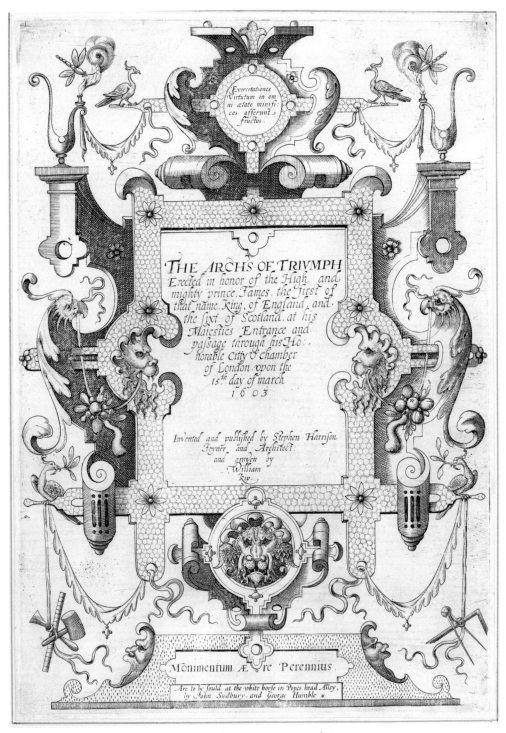

Fig. 1   Title page, *c.*1613 edition

TO THE RIGHT HONORABLE

SIR THOMAS BENNET KNIGHT, LORD
MAIOR OF *THIS CITIE*, *THE RIGHT* WORSIP-
full the Aldermen his Brethren, and to those VVorshipfull
Commoners, elected Committies, for the Mana-
ging of this Businesse.

HE loue which I beare to your *Honour* and VVorships : and the duty wherewith I am bound to this honourable Citie, makes me appeare in this boldnesse to you; To whome I humbly Consecrate these fruites of my inuention, which *Time* hath nowe at length brought foorth, and ripened to this perfection. That Magnificent *Royalty*, and glorious Entertainement, which you your selues for your part, out of a free, a cleare, and verie bounteous disposition, and so many thousands of woorthie Citizens, out of a sincere affection and loyalty of his Maiestie, did with the sparing of no cost, bestowe but vpon one day, is here newe wrought vp againe, and shall endure for euer. For albeit those Monuments of your *Loues* were erected vp to the Cloudes, and were built neuer so strongly, yet now their lastningnes should liue but in the tongues and memories of men : But that the hand of Arte giues them here a second more perfect beeing, aduaunceth them higher then they were before, and warrants them that they shall doe honour to this Citie, so long as the Citie shall beare a name. Sory I am that they come into the world no sooner : but let the hardnesse of the labour, and the small number of handes, that were busied about them, make the faulte (if it bee a faulte) excusable. I would not care if these vnpainted *Pictures* were more Costly to me, so that they might appeare curious enough to your Lordship and VVorships; yet in regard, that this present Age can lay before you no President that euer any in this land performed the like, I presume these my endeuours shall receiue the more worthie liking of you. And thus Dedicating my Labours and Loue to your honourable and kinde Acceptations, I most humbly take my leaue, this 16 of *Iune* 1604.

Most affectionately deuoted to your
Lordship and Worships,

Stephen Harrison.

B.

Fig. 2   Dedication to the Lord Mayor

Babell that stroue to weare
A Crowne of Cloudes, and vp did reare
 her forehead hye,
With an ambitious lust to kisse the skie,
Is now or dust, or not at all,
 proud Nymrods wall,
And all his Antique monuments,
Left to the world as presidents,
Cannot now shew (to tell where they did stand,)
So much in length as halfe the Builders hand.

The Mansolæan tombe;
The sixteene curious gates in Rome,
 which times preferre,
Both past and present : Neroes Theater,
That in one day was all gilt o're :
 Ad to these more,
Those Columnes, and those Pyramids, that won
Wonder by height : the Colosse of the Sun :
Th'Ægyptian Obelisks : are all forgotten :
Onely their names grow great : themselues be rotten.

Deare friend! what honour then
Bestow'st thou on thy Country men?
 Crowning with praise,
By these thy labors, (as with wreathes of bayes)
this royall City : where now stand,
 (built by thy hand)
Her Arches in new state, so made,
That their fresh beauties n'ere shall fade :
Thou of our English Triumphes rear'st the Fame,
Boue those of old; But aboue all, thy name.

 Tho. Dekker.

Ode.

Triumphes were wont with swet and bloud bee crown'd :
 To euery brow
 They did allow,
The liuing Laurer which begirded round
Their rusty Helmets, and had power to make
The Souldier smile, while mortall wound did ake.

But our more ciuill passages of state
 (like happy feast
 of In'-urd rest
Which bels and woundlesse Canons did relate,)
Stood high in Ioy : since warlike Triumphes bring,
Remembrance of our former sorrowing.

The memory of these should quickly fade,
 (for pleasures streame
 is like a dreame.
Passant and fleet as is a shade,)
Vnlesse thy selfe which these faire Models bred,
Had giuen them a new life when they were dead.

Take then (good Country man and friend) that merit,
 which folly lends.
 (not iudgement sends,)
To forraine shores for strangers to inherit:
Perfection must be bold with front vpright,
Though Enuy gnash her teeth whilst she would bite.

 Ioh. Webster.

Fig. 3   Odes by Thomas Dekker and John Webster

Fig. 4   First arch, Londinium, in Fenchurch Street

The Deuice called Londinium.

THefe fiue Triumphall Arches *were firft taken in hand in the beginning of Aprill* 1603. *prefently after his Maiefty was proclaimed. It being expected that his paſſage would haue bene through his honourable City and Chamber to his* Coronation *vpon Saint Iames his day following : But by reaſon of the ſickneſſe, it pleaſed his Maieſtie to be ſolemnely Crowned at* Weſtminster *, without ſight of theſe Triumphs : Notwithſtanding the buſineſſe being ſet on foote, went on with all expedition ; till Bartholmew-tide, and then ceaſed becauſe of the great mortalitie,* 40. *dayes more was giuen for preparing of this Triumphall Arch . In which time, the ſtreetes for that purpoſe were diligently ſurueyed, heights, breadts and diſtances taken, as it were to make Fortifications for the Solemnities : Seuen peeces of ground, like ſo many fields for a battell) were plotted forth, vpon which theſe Triumphes ſhould be erected : The gladſome and long-deſired Morning at length is come, In which the Streetes ſeeme to bee paued with people, that in heapes flocke together, to behold their proud heads that were aduanced in this manner.*

 THE firſt *Pegme* was erected in *Fanchurch-ſtreete,* the backe of it ſo leaning on the Eaſt ende of the Church, that it ouer-ſpread the whole ſtreete. And thus we deſcribe it.

It was a *Flat-ſquare,* builded vpright : the *Perpendicular-line* of the whole *Frame,* (that is to ſay, the diſtance from the bottome to the top,) as the *Ground-line,* is (alſo in this, ſo in all the reſt) to be found out and tried by the *Scale,* diuided by 1. 2. 3. 4. and 5. and ſet at the lower end of the Peece : By which figures feete are repreſented : So that in all the deſcriptions, where mention is to bee made of *Heights , Breadths ,* or any other Commenſurable proportions , you ſhall find them left thus — with a blancke, becauſe we wiſh you rather to apply them to the Scale your ſelfe, then by ſetting them downe, to call either your ſkill or iudgement in queſtion.

And note withall, that the *Ground-plot* hath not the ſame *Scale* which the vpright hath, for of the two *Scales,* which you ſee annexed, the *Leſſer* is of the *Ground,* and ſtandeth in the *Ground-plot,* the *Greater,* for the *Edifice* or *Building* it ſelfe.

This Gate of *Paſſage,* then (into which his Maieſty made his firſt entrance) was deriued from the *Tuſcana* (beeing the principal pillar of thoſe 5 vpon which the *Noble Frame of Architecture* doth ſtand,) for the *Tuſcane Columne* is the ſtrongeſt & moſt worthy to ſupport ſo famous a Worke, as this *Fabricke* was, conſidering that vpon his *Ruſticke Pillars,* the goodlieſt *Houſes, Turrets, Steeples &c.* within this City, were to be borne : And thoſe Models, ſtood as a *Coronet* on the forehead or Battlements of this *Great* and *Magnificent Edifice.*

The cheekes or ſides of the Gate, were (as it were) doubly guarded with the Portraitures of *Atlas* King of *Mauritania,* who (according to his owne ſhortneſſe and thickneſſe) from the *Symetry* of his foote, cauſed a pillar to be made, whoſe height with *Baſe* and *Capitall* was 6. times the thickneſſe in height. And ſo is this of ours, bearing the name of *Tuſcans,* as we ſayd before, and reaching to the very point of the Arch, from whence wee did deriue *Dorica* which bore vp the *Architine, Frize,* and *Coronixe,* and was garniſhed with *Corbels* or *Croxtels* fitting ſuch worke, beſides the beauty of *Pyramids, Beaſts, Water, Tables,* and many other inrichments, which you may find expreſt in the Peece it ſelfe.

From a Gallery directly ouer the gate, the ſound of loud Muſicke (being the *Waites* and *Hault-boyes* of the City) was ſent forth.

At the foot of the Battlemēts was in *Capitall* letters inſcribed this word *Londinium,* & beneath that, theſe words *Camera Regis.*

In this *Pegme* or *Arch Triumphall,* were placed 12. perſonages, of which ſhe that had the preeminence to ſit higheſt, was cald *Monarchia Britannica.*

At her feete ſate Diuine *Wiſedome.*

On her right hand ſate three of the daughters { *Veneration,* } On her left, the other three, viz. { *Gladneſſe,* *Promptitude,* } { *Louing Affection,* of *Genius Vrbis,* whoſe names were { *Vigilance :* } { *Vnanimitie.*

Beneath all theſe ſtood the *Genius* of the Citty, richly attirde, being ſupported on the right hand by a perſon figuring *The Councell of the City,* and on the left by a perſon figuring the *Warlike force of the City.*

Directly vnder theſe, in an *Abacke* thruſt out before the reſt, lay *Thameſis* the Riuer, leaning his Arme vpon a *Gourde,* out of which, water with liue fiſhes were ſeene to runne forth, and play about him.

The ſpeakers were onely *Thameſis* and *Genius,* who vttered theſe ſpeeches following on the other ſide.

C. THE

Fig. 5 Description of Londinium

The ſpeeches of Gratulation.

GENIVS.

Ime, Fate, and Fortune haue at length conſpir'd,
To giue our Age the day ſo much deſir'd. (yeares,
What all the minute ..., weekes, moneths, and
That hang in file vpon ... ſiluer haires,
Could not produce, beneath the Britane ſtroke,
The Roman, Saxon, Dane, and Norman yoke,
his point of Time hath done. Now London reare
thy forehead high, and on it ſtriue to weare
thy choiceſt Gems: Teach thy ſteepe Towers to riſe
higher with people: Set with ſparkling eyes
thy ſpacious windowes: and in euery ſtreete,
let thronging Ioy, Loue, and Amazement meete.
Cleaue all the aire with ſhowtes, and let the cry
ſtrike through as long, and vniuerſally
as thunder; For, thou now art bliſt to ſee
That ſight, for which thou didſt beginne to be.
When Brutus plough firſt gaue thee infant bounds,
And I, thy GENIVS walk't auſpicious rounds
In euery furrow; Then did I forelooke,
And ſaw this day mark't white in Clotho's booke.
The ſeuerall Circles, both of change and ſway,
within this Iſle, there alſo figur'd lay:
Of which the greateſt, perfecteſt, and laſt
was this, whoſe preſent happineſſe we taſte.
why keepe you ſilence Daughters? What dull peace
Is this inhabites you? Shall office ceaſe
In th'aſpect of him, to whom you owe
More then you are, or can be? Shall TIME knowe,
his Article, wherein your flame ſtood ſtill,
And not aſpir'd? N... heauen auert an ill
That blacke looke. Ere pauſe poſſeſſe your breaſts
Wiſh you more of Plagues: "Zeale when it reſts,
Turnes to be ague. Vp thou tame RIVER, wake,
And from thy liquid limbes this ſlumber ſhake:
Thou drown'ſt thy ſelfe in inofficious ſleepe;
And theſe thy ſluggiſh waters ſeeme to creepe,
Rather then flow. Vp, riſe, and ſwell with pride
Aboue thy bankes. "Now is not euery Tyde,

THAMESIS.

To what vaine end ſhould I contend to ſhow
My weaker powers, when Seas of pompe o'reflow
The Citties face: and couer all the ſhore
With ſands more rich than Tagus wealthy ore?
When in the flood of Ioy, that comes with him,
He drownes the world; yet makes it liue and ſwimme,
And ſpring with gladneſſe: Not my fiſhes heere,
Though they be dumbe, but do expreſſe the cheere

GENIVS.

INdeed, true Gladneſſe doth not alwayes ſpeake:
Ioy bred and borne but in the tongue, is weake.
Yet (leaſt the feruor of ſo pure a flame,
As this my City beares, might looſe the name,
Without the apt euenting of her heate)
Know greateſt IAMES (and no leſſe good, than great,)
In the behalfe of all my vertuous Sonnes,
Whereof my eldeſt there, thy pompe forerunnes,
(A Man without my flattering, or his Pride,
As worthy, as hee's bleſt to be thy guide)
In his graue name, and all his Brethrens right,
(Who thirſt to drinke the Nectar of thy ſight)
The Counceſſ, Commoners, and Multitude;
(Glad, that this day ſo long deny'd, is view'd)
I tender thee the heartieſt welcome, yet
That euer King had to his Empires ſeate:
Neuer came man, more long'd for, more deſir'd:
And being come, more reuerenc'd, lou'd, admir'd:
Heare, and record it: "In a Prince it is
"No little vertue, to knowe who are his.
With like deuotions, do I ſtoope t'embrace
This ſpringing glory of thy Godlike race;
His Countries wonder, Hope, Loue, Ioy and Pride:
How well dooth he become the royall ſide
Of this erected, and broad ſpreading Tree,
Vnder whoſe ſhade may Brittane euer be.
And from this branch, may thouſand branches more
Shoote o're the Maine, and knit with euery ſhore
In bonds of Mariage, Kinred, and Increaſe;
And ſtile this Land, the Nauill of their peace.
This is your Seruants wiſh, your Cities vow,
Which ſtill ſhall propagate it ſelfe, with you;
And free from ſpurres of Hope, that ſlow minds moue:
"He ſeekes no hire, that owes his life to Loue.
And heere ſhe comes that is no leſſe a part
In this dayes greatneſſe, then in my glad heart.
Glory of Queenes, and Glory of your Name,
Whoſe Graces do as farre out-ſpeake your Fame,
As Fame doth ſilence, when her Trumpet rings
You Daughter, Siſter, Wife of ſeuerall Kings:
Beſides Alliance, and the ſtile of Mother,
In which one title you drowne all your other.
Inſtance, be that faire ſhoote, is gone before
Your eldeſt Ioy, and top of all your ſtore,
With thoſe, whoſe ſight to vs is yet deni'd,
But not our zeale to them, or ought beſide
This City can to you: For whoſe eſtate
She hopes you will be ſtill good Aduocate
To her beſt Lord. So, whilſt you mortall are,
No taſte of ſower mortalitie once dare

Fig. 6   Joyous speeches delivered by figures on Londinium

[This page has been left blank to retain the original presentation of designs (on versos) and related text (on rectos).]

Fig. 7　Second arch, erected by Italians in Gracechurch Street

The Italians Pegme ſtood in Gracious-ſtreete.

HE ſecond *Triumphall Arch* was erected by the *Italians* : the coſt theirs : the Inuention their owne : It tooke vp the whole breadth of *Gracious-ſtreete* (on which it ſtood) being —— foote : the height of it was —— foote . The lower parte of this *Building* , was a large ſquare , garniſhed with foure great *Corinthia Columnes* : In the midſt of which ſquare, was cut out a faire and a Spacious hie gate , Arched, being —— foote in the *Perpendicular-line*, and —— in the *Ground-line* : directly ouer the gate were aduaunced the Armes of the *Kingdome*, the Supporters whereof were fairely cut out to the life.

On the top of this firſt ſquare (beeing flat) was erected another Square which bare in the fore ſide foure more leſſer *Columnes* , on which were all the garniſhments belonging to thoſe pillars : as namely , the architriue frize and Corniſh, on which Square was placed a great *Canted Pedeſtall*, which with his moldinges did diminiſh vpwards to ſmaller *Cants*, on which top was fixed a *Perſonage* carued or molded out to the life, her left hand leaning on a ſword, with the point downeward, and her right hand reaching forth a *Diademe*, which,

ſhee ſeemde by bowing of her knee and head, to beſtow vpon his *Maieſtie.*

On the foure Corners of this vpper parte, ſtoode foure naked *Portraictures* (in great) with artificiall trumpets in their hands.

All which Shapes that were erected in moſt liuely colours, together with *Pyramides*, long Streamers, Galleries, and all other inrichments belonging to this *Archtriumphant* : I referre you to the Modell or Peece it ſelfe, for the *Front* of it, as the next leaſe will ſhewe you, ſo likewiſe proportionall was the backe ſide to the fore-*Front*.

The *Italians*, were placed within two little Galleries very richly and ſtately hung, vnder the Arch of the *Paſſage* : Inwhoſe behalſe, thus much Latine was deliuered.

The Italians Speech.

Salue, *Rex magne, ſalue . Salutem Maieſtati tuæ Itali, fœliciſsimum Aduentum læti, fœlices ſub te futuri, precamur. Ecce hic Omnes, Exigui Munere, pauculi Numero : ſed magni erga Maieſtatem tuam animi ,multi obſequij . At nec Atlas, qui Cælum ſuſtinet, nec ipſa Cæli Connexa , altitudinem attingant meritorum Regis optimi , Hoc eſt, eius quem de Teipſo expreſsiſti doctiſsimo (Deus !) & admirabili , penicillo , Beatiſsimos populos ,vbi & Philoſophus regnat , & Rex Philoſophatur . Salue ; Viue Rex Potentiſsime, fœliciter. Regna, Rex ſapientiſsime , fœliciter. Itali optimus O nnes, Itali clamanus Omnes, Omnes, Omnes.*

The ſame in Engliſh.

ALL haile mightie Monarch ! wee (the *Italians*) full of Ioy to behold thy moſt happie preſence, and full of hopes to inioy a felicitie vnder thy Royall wing , doe wiſh and pray for the health of thy Maieſtie . Behold, here wee are all; meane in merite : fewe in number : but towardes thy Soueraigne ſelfe , in our loues great,in our duties more . For neither *Atlas*, who beares vp heauen , no nor the Arched roofe it ſelfe of heauen , can by many-many degrees reach to the toppe and glorious height of a good and vertuous Kinges deſeruings. And ſuch a one is he , whome (Good God!) moſt liuely , moſt wiſely , and in wonderfull colours, thou didſt then pencill downe in thine owne perſon, when thou ſaydſt thoſe people were bleſt, where a Philoſopher rules , and where the Ruler playes the Philoſopher. All haile thou royalleſt of Kinges; liue thou mightieſt of Princes : Reigne thou wiſeſt of Monarches in all proſperitie : theſe are the wiſhes of vs *Italians* : the hearty wiſhes of vs all : All, euen All.

D.

Fig. 8 Description of the Italians' arch

Fig. 9   Third arch, built by the Dutchmen in Cornhill

The Pegme of the Dutchmen.

HE third welcome that his Maiesty receiude, was from the *Belgians*, who had builded a stately *Triumphall Arch*, to entertaine him in, and thus was it contriude.

So wide did the bodie of it extend it selfe, that it swallowed vp the breadth of the whole streete, neere the *Royall Exchange in Cornehill*. The *Passage* of state was a gate, comely, and large, ascending ——foote in heigth, and ——foote in the breadth, neatly Arched, and graced with two lesser *Posternes* on the sides, whose dimensions you may behold in the modell.

Sundry inscriptions were in golden Letters to bee seene, both ouer the Gate, and in the *Tables*, fild with excellent Pictures; as the King in his Imperiall Robes: with other *Portraictures* of Princes, and Poeticall Emblemes of Peace, &c. On the back part also were peeces, wherein were drawne the people of the Seuenteene *Prouinces* at their Husbandry; their *Exchange*: their *Mart*: Also seuenteene children on the fore side, representing the seuenteene *Prouinces*, sate in degrees, each of them hauing a Scutcheon in his hand, figuring his *Prouince*.

On the shoulders of this *Belgicke body*, stood rowes of *Balysters* with *Pedistals*, that supported Lyons rampant, bearing vp Banners: And aboue them in the midst of another square about with *Balysters* likewise, was aduanced a woman (figuring *Diuine Prouidence*, her feete fastned to a great *Pedestall*, whose toppe was curiously connexed and knit together with the tailes of two *Dolphins*.

Other Garnishments there were that gaue illustration and beauty to this building, as *Columnes, Pyramids, &c.* whose proportions your eye may measure on the other side. The speech, wherein the loue of these Strangers was testified, was deliuered by a boy in Latine, and is thus much in English.

The speech of the Dutchmen.

GREAT King, those so many Scepters, which euen fill thy right hand, are all thine owne, onely by the Prouidence of heauen. Behold, heauen it selfe laughes to see thy Subiects smile, and thunder out loud Plaudities, to heare their Aues. This honor of Soueraignty beeing at the beginning of the world bestowed but vpon few, vpon the heads of few were the cares of a Crowne set, for to sway onely but one Empire (happily) as it is a labour hard: So none can vndergoe the waight but such as are mightie: But (with a becke as it were) to controle many Nations (and those of different dispositions too) O! the Arme of man can neuer do that, but the finger of God. God therefore (that guides the Chariot of the world) holds the Raynes of thy Kingdome in his owne hand: It is hee whose beames lend a light to thine. It is hee that teacheth thee the Art of Ruling, because none but hee made thee a King. And therefore as thou growest in yeares, thou waxest old in Vertues: of all thy Vertues, Religion sitting highest. And most worthy; for by Religion, the hearts of barbarous Nations are made soft: By Religion, Rebellion hath a yoke cast about her necke, and is brought to beleeue, that those Lawes to which thou submittest euen thy royall selfe, are most easie. With Religion Iustice keepes companie, who once fled from this prophane world, but hearing the name of King Iames she is againe returned. By her side sits her sister Fortitude, whose life is readie (in Heroike actions) to bee spent for the safety of thy people. Besides to make these Vertues full, Apollo and the Muses, resigne, the one his Golden lyre, the other their Laurell, to thy royall hands, whilest Plenty (daughter to Industry) layes the blessings both of Countrey and Cittie in heapes at thy feete. These are the gifts of heauen: the fame then spreading it selfe so farre, that (to wonder at them) both the Poles seeme to come together. We (the Belgians) likewise come, to that intent: a Nation banisht from our owne Cradles, yet nurst and brought vp in the tender bosome of a Princely mother, Eliza. The loue which we once dedicated to her (as a Mother) doubly do We vowe it to thee, our Soueraigne, and Father: Intreating wee may bee sheltred vnder thy wings now, as vnder hers: Our Prayers beeing, that he who through the loynes of so many Kingdomes, may likewise multiply thy yeares, and lengthen them out to the age of a Phœnix: And that thy Queene (who is one part of thy selfe) with thy Progeny (who are the second hopes of thy people,) may both gine too, and receiue from, thy Kingdome Immortall glory.

E.

Fig. 10 Description of Dutchmen's arch

Fig. 11   Fourth arch, 'New Arabia Felix', at east end of Cheapside

The Deuice called,

Noua fœlix Arabia, The new Arabia fœlix.

THIS *Pegme* prefented it felfe aboue the great Conduit in *Cheape:* and caried the name of the *New Arabia*, vnder which title the whole Ifland of *Britannia* was figured.

This was beautified with a large Gate in the midft : On each fide was cut out a *Pofterne*, either of which was ―foot wide, and ―foot high:before which *Pofternes* two *Portals* were built from the fame, hauing their fides open foure feuerall wayes, and feruing as *Pedeftals* (of *Rufticke*) to fupport two great *Pyramids*, whofe bafes were held vp with foure great *Bals*, and foure Lyons.

This *Mechanicke body* had other dead limmes, (which you may behold cut out on the other fide.) The liuely and ftirring parts were thefe. *viz.*

In the moft eminent place was aduanced a perfon, reprefenting *Arabia Britannica*, and within a *Nefte* (beneath her) ftood *Fame*.

Directly vnder her in a wide hollow fquare, were exalted fiue greene Mounts, the one fwelling aboue the other; vpon which the fiue *Senfes*, (*Hearing, Seeing, Feeling, Smelling* and *Tafte*,) late heauily drooping : before which Mounts, an Artificiall *Lauer* was erected, called the Fount of *Vertue*; out of which (from fundry pipes) vpon his *Maiefties* approch, ranne wine very plenteoufly.

At the foote of this Fount lay *Detraction* and *Obliuion*, Sleeping till his Maiefties approch; but beeing arriued at the place, and the *Trompe of Fame*, ftarting vp the *Senfes*, they two likewife awaked, doing their beft, with clubs to beate downe the Fount, but were hindered by the *Senfes*, and a perfon reprefenting *Circumfpection*.

Vpon feuerall *Afcenfions*, (and clofe adioyning to the *Pyramids*,) were feated at one fide, the three *Graces*, and on the other fide the three *Howres*.

The fpeakers were *Fame, Howres, Euphrofine* (one of the *Graces*) and *Circumfpection*, who was mounted on a Stage, raild round about with *Pilaftres*, beeing drawne foorth fome thirtie foote in length from the other Building . And thus founded their voyces.

FAME.

Vrne into yce mine eye-bals whilft the found,
Flying through this brazen tromp, may back rebound,
To ftop Fames hundred tongues, leauing them mute,
As is an vntoucht bell, or ftringleffe Lute,
For Vertues Fount, which late ran deepe and cleere,
Dries : and melts all her body to a teare :
You Graces : and you Houres that each day runne,
On the quicke errands of the Golden Sunne,

Hereupon *Fame* founding her Trumpet, the *Sences* ftart vp, *Circumfpection* appeares, vttering thus much to the K ng.

Great Monarch of the Weft, whofe glorious Stem,
Does now fupport a triple Diadem,
Weying more then that of thy graund Graund-fire, (Brute,)
Thou that mayft make a King thy Subftitute,
And doeft befides the Red-rofe and the white,
With the rich flower of France, thy garland dight,
Wearing aboue kings now, or thofe of old,
A double Crowne, of Lawrell and of Gold,
O let my voyce paffe through thy Royall eare,
And whifper thus much, that we figure here.
A new Arabia, in whofe fpiced Neft,
A Phœnix liu'd, and dide in the Sunnes breft,
Her loffe made Sight, *in* Teares *to drowne her eyes,*

O *fay !* to Vertues *Fount what has befell,*
That thus her Veines fhrinke vp.

GRACES ― HOWRES.

We cannot tell.

EVPHROSINE.

Behold the fiue-fold guard of Senfe, *which keepes*
the facred ftreame, fits drooping : neare them fleepe,
Two horrid monfters: Fame, *fummon each fenfe,*
To tell the caufe of this ftrange Accidence.

Detraction and Obliuion awaken, and vanifh, whileft Cir-

The Eare grew deaffe, Tafte *like a Sick-man lyes,*
Finding no rellifh : Euery other Sence
Forgat his office, Worth and excellence;
Whereby this Fount of Vertue *gan to freeze,*
Threatned to be drunke vp by two enemies,
Snaky Detraction, *and* Obliuion,
But at thy glorious prefence both are gone.
Thou being that facred Phœnix, *that doth rife,*
From th'afhes of the firft, Beames from thine eyes
So vertually fhining, that they bring
To Englands new Arabia, a new fpring :
For Ioy whereof, Nymphes, Sences, Howre s *and* Fame,
Eccho-loud Hymnes to his Imperiall name.

At the end of this fpeech, a fong (to an excellent Muficke) was deliuered, which being finifht, his Maieftie went on.

F.

Fig. 12 Description of 'New Arabia Felix'

Fig. 13   Fifth arch, 'Garden of Plentie', at west end of Cheapside

The Deuice called,

Hortus Euporiæ, Garden of Plentie.

THE fift *Pegme* was a sommer Arbor, and seemed to growe close to the little *Conduit in Cheape*, which ioyning to the backe of it, serued (or might bee supposed to haue bene) as a Fountaine to water the fruits of this *Garden* of Plenty.

This greene bower spread it selfe likewise (as all the rest did) ouer the whole breadth of the streete; hauing two Gates arched and grated Arbor-wise, to the height of —— feete, and breadth of ——: the sides of which gates were borne vp with foure great *French termes*, standing vpon *Pedestals*, which conteined in their full height —— foote. Betweene these open *Passages* were a paire of staires mounted, at the bottome of which (on two pillers) were fixed two *Satyres*, carued out in wood. Both the roote and sides of these Gates, were Artificially hung with Pompions, Cowcumbers, Grapes, Cherries, Peares, Apples, and all other fruits, which the land bringeth foorth. The vpper part also (which was closed with three round tops, *Fortune* standing on the midst of the three) was garnished with lesser fruits, and with all sorts of Flowers, made by Art.

The whole Frame of this sommer house, stood (at the Ground-line) vppon —— foote, the *Perpendicular*, stretching it selfe to —— .

Peace and *Plentie* had the highest places in this Bower, and sate together: directly vnder them, sate two other persons, representing Gold and Siluer, supporting the Globe of the world betweene them: On each side of them sate two other persons, the one *Pomona*, Goddesse of Fruits, the other *Ceres*, Goddesse of Corne.

Vpon two large *Descents* (a little belowe these) were placed at one ende the nine *Muses*, at the other end the seuen liberall Sciences.

Syluanus, and his followers, (who vpon sight of his Maiestie, played vpon Cornets) gaue entertainement to his Maiestie, in these speeches following.

The speech.

MOST happie Prince, pardon me, that beeing meane in habite, and wild in appearance (for my richest liuery is but leaues, and my stateliest dwelling but in the woods) thus rudely with piping Syluanes, I presume to intercept your Royall passage. These are my walkes, yet stand I not here to cut off your way, but to giue it a full and a bounteous welcome, beeing a messenger sent from the Lady Eirene my mistresse; those that sleepe vnder the warmth of her winges adore her by the Sacred and Celestiall name of Peace; her daughter Euporia (well knowne by the name of Plenty) is at this present with her, (being indeed neuer from her side:) Vnder yonder Arbor they sit, which after the daughters name is called Hortus Euporiæ (Plenties Bower.) Chast are they both, and both maidens, in memory of a Virgine to whom they were Nurse-children, for whose sake (because they were bound to her for their life) me haue they charged to lay at your Imperiall feete, (being your hereditary due) the tribute of their loue. And with it thus to say. That they haue languished many heauy moneths for your presence, which to them would haue bene, (and proud they are that it shall be now so) of the same operation and influence, that the Sunne is to the Spring, and the Spring to the Earth; hearing therefore what treble preferment you haue bestowed vpon this day, wherein besides the beames of a glorious Sunne, two other cleere and gracious Starres shine cheerefully on these her homely buildings: Into which (because no duty should be wanting) she hath giuen leaue euen to Strangers, to be sharers in her happinesse, by suffering them to bid you likewise welcome: By me (once hers, now your vassaile) shee intreates, and with a knee sinking lower then the ground on which you treade, do I humbly execute her pleasure, that ere you passe further, you would deigne to walke into yonder Garden. The Hesperides liue not there, but the Muses, and the Muses no longer than vnder your protection. Thus farre am I sent to conduct you thither, prostratly begging this grace (since I dare not, as being vnworthy, Lackey by your Royall side) that yet these my greene Followers and my selfe may be Ioyfull fore-runners of your expected approch. Away Syluans.

G.

Fig. 14   Description of the Garden of Plenty

Fig. 15   Sixth arch, 'New World', in Fleet Street

The Deuice called,

Cozmoz Neoz, New World.

THE sixt *Triumphall Arch*, was (in the shape which you see it caries on the other side) erected aboue the *Conduit* in Fleetestreete; extending it selfe ouer the whole streete, to the length of —— foote, and in height —— foote : The Gate of it was —— foote wide, and —— foote hie. The two *Posternes* were answerable to those of others set downe before : and were cut out of the two round *Towers* which riz vp in proportionable measures, from the ground on the foreside with battlements and *Ballisters* round enclosing the tops, containing in all their heights —— foote : ouer the Gate, and iust in the midst of the *Builaing*, (which was spacious and left open) a *Globe* was seene to moue being fild with all the estates that are in the land ; And this *Engine* was turned about by foure persons, representing the foure *Elements*, (*Earth*, *Water*, *Aire*, and *Fire*) who were placed so queintly, that the *Globe* seemed to haue his motion euen on the *Crownes* of their heads.

The liuely garnishments to thi *Building* were 23 persons, of which the principall and worthiest was *Astræa* (*Iustice*) who was aduanced o the highest *Seate*. Beneath her in a *Cant* by her selfe, *Arete* (*Vertue*) was placed : and at her feete *Fortune*, who trod vpon the Globe.

In a darke and obscure place (neere *Vertue*) sate *Enuy* : beneath whom, on seuerall *Ascensions* were placed the *Cardinall Vertues*, *Iustice*, *Fortitude*, *Temperance* and *Prudence*; and in an opposite seate, the foure kingdomes, *England*, *Scotland*, *France* and *Ireland*.

Zeal was the Presenter of this *Deuice*, who spake thus.

ZEALE.

THe populous *Globe* of this our English *Ile*,
Seem'd to moue backward at the funerall pile
Of her dead female Maiesty : *All states*
From Nobles downe to Spirits of meaner Fates,
Moou'd opposite to Nature and to Peace,
As if these men had bene Th'antipodes.
But see, the vertue of a regall eye,
Th'attractiue wonder of mans *Maiestie*,
Our *Globe* is drawne in a right line agen,
And now appeare new faces and new men :
The Elements, Earth, Water, Ayre and Fire,
(Which euer c'ipt a naturall desire,
To combat each with other) being at first
Created enemies, to fight their worst,
See : at the peacefull presence of their King,
How quietly they moue without their Sting.
Earth not deuouring : Fire not defacing :
Water not drowning : and the Ayre not chasing :
But propping the quoint Fabricke that here stands,
Without the violence of their wrathfull hands.
Mirror of times, loe, where thy *Fortune* sits
Aboue the world, and all our humaine wits,
But thy hie Vertue aboue that : what pen
Or *Art*, or *Braine*, can reach thy Vertues then ?
At whose Immortall brightnesse and true light,
Enuies infectious eyes haue lost their sight :
Her Snakes (not daring to shoote forth their stings,
Gainst such a glorious Obiect) downe she flings
Their forkes of Venome into her owne mawe,

Whilst her ranke teeth the glittering poysons chawe,
For tis the property of Enuies bloud,
To dry away at euery Kingdomes good,
Especially when she had eyes to view
These foure Maine Vertues which here figure you,
Iustice in causes : Fortitude gainst foes,
Temp'rance in spleene; and Prudence in all those :
And then so rich an Empire, whose faire brest
Containes foure Kingdomes by your entrance blest,
By Brute diuided, but by you alone,
All are againe vnited, and made One :
Whose fruitfull glories shine so farre and euen,
They touch not onely earth, but they kisse heauen,
From whence Astræa is descended hither,
Who with our last Queenes Spirit fled vp thither,
Fore-knowing on the earth she could not rest,
Till you had lockt her in your rightfull brest,
And therefore all estates, whose proper Arts
Liue by the breath of Maiestie, had harts,
Burning in holy Zeales Immaculate fires,
With quenchlesse Ardors and vnstain'd desires.
To see what they now see, your powerfull Grace,
Reflecting Ioyes on euery Subiects face.
These painted flames and yellow-burning stripes,
Vpon this roabe being but as shewes and types,
Of that great Zeale ; And therefore in the name,
Of this glad Citty, whither no Prince euer came,
(More lou'd, more long'd for, lowly I intreate
You'ld be to her as gracious as y'are great :
So with reuerberate shoutes our Globe shall ring,
The Musicks cloze being thus, God saue our King.

H.

Fig. 16   Description of 'New World'

Fig. 17   Seventh arch, Temple of Janus near Temple Bar

The Deuice called,

Templum Iani, Temple of Ianus.

THE seuenth and last *Pegme* (within the Citie) was erected at *Temple-barre*, beeing adioyned close to the Gate: The *Building* was in all points like a *Temple*, and dedicated to *Ianus Quadrifrons*.

Beneath that *Foure-fac'd head* of *Ianus* was aduanced the Armes of the *Kingdome*, with the Supporters cut out to the life: from whence being remoude they now are placed in the *Guild Hall.*

The wals and gates of this Temple were brasse; the Pillars siluer, their *Capitals* and *Bases* gold: All the *Frontispice* (downeward from those Armes) was beutified and supported by twelue rich *Columnes*, of which the foure lowermost, being great *Corinthian* pillers, stood vpon two large *Pedestals*, with a faire *Faux* ouer them in stead of *Architriue*, *Frieze* and *Cornice.* Aboue them, eight *Columnes* more, were likewise set, two and two vpon a large *Pedestall*; for as our worke began (for his Maiesties entrance) with *Rustieke*, so did wee thinke it fit, that this our *Temple*, should end with the most famous *Columne*, whose beauty and goodlinesse is deriued both from the *Tuscane*, *Doricke*, *Ionicke* and *Corinthian*, and receiued his full perfection from *Titus Vespasian*, who aduanced it to the highest place of dignitie in his *Arch Triumphall*, and (by reason that the beauties of it were a mixture taken from the rest) he gaue it the name of *Composita* or *Italica:* within the *Temple* stood an Altar, with burning *Incense* vpon it, before which a *Flamin* appeares, and to the *Flamin* comes the *Genius* of the City. The principall person in this Temple, was *Peace.* At her feete lay *Warre* groueling. At her right hand stood *Wealth.* On the same hand likewise, but somewhat remote, and in a *Cant* by her selfe, *Quiet* was seated, the first hand-maide of *Peace*, whose feete stood vpon *Tumult.* On the left hand (at the former distance) *Liberty* the second hand-maide of *Peace* had her place, at whose feete *Seruitude* lay subiected. Beneath these (on distinct degrees) sate two other hand-maides of *Peace*, *Safety* and *Felicity*, *Safety* trampling vpon *Danger* and *Felicity* vpon *Vnhappinesse, Genius* and *Flamin* spake thus much.

GEN. STay, what art thou, that in this strange attire,
Darst kindle stranger, and vnhallowed fire
Vpon this *Altar*? FL. Rather what art thou
That darst so rudely interrupt my vowe?
My habite speakes my name. GE. A *Flamin:* FL. *Yes*,
And Martialis cald. GE. I so did gesse
By my short view, but whence didst thou ascend
Hither? or how? or to what mysticke end?
FL. The noise, and present tumult of this *Day*,
Rows'd me from sleepe, and silence, where I lay
Obscur'd from light, which when I wakt to see,
I wondring thought what this great pompe might be.
When (looking in my *Kalender*) I found
The *Ides* of *Marche* were entred, and I bound
With these, to celebrate the Geniall feast
Of Anna stil'd Perenna, Mars his guest,
Who, in this Month of his, is yearely cal'd
To banquet at his *Altars*; and installd,
A Goddesse with him, since she fils the Yeare,
And knits the oblique scarfe that gyrts the sphere.
Whilest foure fac'd *Ianus* turnes his vernall looke
Vpon their meeting howers, as if he tooke
High pride and pleasure. GE. Sure thou still dost dreame,
And both thy tongue and thought rides on the streame
Of *Phantasie:* Behold here Het nor Shee,
Haue any Altar, Fane, or Diety.
Stoope; read but this Inscription: and then view
To whome the place is consecrate. Tis trew
That this is *Ianus* Temple, and that now
He turnes vpon the Yeare his freshest browe;
That this is Mars his moneth, and these the Ides,
Wherein hit Anne was honored, Both the Tides,
Titles, and Place, we knowe: But these dead rites
Are long since buried, and new power excites
More high and hartie flames. Loe, there is he,
Who brings with him a greater Anne then shee:
Whose strong and potent vertues haue defac'd
Sterne Mars his statues, and vpon them plac'd
His, and the worlds blest blessings: This hath brought
Sweete Peace to sit in that bright state she ought
Vnbloudy, or vntroubled; hath forc'd hence
All tumults, feares, or other darke portents,
That might inuade weake minde; hath made men see
Once more the face of welcome Liberty:
And doth (in all his present acts) restore

That first pure world, made of the better Ore.
Now Innocence shall cease to be the spoile
Of rauenous Greatnesse, or to steepe the soile
Of raised Pesantrie with teares, and bloud;
No more shall rich men (for their litle good)
Suspect to be made guiltie; or vile Spies
Enioy the lust of their so murdering eyes:
Men shall put off their Yron minds, and hearts;
The Time forget his olde malicious artes
With this new minute; and no print remaine
Of what was thought the former ages staine.
Backe Flamin, with thy superstitious fumes,
And sense not heere; Thy ignorance presumes
Too much; in acting any Ethnick rite
In this translated Temple: Heere no wight,
To sacrifice saue my deuotion comes,
That brings in steed of those thy Masculine gummes.
My Cities heart; which shall for euer burne
Vpon this Altar, and no Time shall turne
The same to ashes: Heere I fixe it fast,
Flame bright, flame high, and may it euer last.
Whilest I, before the figure of thy Peace,
Still tend the fire; and giue it quicke increase
With prayers, wishes, vowes; whereof be these
The least, and weakest: that no Age may leese
The memory of this so rich a day;
But rather, that it henceforth yearely may
Begin our spring, and with our spring the prime,
And first account of Yeares, of Months, of Time:
And may these Ides as fortunate appeare
To thee, as they to Cæsar fatall were.
Be all thy Thoughts borne perfect, and thy Hopes
In their euents still crown'd beyond their scopes.
Let not wide Heauen that secret blessing know
To giue, which she on thee will not bestow.
Blind Fortune be thy slaue; and may her store
(The lesse thou seest it) follow thee the more.
Much more I would: but see, these brasen Gates
Make hast to close, as vrged by thy Fates;
Here ends my Cities office, here it breakes:
Yet with my tongue, and this pure heart, she speakes
A short farewell; and lower then thy feete,
With feruent thankes, thy roy all paines doth greete.
Pardon, if my abruptnesse breed disease;
He merits not t'offend, that hasts to please.

I.

Fig. 18   Description of the Temple of Janus

Lectori Candido.

EADER, The limmes of thefe great *Triumphall* bodies (lately difioynted and taken in funder) I haue thou feeft (for thy fake) fet in their apt and right places againe: fo that now they are to ftand as perpetuall monuments, not to be fhaken in peeces, or to be broken downe, by the malice of that enuious deftroyer of all things, *Time*. VVhich labours of mine, if they yeeld thee either profit or pleafure, thou art (in requitall thereof) to pay many thankes to this honourable Citie, whofe bounty towards me, not onely in making choife of me, to giue directions for the intire workmanfhip of the fiue *Triumphall Arch's* builded by the fame, but alfo (in publifhing thefe *Peeces*,) I do here gladly acknowledge to haue bene exceeding liberall.

Nor fhall it be amiffe in this place to giue thee intelligence of fome matters (by way of notes) which were not fully obferude, nor freely inough fet downe in the Printed Booke of thefe *Triumphes*: amongft which thefe that follow are chiefeft.

His Maieftie departed from the *Tower* betweene the houres of 11. and 12 and before 5. had made his royall paffage through the Citie, hauing a *Canopie* borne ouer him by 8. Knights.

The firft *Obiect* that his Maiefties eye encountred (after his entrance into *London*) was part of the children of *Chrifts Church Hofpitall*, to the number of 300. who were placed on a Scaffold, erected for that purpofe in *Barking Church-yard* by the *Tower*.

The way from the *Tower* to *Temple-Barre* was not onely fufficiently grauelled, but all the ftreetes (lying betweene thofe two places) were on both fides (where the breadth would permit) raild in at the charges of the Citie, *Paules Church-yard* excepted.

The *Liueries* of the *Companies* (hauing their Streamers, Enfignes, and Banerets fpred on the tops of their railes before them) reached from the middle of *Marke Lane*, to the *Pegme* at *Temple Barre*.

Two *Marfhals* were chofen for the day, to cleere the paffage both of them being well mounted, and attended on by fixe men (futeably attirde) to each *Marfhall*.

The Conduits of *Cornehill*, of *Cheape*, and of *Fleeteftreete*, that day ran Claret wine very plenteoufly: which (by reafon of fo much excellent Muficke, that founded foorth not onely from each feuerall *Pegme*, but alfo from diuerfe other places) ran the fafter and more merrily downe into fome bodies bellies.

As touching the Oration vttered by Sir *Henry Mountague* (Recorder of the City) with the gifts beftowed on the King, the Queene, and the Prince (beeing three Cups of gold) as alfo, all fuch fongs, as were that day fung in the feuerall *Arch's*, I referre you to the Booke in print, where they are fet downe at large.

And thus much you fhall vnderftand, that no manner of perfon whatfoeuer, did disburfe any part towards the charge of thefe fiue *Triumphes*, but onely the meere Citizens being all free-men; heretofore the charge being borne by fifteenes and the *Chamber of London* (as may appeare by auncient prefidents) but now it was leauied amongft the Companies. The other two *Arch's* erected by Merchant-Strangers (viz. the *Italians* and *Dutchmen*) were only their owne particular charge.

The Citty elected 16. Committies to whom the managing of the whole bufineffe was abfolutely referred: of which number 4. were Aldermen, the other 12. Commoners, viz. one out of each of the 12. Companies. Other Committies were alfo appointed as ouer-feers and furueyors of the worke. *Farewell*.

Imprinted at London by Iohn Windet,

Printer to the Honourable Citie of London, and are to be fold at the
Authors houfe in Lime-ftreet, at the figne of the *Snayle*. 1604.

K.

Fig. 19   Address to the Honest Reader

Fig. 20 Blank verso of Fig. 19 with seventeenth-century inscription.

VIII.   NOT THE ROYAL EXCHANGE

By DEREK KEENE

Sᴵɴᴄᴇ about 1600 a plan among William Cecil's collection at Hatfield House has been identified as one of London's Royal Exchange, erected between 1566 and 1569 and destroyed in the Great Fire of 1666.[1] In fact, the plan concerns not the Royal Exchange, but an earlier proposal for an exchange on another site. This essay compares that proposal with what is known of the Antwerp 'New Bourse' (begun in 1531 and opened for trading in 1533),[2] of other public buildings in Antwerp, and of the Royal Exchange itself, the design of which was inspired by Antwerp models. Key features of these structures are summarised in the Table below. Also considered are the means by which Cecil (d. 1598) acquired the plan and its relationship to the design of the Royal Exchange.

Filling a vellum sheet measuring 519mm by 744mm, the plan (Fig. 1) is simple and precise in style. The text on its original version consisted of three sets of small Arabic numerals: one on the scale (totalling 185 units, probably English feet) marked out along the outside of the south wall of the building,

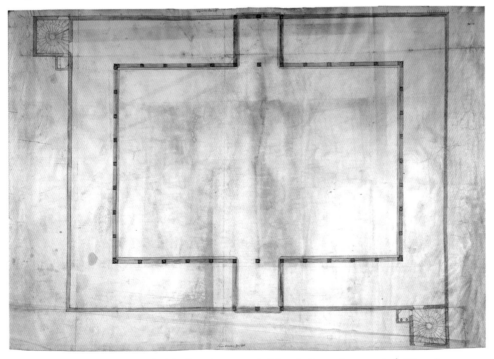

Fig. 1.   The Hatfield plan (see text). North is at the top (cf. Fig. 3).
By kind permission of the Marquess of Salisbury.

and two on the spiral staircases, each of which contains forty steps (Fig. 2).
The plan lacks explicit orientation, but texts added in the mid sixteenth
century demonstrate that the staircase turret with an irregular outline was
on the south side.

   The building shown is rectangular, with an exterior wall which encloses
colonnaded loggias opening on to a courtyard. Broad entrances occupy two
bays in the middle of each of the longer sides. One of the two staircase
turrets projects westward at the north-west corner and the other southward
at the south-east corner. The oblique alignment of the south wall of the latter
is not matched elsewhere in the structure, and was presumably intended to
allow it to fit within the available site, probably constrained by a street on
that side (Fig. 3). In the angles between the turrets and the outer wall are
two latrines, each containing a pair of seats and a corner feature which may
have been served as a bin for earth. The outer walls, including those of the
turrets and latrines, are coloured with a pink wash, probably indicating
those parts of the structure to be built of brick. The inner parts and the entry
thresholds are coloured in three shades of blue. The darkest is used for the

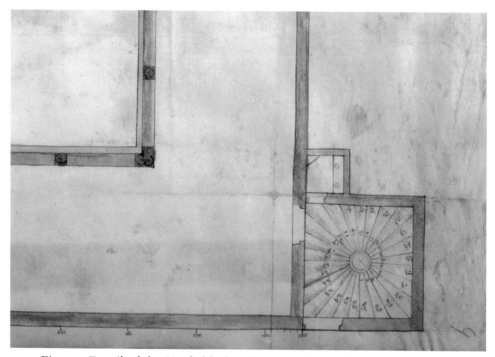

Fig. 2.   Detail of the Hatfield plan showing the north-west stair turret,
latrine, the west end of the scale of feet, and clustered columns of feet,
at the corner of the arcade. South is at the top.
By kind permission of the Marquess of Salisbury.

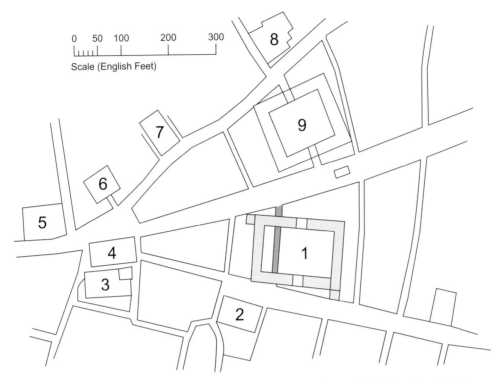

KEY: 1, approximate position of the building shown on the Hatfield plan (identified by pale tone) and Pope's Head Alley (identified by dark tone); 2, church of St Mary Woolnoth; 3, church of St Mary Woolchurch; 4, the Stocks Market House; 5, church of St Mildred Poultry; 6, Posthouse; 7, church of St Christopher le Stocks; 8, church of St Bartholomew by the Exchange; 9, the Royal Exchange.

Fig. 3. The building on the Hatfield plan shown in relation to the Royal Exchange and the surrounding area; plan based on John Leake's *Exact Surveigh* compiled soon after the Great Fire of 1666. North is at the top.

round columns, their square bases, and the four sets of three clustered columns and their bases at the corners of the courtyard.[3] A paler shade denotes the wall on which the column bases stood. The palest shade is used for what appears to be a step in front of that wall (also a feature of the Royal Exchange and indicating that that the floor within the loggias was at a higher level than the surface of the courtyard), and for the external thresholds. The blue may indicate that distinctively coloured stones were to be used for these features, as was the case with the Antwerp New Bourse and the Royal Exchange.[4] The stair turrets were accessible only from outside the building, while the latrines were accessible only from within, beneath the stairs. If the steps in the staircases were about seven inches high, the stairs would have risen to more than 23 feet, presumably to galleries above the loggias, which were probably a little higher than they were wide.

Resemblances both to the Antwerp New Bourse and to the Royal Exchange, demonstrate that the building shown on the plan was intended to be an exchange, a protected space where merchants assembled twice a day to do business. The latrines were for the use of traders during the hours of 'Change, while the upper storey was probably intended to accommodate the sale of luxury goods throughout the day, as was also the case at the New Bourse and at the Royal Exchange, where access was also from outside. The plan has no indications of cellars.

That the plan does not depict the Royal Exchange is clearly demonstrated by differences in layout, dimensions, and numbers of arches and columns, and there were similar differences between these two buildings and the Antwerp New Bourse (see Table). Moreover, the notes added to the plan demonstrate that the building did not occupy the site of the Royal Exchange:

1. along the southern edge of the plan: *Lombartt strette* (**Lombard Street**)
2. along the northern edge: *Corneywalle* (**Cornhill**)
3. at the south-eastern corner, perhaps in a different hand: *Sr Martyn bouse howsse*.

The Royal Exchange did not lie between Lombard Street and Cornhill, but in the next block to the north, between Cornhill and Threadneedle Street (Fig. 3). The house to the east on the plan was that of Sir Martin Bowes (d. 1566), a prominent goldsmith, Master of the Mint from 1533 to 1540, knighted in 1540–1, and Lord Mayor for 1545–6. He lived in Lombard Street, in the parish of St Mary Woolnoth and Langbourne Ward, probably in the house near Birchen Lane, which Stow later described as having been built by Bowes with a 'fair forefront' and a back gate near the Conduit in Cornhill (Fig. 3).[5] The additions to the plan, if all of the same date, were presumably made between 1540–1, when Bowes was knighted, and 1566, when work on the Royal Exchange began.

These landmarks and the dimensions indicated by the scale demonstrate that the exchange depicted was intended to occupy a site towards the west end of Lombard Street. When plotted on to the map of the city compiled immediately after the Great Fire by John Leake and others, the dimensions (if in English feet) suggest that the site extended westwards from just west of what in 1666 was known as Exchange Alley to beyond Pope's Head Alley (Fig. 3). Plotting the same dimensions on to Ogilby and Morgan's map of the city as rebuilt by 1676 suggests that the intended site may have been further to the east and bounded by Pope's Head Alley on the west. The difference between these two possible positions is slight and could be accounted for by the surveying of the maps or by a widening of Cornhill and/or Lombard Street undertaken between 1666 and 1676.[6]

The plan evidently concerned a proposal made in the 1530s to build a bourse in Lombard Street, the long-established site for international trading and financial exchange, which at that time took place in the open street at fixed times of day.[7] Presumably inspired by the opening of the New Bourse in Antwerp, the proposal replaced an earlier scheme to set up a bourse at Leadenhall, the city's Common Council having decided in 1535 that the exchange should remain in Lombard Street. In July 1537 the Court of Aldermen expressed its support of a plan to build an exchange on the site of the Pope's Head, a substantial stone structure on the north side of Lombard Street, immediately east of Pope's Head Alley. This site had long been associated with international finance and in the fourteenth century had belonged to the Florentine Society of the Bardi, who when they were responsible for the exchange of bullion and foreign coin had probably run it from there. In 1537 a plan for the new exchange on this site was shown to Thomas Cromwell, but acquiring the title and sufficient money for building presented problems, and the scheme was dropped in 1539.[8]

During the 1540s the pressure from English merchants to have an exchange in London on the lines of the Antwerp Bourse probably grew, for since the 1470s the Merchant Adventurers had received increasing support from the Antwerp authorities in developing commercial facilities there, especially as the focus of business and finance shifted away from the river Scheldt to the vicinity of the New Bourse. After a short move inland in 1518 the English traders were in 1550 provided with their own 'English Bourse' for which in that year the Antwerp authorities agreed to put up a wooden arcade 10 to 12 feet wide and resting on wooden and stone pillars. This structure adjoined a bridge (*Mindernbroeders brugge*) leading across a canal towards the convent of the Friars Minor and is represented in an engraving entitled *Vne nouvelle Bourse pour la Nation Angloise a bastir deuant le refectoire de Cordeliers*, a stylish building with two stories of loggias and an elegant tower surrounding three sides of a courtyard, the fourth side of which was open to the bridge.[9] This scheme may not have been completed, although Lodovico Guicciardini later described the structure as the *gratiosa piazza della Borsa de gli Inghlesi,* where in 1550 a *bella loggieta* had been built for their contemplation; he also described how in the course of business Thomas Gresham had used the English Bourse in conjunction with the New Bourse.[10] Soon after 1550 the English were occupying as their residence the palatial Hof van Liere, situated a few blocks to the north of the New Bourse and later known as the *Engels Huis*. The Antwerp authorities had recently acquired and repaired it for this purpose, the deal being finalised in 1558. In 1557 the Merchant Venturers petitioned in England for a bourse to be made near Lombard Street. This project, however, made no further progress until 1565, when Gresham offered to pay for the building of a bourse 'more fair and more costly builded in all points than is the bourse of Antwerp', if the

City of London provided a site.[11] At first the City settled on another site between Lombard Street and Cornhill, well to the east of that considered in 1537–8 and comprising a block of property which Sir John Percyvale by his will of 1503 had left to the Company of Merchant Taylors for charitable purposes. The Company fended off this approach from the City authorities, who settled on a site to the north of Cornhill early in 1566, when the planning and design of the Royal Exchange presumably were finalised.[12]. The Hatfield plan concerns the earlier of the two sites previously under consideration in Lombard Street.

The building on the plan, the Antwerp New Bourse, and the London Royal Exchange, each occupied approximately the same area of ground, included loggias arranged around courtyards of approximately the same size and proportions, and had two impressive entries. All three had upper rooms to which there was access directly from the street. The Hatfield plan, however, concerns a scheme that more closely resembled the Antwerp New Bourse than the Royal Exchange, since it consisted simply of a courtyard and loggias within an enclosing wall, while the more ambitious design of the Royal Exchange also included outer ranges of three storeys with shops and warehouse entries facing the street.[13] The New Bourse, in an elaborate late Gothic style with Moorish (*mudéjar*) characteristics and richly decorated, was closely modelled on the smaller 'Old Bourse', erected in 1515 following plans drawn up by the same city architect in the street now known as Oude Beurs, where it survives today.[14] By the 1530s this style may have begun to seem old fashioned, especially by comparison with *cortili* recently erected in Italy. Whoever was responsible for the Hatfield plan seems to have been aware of this and introduced several innovations. The columns around the courtyard of the intended building were round and stood on square bases, in contrast to the polygonal Gothic bases at the New Bourse. Instead of the single columns, slightly heavier than the rest, at the four corners of the New Bourse, there were four clusters of three columns. Nothing is known of the structure above ground level, but the spacing between the columns on the plan (11ft centres) appears to have been less than at the New Bourse (perhaps 13.5ft centres), implying arches of a different design (perhaps round arches in classical style) to that of the three-lobed Gothic arches at the New Bourse.

The design of the Royal Exchange (1566–9) appears to have been largely the work of Hans Hendryk van Paesschen (*alias* van Passe), a talented and well-known architect, sworn surveyor of the city of Antwerp, and frequently described as 'master'. Having been commissioned by Gresham to work on the London exchange, he spent much time there during these years. At the same time he was also responsible for major contributions to the design and building of prominent structures in his home city, including the Town Hall (1561–6) and the Hansa House (1564), the latter a large and imposing edifice, about 244 English feet in length, which provided warehousing and accommodation for Hanseatic merchants.[15] Both of these buildings were notable, along with the Royal Exchange but in contrast to the New Bourse, for the ordered classicism of their design. Van Paesschen, indeed, has been claimed as uniquely significant for introducing Italian architectural classicism to northern Europe and as being the only architect of his generation there to be comparable to Serlio, Palladio, or de l'Orme. In Britain, he certainly undertook several commissions in addition to the Exchange. His work in Denmark is well documented and he was probably responsible for buildings elsewhere in the Baltic region, where commercial links with Antwerp were strong. Traditionally, the Town Hall and the Hansa House in Antwerp have been attributed to the sculptor Cornelis Floris de Vriendt, but it seems more likely that the two of them worked together, van Paesschen supplying the overall design, while de Vriendt dealt with sculpture and contacts with clients. Van Paesschen, born c.1515, probably studied in Italy, possibly under Antonio da Sangallo the younger (d. 1546).[16] Guicciardini mentioned him as the architect of both the Hansa House and the Royal Exchange, and as one of those Antwerp artists who had visited Italy and transmitted to northern Europe what they had learned there.[17]

So far as the design of the Royal Exchange is concerned, the influence of the Hansa House was stronger than that of the New Bourse, being apparent in the double-pile plan around the courtyard, in the two symmetrically opposed entries, and in the details of the roofs, the fenestration and the shop and cellar doorways of the ranges facing the streets. Common features of the Antwerp buildings associated with van Paesschen were heavy overhanging eaves, dormer windows, and the placing of symbolic images at prominent points on and above the roof: eagles at the Town Hall, imperial double-headed eagles at the Hansa House, and Gresham's grasshopper emblem at the Royal Exchange.

The colonnades at the Royal Exchange had a distinctively Italian appearance,[18] as did their three-storied counterparts within the Hansa House.[19] A notable feature of the Royal Exchange was van Paesschen's use of clusters of three columns at the corners of the courtyard, in the same manner as on the Hatfield plan. Moreover, the Amsterdam Bourse, completed in 1608 and closely modelled on the London Exchange, had similar clusters of columns at the corners.[20] By contrast, earlier Italian architects such as Bramante (d. 1514) had used a single column or engaged columns in such positions, as had also been the case at the New Bourse. Sangallo, however, included clusters of three columns in a design drawn up after 1527,[21] and they were later to be an occasional feature of Palladio's work.[22]

There seems, therefore, to have been a connection between the Hatfield plan and the design of the Royal Exchange. One possibility is that van

Paesschen was the author of the plan, in which he incorporated elements learned from Sangallo or a similar source. That is unlikely, however, since in 1537, when the Lombard Street exchange was proposed, van Paesschen – if his date of birth has been estimated correctly – would have been no more than twenty-two years old. Moreover, what has been claimed as his earliest known work, contributions to the design of triumphal arches, dates to 1549. The engraving of the proposed English Bourse in Antwerp, constructed in 1550, shows a building with similarities to van Paesschen's later Antwerp buildings, including the roof, pinnacles, dormer windows, and an elegant tower with classical features resembling those at the Hansa House (1564) and the Royal Exchange (1566–9). The English Bourse may have been the first of van Paesschen's projects for English clients, but the supports for the internal corners of the loggias enclosing the courtyard were single columns rather than clusters of three.

Van Paesschen may have seen and used the Hatfield plan as an indication of earlier ideas concerning the design of the London bourse. If so, he presumably acquired it before 1566 from Thomas Gresham, who could have inherited it from his father, Richard, who as mayor had possessed the plan in 1537–8.[23] Van Paesschen, or an assistant, may have been responsible for annotating the plan so as to indicate that the project had concerned a different site. Certainly, the exotic spellings of the street-names on the plan suggest that the writer was unfamiliar with London and that his first language was not English.

It was presumably after the completion of the Royal Exchange that the plan came into the possession of William Cecil, well-known for his interest in maps and plans, either as a gift from Gresham, with whom he had a close association, or from van Paesschen himself, who while in England undertook domestic projects both for Cecil (at Burghley House and Theobalds) and for Gresham (at his London house – later Gresham College – and at Osterley Park).[24]

While van Paesschen is unlikely to have been the author of the Hatfield plan, he may have derived from it distinctive features of his design, including the clustered columns and perhaps the overall style of the colonnade. The plan seems associated with the first phase of the reception of classical architectural principles in Antwerp, which took place during the 1530s and was marked by translations from Vitruvius and Serlio and a particular interest in the form and use of columns.[25] The author of the plan has not yet been identified, but he was probably one of those artists from Antwerp who visited Italy at that time. He was presumably known to the English merchants in Antwerp who commissioned from him a plan for a bourse in London, which perhaps eventually became one of the sources for van Paesschen's work on the Royal Exchange. In this and other respects van Paesschen's role in Royal Exchange project – coordinating ideas and skills from a variety of sources and stamping them with a mark of his own – was characteristic for the period and resembled that which he recently had played in the design and building of Antwerp Town Hall.

TABLE: points of comparison between the Antwerp New Bourse, the Hatfield House Plan, and the Royal Exchange in London

Characteristics	Buildings		
	Antwerp, New Bourse, built 1531[26]	Hatfield House Plan, c. 1537[27]	London, Royal Exchange, 1566[28]
Plan	Single-pile ranges enclosing courtyard[29]	Single-pile ranges enclosing courtyard	Double-pile ranges enclosing courtyard[30]
External dimensions (excl. turrets)	180 ft N/S by 140 ft E/W[31] [169 ft N/S by 132 ft E/W]	185 ft E/W, by 135 ft N/S [197 ft by 143 ft]	170 ft E/W; 150 ft N/S.[32] Or 190 ft E/W; 155 ft N/S[33]
Dimensions and details of courtyard	Possibly approx. [121 ft by 108 ft].[34] Two steps down from loggia to courtyard	138 ft E/W; 91 ft N/S [147 ft by 97 ft]. Two steps down from loggia to courtyard	135 ft E/W, by 100 ft N/S.[35] 80 paces (200 ft?) by 60 paces (150 ft?).[36] 115 ft by 80 ft.[37] Held 4,000 merchants.[38] Two steps down from loggia to courtyard
Width of galleries or ranges	Possibly 21 ft [20 ft]	Internal: 20 ft [21 ft]	External: E/W ranges, 20 ft; N/S ranges, 24 ft.[39] Width of loggia noted as 6 or 7 paces (15 or 17.5 ft).[40] A modern reconstruction suggests 15 ft[41]
Entries	2 offset on N and S sides[42]	2 opposed on N and S sides	2 opposed on N and S sides[43]

Entries: width and number of columns	6 columns (including two central)	20 ft [21 ft]; 6 columns (including two central)	20 ft.[44] 6 columns. In 1578 it was noted that the portals (denoting the outer side of each entry) each had 3 great columns 14 ft high and of jasper marble, and thresholds in same marble[45]
Turrets	Perhaps originally 4, of which 2 destroyed by 1565.[46] Both surviving staircase towers entered from the street and set against the outside wall: one, with an elaborate spire and a bell-cote, was just E of the S entry; the other, with a sundial facing S, was a bay W of the N entry[47]	2, both staircase towers 18–20 ft [19–21 ft] square and entered from the street (one at NW corner; the other at SE corner)	1 staircase tower entered from Cornhill; set externally just E of the S entry; with two musicians' galleries, a clock and a bell-cote resembling S tower at Antwerp Bourse; similarities to classical design of towers at English Bourse and Hansa House[48]
Stairs	Probably both spiral and entered from the street	Both spiral stairs, with 40 steps each, entered from the street	25 or 30 steps leading up to the first-floor gallery in flights of 7; probably accommodated within the tower and entered from the street[49]
Number of arches around courtyard (including entries)	11 on each long side (N/S); 8 on each short side (E/W); 38 in all[50]	12 on each long side; 8 on each short side; 40 in all	10 on each long side; 7 on each short side; 34 in all[51]

Number of columns around courtyard (from number of arches, counting each cluster of columns at corners as one)	38 43 of *pierre bleuë* noted in 1610 and later[52]	40	34 In 1578 36 big columns of *piere bize*, each 12 ft high, were noted, with 36 others of jasper marble above them[53]
Spacing of columns (centres)	Perhaps 13.5 ft centres in English feet and probably greater than in the Hatfield plan and at the Royal Exchange	11 ft [12 ft] centres; 10 ft [11 ft] interval between bases	Intervals of 4 paces (10 ft)[54]
Number of storeys and windows (the dormers may have lit the storey above the loggias rather than a separate attic)	2 plus attic: loggia, storey above (perhaps no more than 8 windows on to courtyard); attic with 1 dormer per bay [55]	2, perhaps similar to Antwerp New Bourse	3 including cellar, loggia, storey above loggia (4 windows on to courtyard), attic with 1 dormer per bay as in Antwerp New Bourse[56]

1. Hatfield House Archives, CPMII I.9, referred to here as 'the Hatfield plan'. See R. A. Skelton and J. Summerson, *A Description of Maps and Architectural Drawings in the Collection made by William Cecil First Baron Burghley, now at Hatfield House* (Oxford: Roxburghe Club, 1971), p. 82 (cat. 77), where Summerson identified it as the Royal Exchange, on the basis of endorsements of c.1600 and later. The plan, with the same identification, was reproduced in *The Royal Exchange*, ed. A. Saunders (LTS 152, 1997), p. 38.
2. J. Denucé, 'De Beurs van Antwerpen: oorsprong en erste entwikkeling 15e en 16e eeuwen', *Antwerpsch Archievenblad*, Tweede Reeks, 6de Jaargang (Antwerp, 1931), pp. 81–145, at pp. 88–91; J Materné, 'Schoon ende bequaem tot versamelinghe der coopheden: De Antwerpse beurse tijden de gouden zestiende eeuw', in *Ter Beurze: Geschiedenis van der aanhandel in België, 1300–1900*, ed. G. de Clercq (Bruges and Antwerp, 1992), pp. 51–84, at pp. 55–6.
3. The clustering of columns at the corners is a distinctive and innovative feature, discussed below.
4. *Royal Exchange*, ed. Saunders, Fig, 10; L. Grenade, *The Singularities of London, 1578*, ed. D. Keene and I. W. Archer (London Topographical Society 175, 2014), pp. 115–16, 235.
5. J. Stow, *A Survey of London*, reprinted from the text of 1603, with Introduction and

notes by C. L. Kingsford, 2 vols. (Oxford, 1908, reprinted with additions, 1971), i, 192, 203; C. E. Challis, 'Bowes, Sir Martin (1496/7–1566)', *Oxford Dictionary of National Biography* (2004); online edn., Jan 2008; *Two Tudor Assessment Rolls for the City of London: 1541 and 1582*, ed. R. G. Lang (London Record Society 29, 1993), no. 127.

6.   *An exact svrveigh of the streets and lanes and chvrches contained within the rvines of the city of London first described by Iohn Leake* [et al] in December 1666, engraved by Wenceslas Hollar (1667); *A new and accurate map of the city of London*, surveyed by John Ogilby and William Morgan (London, 1676). For these, see J. Howgego, *Printed Maps of London circa 1553–1850* (2nd edition, London, 1978), nos. 21 and 28.

7.   D. Keene, 'The setting of the Royal Exchange: continuity and change in the financial district in the city of London, 1300–1871', in *Royal Exchange*, ed. Saunders, pp. 253–71, at pp. 255–6.

8.   Stow, *Survey*, i, p. 201, ii, p. 307; J. Imray, 'The origins of the Royal Exchange' in *Royal Exchange*, ed. Saunders, pp. 20–35, at pp. 22–5; Keene, 'Setting', pp. 255–6.

9.   L. Voet, *Antwerp: the Golden Age; the Rise and Glory of the Metropolis in the Sixteenth Century* (Antwerp, 1973), pp. 258–62; fully documented in O. De Smedt, *De Engelse Natie te Antwerpen in de 16^e Eeuw (1496–1522)*, 2 vols. (Antwerp, 1950–4), vol. 2, pp. 128–57. The engraving of the English Bourse is reproduced in *Royal Exchange*, ed. Saunders, p. 49, where it is identified as the Royal Exchange. The Virgilius Bononiensis map of Antwerp (1565) depicts the site as an open area enclosed by a fence or wall. This site is identified in Hugo Soly's notes accompanying the reproduction of the map in L. Voet et al., *De Stad Antwerpen van de Romeinse Tijd tot de 17de Eeuw* (Gemeendkredit van België, 1978), in folder at end.

10.   *Descrittione di m. Lodovico Gviicciardini patritio Fiorentino, di tutti i Paesi Bassi, altrimenti detti Germania inferiore: con piu carte di geographia del paese, & col ritratto naturale di piu terre principali* (Antwerp, 1567), p. 67. Successive Antwerp editions of this work are cited as Guicciardini, *Descrittione* (with date); Guicciardini, *Descrittione* (1588), p. 169.

11.   Imray, 'Origins', pp. 25–7.

12.   Imray, 'Origins', pp. 26–8; M. Davies and A. Saunders, *The History of the Merchant Taylors' Company* (Leeds, 2004), p. 111; for the site of Percyvale's property, see *Calendar of Wills proved and enrolled in the Court of Husting, London, A.D. 1258–A.D. 1688*, ed. R. R. Sharpe, 2 vols. (London, 1889–90), ii, p. 605.

13.   *Royal Exchange*, ed. Saunders, Fig. 9.

14.   Denucé, 'De Beurs', pp. 87–91.

15.   For contemporary descriptions and illustrations of these buildings, see Guicciardini, *Descrittione* (1567), p. 80 and (1581), pp. 122–3, 160–2; Caroli Scribani, e Societate Jesv, *Origines Antverpensivm* (Antwerp, 1610), pp. 118–22.

16.   See H. Hymans, *Henri van Paesschen et l'Ancienne Bourse de Londres* (Antwerp, 1908) and *Allgemeines Lexikon der Bilden Künstler von der antike bis zur Gegenwalt, begrundert von Ulrick Thieme und Felix Pecker*, vol. 26 (Leipzig, 1932), p. 282–3; and in their most recent version *The Grove Encyclopedia of Northern Renaissance Art*, 3 vols (Oxford, 2009), ed. G. Campbell, iii, p. 29; J. Stevens Curl, *A Dictionary of Architecture and Landscape Architecture*, 2nd edition (Oxford), 2006, and the sources there cited. J. F. Millar, *Classical Architecture in Renaissance Europe, 1419–1585* (Williamsburg Va., 1987), makes a fundamental contribution, although many of his conclusions rely on stylistic similarities alone.

17.   Guicciardini, *Descrittione* (1588), pp. 92, 107–8, 132.

18.   *Royal Exchange*, ed. Saunders, Figs 10, 17.

19.   A sixteenth-century engraving reproduced in *Antwerp: story of a metropolis*, ed. J. Van der Stock (Ghent, 1993) p. 238 shows a two-storey loggia above lower storeys occupied

by warehousing, but a larger painting of a similar view *c*.1700 shows three-storey loggias along part of that side of the quadrangle (*Deutsche Marinemalerei: Schiffsdarstellung, maritime Genrebilder, Meeres- und Küstenlandschaften*, ed. H. J. Hansen (Hamburg, 1977), p. 79; reproduced at http://en.wikipedia.org/wiki/Hanseatic_League.

20. For the corner columns in the Amsterdam Bourse, see the engravings by B. A. Bolwert (1609) and by C. J. Visscher (1612), and the oil painting by E. de Witte (1653).

21. A plan for cloisters at Santa Maria della Quercia, Viterbo: *The Architectural Drawings of Antonio da Sangallo the Younger*, ed. C. L. Frommell and N. Adams, 2 vols (Cambridge, Mass. and London, 1994), no. U309a.

22. *Le Fabbriche e i Disegni di Andrea Palladio recolta ed illustrata de Ottavio Bertotti Scamozzi* (Vicenza, 1796), 3 vols reprinted as one, with introduction by J. Q. Hughes (London, 1968), tom. 4, tav. xxxvii, tav. xlvii (villas for Francesco and Lodovico Trissini and for Leonardo Mocenigo).

23. Imray, 'Origins', p. 23.

24. Skelton and Summerson, *Description of Maps*, pp., 77, 82. Gresham College included Italianate colonnades resembling those of the Royal Exchange.

25. As indicated, for example, by Pieter Coecke van Aelst, *Die Inventie der colommen* (Antwerp, 1539), a version of Book IV of Sebastiano Serlio's *Regole Generali di Architettvra* (Venice, 1537).

26. Dimensions in Antwerp feet (1ft=0.2868 m); equivalents in English feet (1ft=0.3048 m) within [...].

27. Dimensions as indicated by measurement from the drawn scale on the plan, probably in English feet; equivalents in Antwerp feet indicated within [...].

28. Approximate dimensions in English feet from Leake, *Exact svrveigh*, which includes the only known plan of the first Royal Exchange; other details from description in Grenade, *Singularities*, pp. 112–18 (English), 233–7 (French) and from engravings by Hogenberg and Hollar (*Royal Exchange*, ed. Saunders, figs. 9, 10, 17, 18).

29. As shown in Petrus van der Borcht's engraving in the 1581 and subsequent editions of Guicciardini, *Descrittione*; see *Antwerp*, ed. Van de Stock (Antwerp, 1993), pp. 170 (cat. no. 23b) and 235 (cat. no. 84).

30. *Royal Exchange*, ed. Saunders, figs. 9, 10, 17 (the Hogenberg and Hollar engravings) and as reconstructed from same in Millar, *Classical Architecture*, pp. 130–6.

31. Denucé, 'De Beurs van Antwerpen', pp. 88–91, gives the dimensions as 51 m by 40 m, presumably derived (using the Antwerp foot of 0.2868 m) from the 180 ft by 140 ft stated by Scribanus, *Origines*, p. 122 and repeated in J. le Roy, *Le Grand Theatre profane du Duché de Brabant* (La Haye, 1730), p. 32. Denucé rounded his result incorrectly: it should have been 51.6 m by 40.2 m (169 by 132 English ft). The Antwerp Bourse burned down in 1581, but was rebuilt according to the original design, so that the measurements and details given here from sources dating after 1581 are probably approximately correct; it was destroyed again by fire in 1858, but not fully rebuilt until 1872: A. Thys, *Histoire des Rues et Places publiques de la ville d'Anvers* (Antwerp, 1873), p. 251; Denucé, 'De Beurs'.

32. The plan in Leake, *Exact surveigh* appears to exclude the houses against the street, apparently built as an integral part of the original project, but perhaps of timber rather than of brick and stone (shown in *Royal Exchange*, ed. Saunders, figs. 9, 18).

33. As reconstructed in Millar, *Classical Architecture*, pp. 130–6.

34. In English feet, estimated by subtracting 48 ft (8 ft for walls and 40 ft for the internal width of the galleries) from the external dimensions.

35. Leake, *Exact surveigh*; the plan appears to have omitted the outer ranges.

36. Grenade, *Singularities*, p. 115.

37. Millar, *Classical Architecture*, pp. 130–6.
38. Grenade, *Singularities*, p. 115.
39. Leake, *Exact surveigh*.
40. Grenade, *Singularities*, p. 115.
41. Millar, *Classical Architecture*, pp. 130–6.
42. The Petrus van der Borcht engraving of 1581 shows eight arches on the north side of the courtyard, the third and fourth of which from the west comprise the entry; the entry on the south side appears to have occupied the two central arches (fourth and fifth from the west). Guicciardini, *Descrittione* (1581), p. 99 noted four *gran' porte*, which probably refers to the four arches of the two entries. Early representations show no more than two entries, but by 1610 (see below n. 27) one of the arches in the north entry had been blocked and an additional entry had been made in the east wall (*Antwerp*, ed. Van der Stock, p. 30, fig. 11).
43. Indicated by Hogenberg's engravings of *c.* 1569 and W. Hollar's engraving of 1644: *Royal Exchange*, ed. Saunders, figs. 9, 10, 17.
44. Leake, *Exact surveigh*.
45. Grenade, *Singularities*, pp. 115–16, 235. The single contemporary image of a portal seen from outside suggests that its outer columns and arches may have been higher than those inside.
46. Denucé, 'De Beurs', pp. 90–1.
47. Shown on the van der Borcht engraving and the Virgilius Bononiensis map of 1565 (*Royal Exchange*, ed. Saunders, pl. IIb).
48. *Royal Exchange*, ed. Saunders, figs. 9, 17, 18
49. Grenade, *Singularities*, pp. 116, 235; Hogenberg engraving (*Royal Exchange*, ed. Saunders, Fig. 9).
50. The van der Borcht engraving shows that each arch had a corresponding dormer window above, from which it is possible to determine the number of arches on the longer sides.
51. See Hogenberg and Hollar engravings: *Royal Exchange*, ed. Saunders, figs. 10, 17.
52. Scribani, *Origines*, p. 122; Le Roy, *Grand Theatre*, p. 32 repeats Scribanus's total of 43 and adds the colour of their stone. The number of arches indicates 38 columns around the courtyard, of which each corner column appears to have been more substantial than the others. Scribanus probably included in his total the originally six columns at outer side of the entries (two free-standing and four free-standing), making an original total of 44, reduced to 43 when one of the arches of the north entry was blocked (see above, n. 17).
53. Grenade, *Singularities*, pp. 115, 234. Grenade probably made an error in counting. The engravings by Hogenberg and Hollar in *Royal Exchange*, ed. Saunders, figs. 10, 17, both of indicate that the four corner columns were composed of two or three (almost certainly three) clustered columns which, if included in the total, would make the total of individual columns to be 38 or 42.
54. Grenade, *Singularities*, pp. 115, 234.
55. Engraving by Petrus van der Borcht.
56. Grenade, *Singularities*, pp. 115, 234.

IX.   JOHN COFFYN AND NEVILL'S COURT, FETTER LANE

By DORIAN GERHOLD

AT the start of the twentieth century, Nevill's Court (formerly Nevill's Alley), between Fetter Lane and Great New Street, was one of the most distinctive and attractive parts of the City of London. It retained several seventeenth-century houses, some of which had survived the Great Fire, and many of them still had small gardens in front (Fig. 1). It was the subject of one of the most evocative of all the detailed plans of London buildings — drawn in 1670 and published by the London Topographical Society in 1928.[1] As well as the plan of 1670, there is much other information, including detailed ground plans of 1793 and 1901–21[2] and photos and drawings. These make it possible to unravel the entire history of a development of largely high-status houses from its origin in the sixteenth and seventeenth centuries to its destruction in the twentieth.

Fig. 1.   Drawing of Nevill's Court, looking east, with the Great House on the right, by J. G. Platt, 1924.

John Coffyn

What makes the plan of 1670 so attractive also makes it an oddity. Unlike almost all other London property plans after about 1620, it is pictorial rather than just a ground plan.[3] In the Society's publication and in the plan from the Crace Collection used by the Society, it is attributed to John Goslyng, about whom nothing else is recorded. A reasonable assumption might have been that Sir Nicholas Bacon, the Suffolk landowner who commissioned the plan, employed a rural surveyor, who therefore used a rural or pictorial style.

In fact, the Crace plan is a copy of an original which survives in the Bodleian Library (Fig. 2).[4] On the original plan the surveyor's name is partly covered by a stain, and Crace seems to have used his imagination to fill the gap. The actual surveyor can be identified partly because his name also appears elsewhere on the plan (in the text in the bottom right-hand corner, but omitted by Crace) and partly on stylistic grounds. He was in fact John Coffyn, well known as one of the most important surveyors of Essex. John Goslyng the surveyor never existed. The stylistic features which identify the plan beyond doubt as Coffyn's are the 'single-line' cartouche, the design of the compass rose, the use of wood blocks for all the text on the map and the use of Gothic type for his own name.[5]

Coffyn drew maps of rural estates, but in this period he lived in London, obtaining commissions in various counties. He was evidently the 'John Coffin', gentleman, of St Andrew Holborn parish who was a witness in a Chancery suit in 1666. The suit related to Sir Dennard Strutt, then living at Little Warley in Essex but holding property in several counties. Coffyn stated that he was 'for diverse yeares a cheife agent of the saide Sr Denner Strutte and imployed by him in ye management of his affaires and having some skill and judgment in the survey and value of landes'.[6] Coffyn was then aged thirty-three, which is consistent with his first extant map having been drawn in 1654 as a joint production with another surveyor, when Coffyn was twenty-one.

Coffyn is named on the plan of 1670 a third time, as he was almost certainly the John Coffyn recorded there as lessee of one of Sir Nicholas Bacon's Fetter Lane houses (later No. 41). The house was in St Dunstan in the West parish, but was only a few yards outside St Andrew Holborn parish, where Coffyn had been living in 1666. The St Dunstan rate lists do not include Coffyn up to and including November 1668, but he is in the next list, of 1671, at what became 41 Fetter Lane, and then continuously to 1678, departing between September 1678 and May 1679.[7] No maps of Coffyn's are known from 1671 to 1678, and thereafter all his maps were of places in south-east Essex, probably indicating that by then there was enough work in just part of a single county to support a surveyor. His Essex home was at

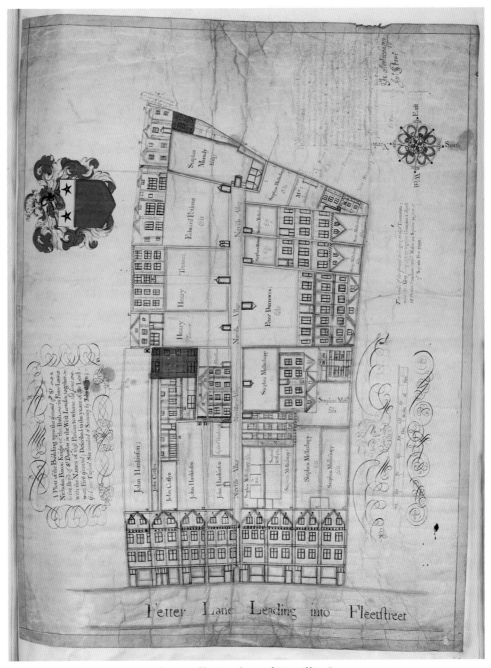

Fig. 2. John Coffyn's plan of Nevill's Court, 1670.
Bodleian Library, University of Oxford, MS Gough Maps 21, fo. 28.

Great Burstead, which may have been where his parents had lived. His last surviving map is from 1699, when he was aged about sixty-six.[8] Thus the peculiarity of the Nevill's Court plan is explained. Bacon commissioned it from one of his own tenants who, though a Londoner, was otherwise exclusively a surveyor of rural estates and was apparently unfamiliar with the London tradition of ground plans.

The Bacon Family and the Creation of Nevill's Court

The arms on the plan are those of Sir Nicholas Bacon, Knight of the Bath, whose seat was Shrublands, in Barham parish near Needham Market in Suffolk.[9] Urban property is generally assumed to be have been held as an investment, without the sentimental attachment inspired by country estates, but when Bacon made his will in 1686, leaving the Nevill's Court and Fetter Lane property to a younger son, he added: 'hopeing as they have been in the family a great while he will keep them in the family'.[10]

In fact, they had been in the family for more than a century. The story begins in 1574, when the premises formed part of the Goldsmiths' Company's large holding between Fetter Lane and Shoe Lane, known as Shoe Lane gardens. This was let out as a series of gardens (forty in 1610), and was not comprehensively developed until 1649–56.[11] It bordered Fetter Lane (then Fewter Lane) only at the point where Nevill's Court was later built. In 1574 Sir Nicholas Bacon, Lord Keeper of the Great Seal, wrote to the Goldsmiths' Company, asking it to grant him its property adjoining Fetter Lane in return for a permanent rent equivalent to what was then being paid — in other words, a fee farm, effectively a freehold but subject to a rent charge, which was a mere £2 a year. The Goldsmiths immediately agreed to this unappealing offer, presumably because of legal or political services Bacon had rendered or was expected to render, or simply because a friend at court was an advantage. The Copperplate Map of *c.* 1555 shows Fetter Lane built up along its whole length, but the property transferred to Bacon was described as 'a peece of ground adioynynge to Fewter Lane', without any mention of buildings, and abutted north on a garden and south on land apparently not built on.[12] The property was intended for Bacon's third son, Edward (1548–1618), to provide him with a London house,[13] and the transfer of land was to both Sir Nicholas and Edward. It was Edward who, through his wife, established his family at Shrublands. The London property passed on Edward's death to his son, Nicholas Bacon of Shrublands (1589–1658), and then to Nicholas's son Philip Bacon (died *c.* 1666), to Philip's brother Sir Nicholas Bacon (*c.* 1622–87), for whom the plan was drawn, and to Sir Nicholas's son Philip in 1687. It was eventually sold by Philip Bacon in or about 1696, after 120 years in the family.[14] The Bacons had other London property acquired by the first Sir Nicholas, in and around Chancery Lane, but this seems not to have inspired the same affection.

Coffyn's plan makes clear that the Bacons' property divided almost equally into a front part, consisting of the Fetter Lane houses and several buildings behind them (some of them facing the alley), and a back part (from Trevers and Burrows eastwards), where there were five substantial dwellings at the time of the Great Fire. Development of the Fetter Lane frontage began under the first Sir Nicholas. His widow told the City's Court of Aldermen in 1579 that her husband 'dyd bargayne for the erectinge of a frame to be sett upp in Fewter Lane', and she sought permission for the carpenters and workmen to set it up despite them not being free of the City, which was agreed to.[15] The back part was developed during Edward Bacon's ownership. When the Fire Court considered the back part in 1668, the two survivors of the five houses (later Nos. 13A to 15) were said to be sixty years old, which dates them to about 1605–10 (Fig. 3). They had been erected on 'a void back piece of ground'. Possibly Edward Bacon's house on the front part was replaced by a row of houses at the same time. John and Francis Gaynsford, who held the lease of the five back houses in 1668, said that they held it in consideration of the houses having been built by their 'ancestors', and that Bacon received £20 rent a year for them.[16] Their father was Richard Gaynsford of Hartfield, Sussex, gentleman, who died in 1653–4, but whether he was the builder is uncertain. By 1653 he was living at Hartfield, but he left goods in two houses in Nevill's Alley.[17] Despite suggestions that the name derives from Ralph Nevill, Bishop of Chichester, who held property

Fig. 3. Nos. 13A to 15 Nevill's Court, 1910. *London Metropolitan Archives, City of London, Collage 48540.*

nearby in the thirteenth century[18] (but otherwise had no connection at all with Nevill's Court), the name seems more likely to come from a builder or lessee called Nevill, but no such person has been identified.[19]

The five houses were timber-built, with lath and plaster walls,[20] and were described in 1668 as 'paper buildings', which

> have bin hardly kept up in repaire and not without great charge and the more for that there is no passage for the water from any of the houses and grounds but into vaults under ground which have bin very chargeable and noysome in emptying as all the said tenants have often complained.[21]

Nevertheless, two of them stood for three centuries, and they were large: in 1666 they had, anti-clockwise from Burrows, eight, eight, six, nine and nine hearths.[22] The two houses which survived the Fire were built against the back boundary, without any windows at the back, and on two of the three other plots the rebuildings after 1666 were against or close to that boundary. The aim had evidently been to create an enclave of substantial houses and give it an air of spaciousness by building them against the outer edge of the site, which allowed for gardens in front of them and a space of over 70 feet between the houses from north to south. Indeed, it was recorded in 1658 as 'Nevills garden otherwise Nevills Alley', and in 1667 as 'Nevills Alley alias Nevills Garden'.[23] It was in effect the courtyard plan, but with individual gardens instead of a communal one or a paved yard. The internal arrangements of the two survivors, which may have been common to all five, can be seen on the plan of 1793 (Fig. 4). They were lobby-entry houses, one room deep, with two rooms on each floor of the house plus service rooms to the side. The lobby inside the front door gave access to the two rooms, and behind it were a staircase, fireplaces and closets. The rooms were about 16 feet from front to back. Lobby-entry houses were unusual in London because most London houses were entered from one of their shorter sides rather than their longer sides as here.[24] Figure 3 shows their central chimneys, and that only the top floor was jettied.

There is a probate inventory of 1676 for the house (later No. 13A) leased in 1654 by Stephen Mundy, an official of the Court of Common Pleas.[25] The ground floor consisted of kitchen and parlour; above that were the dining room and 'young Mr Mundy's chamber'; one floor up again were Mr Mundy's chamber and his wife's chamber; and at the top the maid's garret and back garret. The first six of these rooms had heating, corresponding to the assessment of six hearths. Paper building or not, the house was well furnished, with green hangings in the parlour, gilt-leather hangings and a bed lined with yellow silk in young Mr Mundy's chamber, three tapestries in Mr Mundy's chamber and various pictures. There was a 'back house' of three storeys with one room in each storey (the ground floor possibly being 'the ffoot boys roome'). This was presumably the bay on the

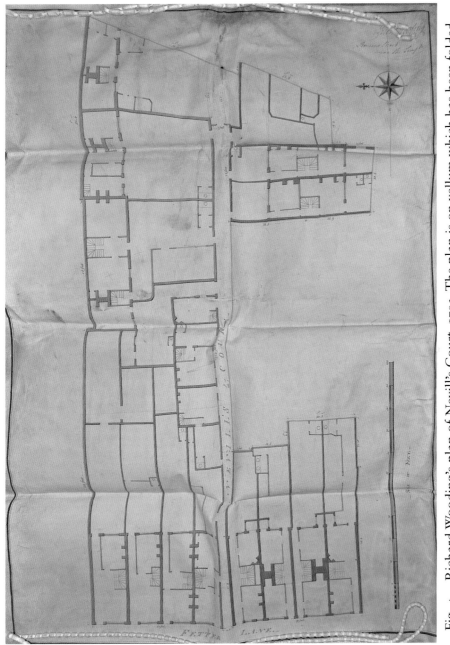

Fig. 4.   Richard Wooding's plan of Nevill's Court, 1793. The plan is on vellum which has been folded, and therefore cannot be photographed flat. The plan ignores the parts of Nevill's Court sold to the Moravian Church. *Courtesy of the Goldsmiths' Company.*

right-hand side of the house (see Figs 3 and 4), probably next to the back kitchen yard recorded in the inventory. In the garden were a table, a rolling stone and a table to dry clothes on. Household goods amounted to £372 (including 819 ounces of plate worth £205), leases to £380, ready money to £304 and debts (some 'desperate') to £1,630, making a total of £2,686.[26] In March 1666 Mundy was living there with his wife, eight children, three clerks and a maidservant; two other women were described as receiving wages and were perhaps servants, too.[27] Edward Potkins at the next-door house was an attorney.[28] Despite the designation 'Alley', Strype was clearly right to describe Nevill's Alley as 'very handsome, and well inhabited',[29] and this was perhaps why Sir Nicholas Bacon was more interested in it than in his other London property. It was perhaps also why the development did not fall foul of the proclamations against new buildings around London. By 1730 it was 'Neville's Alley otherwise Neville's Court'.[30]

In addition to the Gaynsfords' five houses, the rate list of January 1666 records two dwellings on each side of the alley between those houses and the Fetter Lane ones. Those to the north had four and five hearths in 1666, and were the predecessors of Nos. 2 and 3. Those to the south had six and seven hearths, making them almost as large as the Gaynsfords' five houses, and must have been on the site later occupied by Nos. 7 to 9.[31]

The Great Fire and the Rebuilding of Nevill's Court

Hollar and Leake's map and the line on Ogilby and Morgan's map indicating the extent of the Great Fire show the whole of Nevill's Court and its Fetter Lane frontage as having been burnt down in 1666. Fire Court proceedings and the parish rate book tell a different story. Of the Gaynsfords' five houses of 1605–10, three were burnt, including one on the north side of the alley, but Potkins' and Mundy's in the north-east corner survived. The rate list for February 1667 indicates two other survivors, occupied by Richard Henthorn and Robert Perry.[32] Neither are in the pre-Fire lists, but Henthorn is named on the 1670 plan holding land either side of two houses on the north side of the Alley (later Nos. 2 and 3), which identifies those two as the survivors. None of the Fetter Lane houses survived. Evidently the line between burnt and unburnt London was here an untidy one. The gardens may have saved Potkins' and Mundy's houses, but they did not save the adjoining house to the west. Perhaps it was pulled down to create a firebreak, or the fire reached it via buildings behind the Fetter Lane houses, bypassing Henthorn's, or the wind carried burning material across the alley.

Rebuilding began first on the Fetter Lane frontage. Stephen Mellichap, who evidently rebuilt 35–8 Fetter Lane as well as other houses, had two of the plots staked out in August and October 1667. In October 1667 Bacon leased two pieces of ground where houses had lately stood to John

Hankinson, a carpenter of St Giles in the Fields. Judging by their later occupants, these were 39 and 42 Fetter Lane. One of these plots was staked out in November 1667. Hankinson was allowed to build over one half of the passage into Nevill's Court, though a party wall over the alley would have been awkward, and Coffyn's plan and later evidence indicate that No. 39 occupied the whole of the space over the alley. One of the complaints by the Gaynsfords in 1668 was that, whereas there was previously 'a broad lightsome passage' into the alley, Bacon had leased ground on either side of it to workmen 'who have by new building much streightned and darkened the said passage into the alley whereby the houses will be much prejudiced'. The 1670 plan suggests that Hankinson also built 40 Fetter Lane. The houses varied in width, most being 15 feet wide at ground level, but Nos. 38 and 41 being 1 foot 6 inches narrower and No. 42 6 inches wider.[33]

Rebuilding the back part of Nevill's Court required assistance from the Fire Court. In 1668, two of the five houses were still standing, so Bacon was demanding the £20 rent. However, the Gaynsfords had transferred the responsibility for paying that rent to Peter Burrows, whose own house had not survived, so Bacon was threatening instead to levy the rent on Potkins and Mundy, whose leases did not require them to pay rent. The Gaynsfords stated that they lived in the country and were unwilling to undertake the rebuilding, but were willing to surrender their lease. Daniel Parr, who held the south-east house, also surrendered his lease, despite having paid a £50 entry fine not long before the Fire. The rent-free status of Potkins and Mundy was confirmed. Peter Burrows and Robert Tainton (represented by Henry Trevers or Travers, whose name appears on the plan as holder of Tainton's land) were willing to rebuild, and were each to have a 51-year lease from 1668, each paying £4 a year to Bacon during their existing term and £8 a year thereafter. Burrows' plot was staked out in September 1668 and Tainton's in February 1669.[34] The handsome seven-bay house built by Burrows, known much later as the Great House, presumably dated from 1668–9 (Fig. 5). It had ten hearths. Burrows, described as a gentleman, was still living there in 1679, together with wife, child, sister, clerk and two female servants.[35] Burrows and Trevers seem to have built on or near the old building line, but on the site of Parr's house the 1670 plan records that Mellichap built two 'duble houses' (later Nos. 11–12), probably bringing them forward from the old building line and reducing the previous openness. By the time of Coffyn's plan in 1670, the rebuilding of Nevill's Court and its Fetter Lane frontage was complete.

The 1793 plan (Fig. 4) shows that the Fetter Lane houses and Mellichap's 'duble houses' (which evidently meant houses two rooms deep) all had central staircases. These were common around 1660–80, but less so thereafter as builders found a staircase at the back to one side to be more economical.[36] Most had fireplaces and chimney stacks in the party walls, but 36 and 37

Fig. 5.   The Great House,
10 Nevill's Court.
English Heritage.

Fetter Lane had central fireplaces. Nos. 35 to 38 Fetter Lane had what seem to be projecting closets at the back in 1793, but whether these were present in 1670, foreshadowing the later back extensions of terraced housing, is uncertain; they may be shown on the plan as red outlines. Trevers' and Burrows' houses had the one-room deep plan of their predecessors, though Burrows' also had a wing at the back on the west side. Both had central staircases rising from a hall, which was spacious in Trevers' case, and fireplaces in the end walls instead of central fireplaces. A curious feature of most of the new houses was half-width windows. Their purpose was not to light staircases but presumably to provide extra light. They seem to have been unusual, though they were not unique to Nevill's Court and Fetter Lane.[37] Unlike those of the Great House, those of 11 and 12 Nevill's Court and the Fetter Lane houses had gone before any photographs were taken, leaving only traces in the brickwork and the window spacing, suggesting that they were troublesome to adapt for sash windows.

Although Coffyn's plan is highly decorative, it had a serious purpose. It was apparently prompted by Mellichap's rebuilding of the south-east corner. This had resulted in a triangular piece of land being left over, and Mellichap had sub-let it to the holder of adjoining property in Great New Street. Bacon's property was therefore no longer defined on the ground, and he required Mellichap and the sub-lessee to sign the plan to acknowledge that it correctly showed how far his land extended.

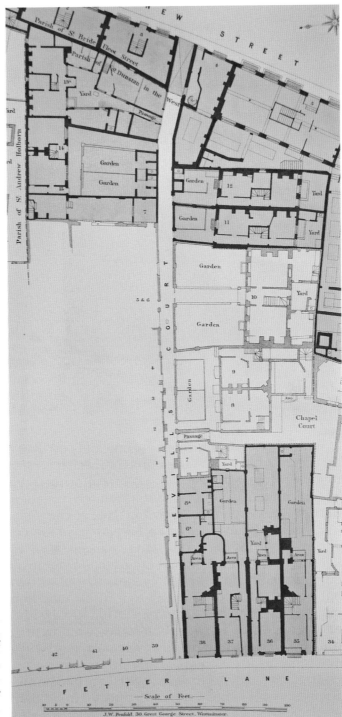

Fig. 6. Plan of the parts of Nevill's Court owned by the Goldsmiths' Company (in red), also showing the parts of Nevill's Court owned by the Moravian Church (uncoloured), 1901. The south-east wing of the Great House was a modern addition. *Courtesy of the Goldsmiths' Company.*

Fig. 7. Nos. 39–42 Fetter Lane
in 1928, with No. 40 in the
process of demolition. No. 41,
second from the left, was
Coffyn's house.
English Heritage.

With what is known about the pre- and post-Fire buildings, we can assess
the accuracy of Coffyn's depictions of them. It is clear that Coffyn was trying
to do something difficult: to combine a pictorial view and a ground plan.
His intention to show facades accurately is demonstrated by comparing
Burrows' house on the plan with Figure 5. The three-and-a-half storeys and
five full bays flanked by two narrow bays are correctly shown, though
apparently there were some later changes to the roof. Even on the Fetter
Lane frontage Coffyn did not draw a uniform row of eight identical houses,
but included minor differences, notably the half-width windows on some
but not others, and a second door in his own house providing access to
buildings at the end of the plot. Although by the time the houses were
photographed in 1928 the half-width windows had gone, the spacing of
windows in Figure 7 shows they had once existed where Coffyn shows them,
just as the brickwork and the spacing of windows does for 11 and 12 Nevill's
Court (Figs 8 and 9). However, not all the buildings are shown so accurately.
The plan is not a bird's-eye view, for Coffyn followed the common practice
of placing the view of each building on the baseline of its facade, with

different buildings being seen from different directions.[38] This worked well for the Great House, but for Potkins' and Mundy's houses, which were tall and set even further back, he had to leave out a storey, as the view of the houses would otherwise have obscured the all-important boundary of Bacon's property. The depictions of these houses are otherwise accurate, though Coffyn's placing of the doors seems odd. For the same reason some other buildings have become an odd collection of windows and walls. Coffyn carefully shows their garden gates.

Showing passages under buildings is difficult on a pictorial plan. Coffyn does this for the passage from Fetter Lane by the use of red lines. He was undoubtedly correct in showing the alley as a dead end, without a passage eastwards into Great New Street. Not only is no such passage shown on Ogilby and Morgan's or Strype's maps either, but when Nevill's Court was created it would not have led anywhere, and when the passage was eventually recorded it passed through what had been Mundy's plot rather than between plots (Fig. 4). A passage to Great New Street existed by the time of Rocque's map in the 1740s, but until 1836 £2 a year was paid to the Goldsmiths in return for it crossing their property. In that year the Goldsmiths agreed to make it a permanent right of way without payment

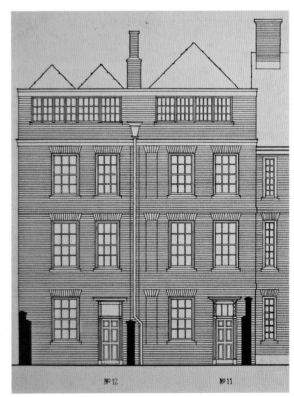

Fig. 8.   Elevation of 11 and 12 Nevill's Court, drawn for the Royal Commission on Historic Monuments. *English Heritage.*

Fig. 9.   Looking east
along Nevill's Court, with
Nos. 11–12 on the right,
c. 1900. *English Heritage.*

of rent, in exchange for the small part of Mundy's plot south of the
passage.[39] As for the passage to Chapel Court to the south, shown by Ogilby
and Morgan but not by Coffyn, this not only passed under No. 8 until the
later rebuilding of that house but was also privately owned rather than a
right of way, so Coffyn perhaps felt justified in leaving it out.[40]

The Later History of Nevill's Court

Philip Bacon apparently sold the Nevill's Court and Fetter Lane property in
1696.[41] The purchaser was Sir William Russell of North Ockenden in Essex,
who died in 1705. His son sold it to Sir Roger Hill of Denham in
Buckinghamshire for £8,000 in 1728. The whole of the land purchased by
Sir Nicholas Bacon remained a single holding until 1787, when 7 to 10
Nevill's Court were sold to the Moravian Church. The remainder was sold
by Hill's descendants in 1804 to Joseph Wolfe, a merchant of Botolph Lane,
for £6,000, and after his death was held in trust for his daughters. It was
split up only in 1900, when the Goldsmiths' Company acquired much of it.[42]

There were some changes on the ground. Nos. 7 to 9 Nevill's Court were
rebuilt in 1808,[43] and 1 Chapel Court on the backland south of No. 9 seems

to have been rebuilt at about the same time. Henthorn's two pre-Fire houses may still have existed in 1793, but were certainly rebuilt between then and 1901, and were added to: in 1803 there were three brick dwellings there, and by 1834 four. The upper two storeys of Trevers' house were rebuilt. Otherwise all or almost all the buildings shown on Coffyn's plan survived into the twentieth century, with the possible exceptions of 5 Nevill's Court and the workshops behind 41 Fetter Lane. There was some infilling: in 1803, in addition to the workshops behind 40 to 42 Fetter Lane, there were workshops or warehouses in front of 6 and 13A Nevill's Court.[44] That at No. 6 was later a single-storey factory and foundry, occupied by George Forrest & Sons, brassfounders, from at least 1895 to 1914. It remained an engineering works until the site was cleared in 1938.[45]

From the 1740s the Moravian congregation was important in the story of Nevill's Court. The Moravians were a Protestant community from the German-speaking area of Moravia, a descendant of the Hussite movement of the fifteenth century, forced into exile from the 1720s. Between 1738 and 1740 the Wesleys were associated with them. From 1740 they used a chapel just south of Nevill's Court, which had existed before the Great Fire and been rebuilt several times. Until 1777, when access was created from Fetter Lane, it could be reached only by the passage from Nevill's Court. The Moravians accommodated sections of their community in communal houses, and from 1744 they rented the Great House, which became known as Congregation House. They built up a substantial block of property, consisting of 7 to 10 Nevill's Court, the chapel, 1 and 2 Chapel Court and 29, 30 and 32 Fetter Lane. However, in the nineteenth century the congregation increasingly moved out to the suburbs, and their Hornsey church of 1908 eventually became their main place of worship in London. In 1908 they offered to sell 8 to 10 Nevill's Court to the Goldsmiths, and they were willing to sell the whole block provided they could retain a lease of their chapel, but nothing came of this. They last held services in the Fetter Lane chapel in 1940, but there is still a Fetter Lane congregation, which worships at Chelsea.[46]

By the twentieth century, Nevill's Court had long since lost any social distinction it had once had, and the houses were let out as lodgings. The Moravians had eight separate tenants in the Great House in 1907, and at least twenty people were living there in 1911.[47] But it was in the twentieth century that Nevill's Court acquired its most famous resident. In 1902 Keir Hardie, the founder of the Independent Labour Party, took lodgings in No. 14. Hardie evidently loved the quirky, old-fashioned character of Nevill's Court, and valued the combination of convenient location and seclusion. As described in 1906, one ascended 'a flight of rickety winding stairs' to find his office on the first floor on the left, above which was 'one large room made into two apartments by heavy green curtains', where Hardie lived when in London. Another account refers to a large room divided by match-board partitions into sitting room, bedroom and kitchen. The Goldsmiths' records indicate that in 1911 Hardie had a room on the ground floor (presumably his office) and two rooms on the second floor. His fellow tenants were, on the first floor, Yorke Smith, an assurance agent, aged thirty, with one room, and Thomas Shields, mount cutter, and his wife Anne, with two rooms they had rented for thirty-two years; on the second floor Miss Mortimer, aged seventy-six, a former domestic servant, with one room; and on the top floor Miss Duncombe and Miss Mayhew, each with one room. In the garden outside Hardie grew Welsh leeks, primroses and gowans. He referred to 'the silence and solitude of my London mansion, which is the envy of all who have seen it', and said that 'I would not exchange residences with his most gracious majesty Edward VII'. To his rooms in Nevill's Court came a wide range of people — 'an Indian prince at one time, a Highland crofter at another, and, of course, his colleagues of the [Independent Labour Party] Council and his own family folk from Cumnock and Cambuslang'. Here also came his great admirer, Sylvia Pankhurst.[48]

By then Nevill's Court was on borrowed time, as the Goldsmiths' Company sought to increase the value of its dilapidated property there. Nos. 35 to 38 Fetter Lane were demolished in 1910.[49] Nos. 13A to 15 Nevill's

Fig. 10.   Keir Hardie in his rooms at 10 Nevill's Court, c. 1912.

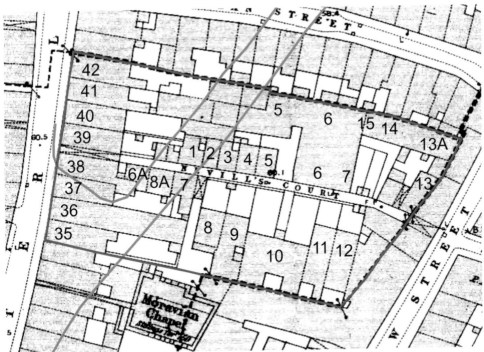

Fig. 11. Nevill's Court and part of Fetter Lane on the OS map of 1874, with the Bacons' plot outlined in red and street numbers as they were in 1900 added. The original numbering was 1 to 6 on the north side and 7 to 12 to the south. Renumbering to take account of extra buildings caused the muddle on the north side. No. 7 (north) was later renumbered 6A. The approximate course of the roadway of the current New Fetter Lane is shown in green.

Court followed in 1911, after a ceiling collapsed at No. 14 and floors had to be shored up; one of the photos of Keir Hardie, evidently taken at No. 14, shows two large posts supporting the ceiling.[50] The demolition caused Hardie to move to new lodgings in the Great House (Fig. 10), given up shortly before his death in 1915.[51] The Goldsmiths' Company purchased more of Nevill's Court and its Fetter Lane frontage, and by 1928 had the whole of what had belonged to the Bacons except the Moravians' properties.[52] From 1904 it was seeking to drive a road through Nevill's Court. The alley would have been widened mainly on the south side but also partly on the north; only the Great House might have survived. The Moravians were willing to acquiesce in the widening, and the City Corporation was willing to build the road, despite regarding it as almost entirely for the benefit of the Goldsmiths' Company, but the obstacles included the owner of 39 Fetter Lane (until 1928) and several lessees and protected tenants. Despite the matter being periodically raised into the 1930s and widening being expected imminently in 1931, no widening ever took place; in 1933 and probably later, protected tenants were still preventing it.[53] Meanwhile several sites were empty, and the tenant of 7 Nevill's Court began an archaeological dig on the adjoining land, which was brought to a conclusion by Mortimer Wheeler in 1932. Roman, Saxon, medieval and later material was found.[54]

When the investigators of the Royal Commission on Historical Monuments visited in 1928, the Great House, 11 and 12 Nevill's Court, the two lower storeys of Trevers' house and 39–42 Fetter Lane were still standing, all with their original staircases and most with panelling.[55] Nos. 39–42 Fetter Lane had gone by 1931, and all the other buildings north of the Court by 1939, though the south side of Nevill's Court remained intact.[56] The final destruction, including that of the Great House, was brought about by incendiary bombs on 11 May 1941. The flames spread from Fetter Lane, and press reports state that the Great House succumbed only after a twenty-four-hour struggle to put them out.[57] A photo taken afterwards shows the external walls and gables still standing,[58] and in other European countries the Great House might have been reconstructed. The Moravians sold their Fetter Lane and Nevill's Court enclave to the Goldsmiths' Company in 1949. By then, instead of a widened Nevill's Court, the City Corporation had decided to create what is now New Fetter Lane (Fig. 11). In about 1955, after three and a half centuries, the last remains of Nevill's Court were obliterated.[59]

Acknowledgements

I am grateful for help from David Beasley, Eleni Bide and Sophia Tobin at the Worshipful Company of Goldsmiths, Lorraine Parsons at the Moravian Church Archive and Library, Nigel Wilkins and others at English Heritage and archivists at London Metropolitan Archives.

1. LTS Publication No. 58 (1928).
2. Goldsmiths' Company (hereafter GC), B IV, City 133 (i), box 3; GC, volumes of plans 1895, etc.
3. The only others seem to be plans of King's Bench Prison, Southwark, c. 1660 (TNA, MPE 1/1090), the Unicorn Inn, Southwark, c. 1680 (Society of Antiquaries), Church Entry, Blackfriars, 1702 (London Metropolitan Archives (hereafter LMA), Collage, record 1650) and properties in Bermondsey, 1711 (Southwark Local History and Archives, West Box D, No. 411).
4. Bodleian Library, Gough Maps 21, fo. 28.
5. For an example, see image for map of Skreens, 1666, in Essex Record Office's online catalogue (http://seax.essexcc.gov.uk); ref. D/DXa 21.
6. TNA, C 24/916, Ward v. Bennett.
7. LMA, P69/DUN2/C/002/MS02969/002 to 004.
8. A. Stuart Mason, 'An Upstart Art: Early Mapping in Essex' (typescript, c. 1996, copy in

British Library), pp. 62, 67; Sarah Bendall (ed.), *Dictionary of Land Surveyors and Local Map-Makers of Great Britain and Ireland 1530–1850*, 2 (1997), p. 105.

9. W. H. Rylands (ed.), *A Visitation of the County of Suffolk ... 1664 ... 1668*, Harleian Society, 61 (1910), p. 131.

10. TNA, PROB 11/387, Sir Nicholas Bacon.

11. Sir Walter Prideaux, *Memorials of the Goldsmiths' Company* (n.d.), pp. 26, 109, 124, 127–8; David Beasley, 'Shoe Lane: The Archivist's Tale', *Goldsmiths Review* (2004/5), p. 12.

12. GC, Court minute book Lii (1573–9), fos. 194, 197; British Library, Add. MS 25590, fos. 58–9. The heading to the latter (Bacon's register of deeds) describes the property as 'certen gardens neare Fewter Lane'. GC, No. 1390, B393, links the 1574 grant to Nevill's Court. The Goldsmiths seem to have begun the building of four houses on the Fetter Lane site but to have changed their minds in 1572 (GC, Court minute book K, L (1566–73), fos. 103, 111, 125, 131, 133).

13. Alan Simpson, *The Wealth of the Gentry 1540–1660* (1963), pp. 56, 77.

14. TNA, C 142/369/158; TNA, PROB 11/287, Nicholas Bacon; TNA, PROB 11/387, Sir Nicholas Bacon; Simpson, *Wealth*, p. 100; below. See also W. C. Metcalfe (ed.), *The Visitations of Suffolk ... 1561 ... 1577 ... 1612* (1882), pp. 109–10; Rylands, *Visitation*, p. 131; Joan Corder (ed.), *The Visitation of Suffolk, 1561* (1981), pp. 158–60; B. D. Henning (ed.), *The History of Parliament: The House of Commons 1660–90*, 1 (1983), pp. 580–1.

15. LMA, COL/CA/01/02/002, fo. 534a.

16. Fire Court decree, in British Library, Add. MS 5074, No. 17, fos. 130, 132. The decree is summarized in Philip E. Jones (ed.), *The Fire Court*, 2 vols. (1966, 1970), vol. 2, pp. 362–4.

17. TNA, PROB 11/240, Richard Gainsford.

18. 'Disappearing London', *London Topographical Record*, IX (1914), p. 34; Walter G. Bell, 'Nevill's Court, Fetter Lane', *London Topographical Record*, XV (1931), p. 91. That the Great House was the town house of the Nevill family until 1744 (Philip Davies, *Lost London 1870–1945* (2009), p. 105) is contradicted by the deeds and rate lists.

19. The second husband of Edward Bacon's sister, Elizabeth, was Sir Henry Nevill of Berkshire (Metcalfe, *Visitations*, p. 109), but no evidence has been found linking him to Nevill's Court.

20. Bell, 'Nevill's Court', p. 88.

21. British Library, Add. MS 5074, No. 17, fo. 132.

22. Matthew Davies et al. (eds.), *London and Middlesex 1666 Hearth Tax*, British Record Society Hearth Tax Series, 9, part 2 (2014), p. 762.

23. TNA, PROB 11/387, Sir Nicholas Bacon; LMA, GL ADMSS 1019.

24. John Schofield, *Medieval London Houses* (1994), pp. 53, 60.

25. LMA, P69/DUN2/C/002/MS02969/002, p. 401.

26. TNA, PROB 5/5791.

27. LMA, P69/DUN2/C/002/MS02969/002, p. 401.

28. T. C. Wales and C. P. Hartley (eds.), *The Visitation of London begun in 1687*, part 1 (Harleian Society, 2004), p. 35.

29. John Strype, *A Survey of the Cities of London and Westminster* (1720), p. 282.

30. GC, B IV, City 133 (i).

31. LMA, P69/DUN2/C/002/MS02969/002, p. 343; Davies, *London and Middlesex 1666 Hearth Tax*, p. 762.

32. British Library, Add. MS 5074, No. 17, fo. 132; LMA, P69/DUN2/C/002/MS02969/002, p. 480. See also LMA, COL/CHD/LA/03/025/009/009.

33. *Survey of the Building Sites in the City of London after the Great Fire of 1666*, LTS Publication No. 101, II (1964), pp. 21, 39, 42; ibid., LTS Publication No. 97, III (1962), p. 69; LMA, GL ADMSS 1019; GC, B IV, City 133 (i), box 3, sale catalogue 1803.

34. *Survey of the Building Sites*, II, p. 146; ibid., LTS Publication No. 98, IV (1962), p. 126.
35. TNA, E 179/252/23, m. 97; LMA, P69/DUN2/C/002/MS02969/004.
36. A. F. Kelsall, 'The London House Plan in the Later 17th Century', *Post-Medieval Archaeology*, 8 (1974), pp. 80, 88–90.
37. T. M. M. Baker, *London: Rebuilding the City after the Great Fire* (2000), pp. 56, 62, 141, 163.
38. See A. C Edwards and K. C. Newton, *The Walkers of Hanningfield* (1984), pp. 81–2.
39. GC, B IV, City 142 (i), 1897 plan.
40. Moravian Church Archive (hereafter MCA), indenture 1870; GC, B IV, City 133 (i), box 1, 1724 deed. Ogilby and Morgan were almost certainly wrong in showing the chapel passage continuing to Great New Street.
41. GC, B393, No. 1910 (rent book, 1694–1712). GC, Warden's accounts 1697–1707, continue to record payments from 'Bacon Esq' until 1705–6. The transfer definitely took place before Russell's death not later than June 1705 (TNA, PROB 11/483, Sir William Russell; GC, B IV, City 133 (i), deed of trust 1728).
42. GC, B IV, City 133 (i) and (ii). The Goldsmiths' deeds indicate the transfer of only 7, 9, 10 and the passage under 8 to the Moravians in 1786–8, whereas the Moravians' deeds indicate the transfer of 8 to 10, occupying on the plan the sites of 7 to 10 (MCA, C/36/25/9); the building lease for 7–9 states that the former premises were known as 7 and 9 (MCA, C/36/23/1); possibly 8 and 9 had been combined before 1786.
43. MCA, C/36/23/11/1.
44. GC, B IV, City 133 (i), box 3, sale catalogue 1803; LMA, P69/DUN2/C/017/MS02974/002; English Heritage, notes made for RCHM in March 1928 by A. T. Phillips.
45. *Post Office London Directory* (1895, 1914); GC, B IV, City 133 (iii).
46. Colin Podmore (ed.), *The Fetter Lane Moravian Congregation London 1742–1992* (1992), pp. 2, 3, 6–7, 13–14, 21, 22, 24; MCA, C/36/25/9; GC, B IV, City 142 (v).
47. MCA, C/36/23/18; 1911 census.
48. William Stewart, *Keir Hardie: A Biography* (1921), pp. 188–91; *The Sunday Oregonian*, 30 December 1906; Kenneth O. Morgan, *Keir Hardie: Radical and Socialist* (1975), pp. 126, 165; GC, B IV, City 142 (v); 1911 census.
49. MCA, C/36/25/17.
50. GC, B IV, City 142 (v); *London Topographical Record*, IX (1914), p. 33; National Library of Scotland, Dep. 176, Box 3.
51. Morgan, *Keir Hardie*, p. 126; Shirley Harrison, *Sylvia Pankhurst* (2012), p. 261.
52. GC, B IV, City 142 (i); GC, B IV, City 134 (ix).
53. GC, B IV, City 134 (ix); GC, B IV, City 142 (v).
54. GC, B IV, City 142 (iii); *Notes and Queries*, 180 (January–June 1941), p. 453.
55. Royal Commission on Historical Monuments (England), *An Inventory of the Historical Monuments in London*, 4, *The City* (1929), p. 164; English Heritage, notes made for RCHM in March 1928 by A. T. Phillips.
56. GC, B IV, City 133 (v); GC, B IV, City 134 (vii).
57. *The Moravian Messenger*, new ser., 51, no. 9 (September 1941), pp. 102–4; GC, B IV, City 142 (iii), cutting of 20 May 1941 (unknown paper).
58. MCA, C/36/27/14/3.
59. GC, B IV, City 133 (v); GC, B IV, 134 (xii).

X.   A NEW DISCOVERY, A PORTION OF THE LOST CHISWICK ENCLOSURE MAP

By TRACEY LOGAN

A RECENTLY discovered section of Chiswick's Enclosure Map, missing for over half a century, shows how some enclosed lands were bartered between the Duke of Devonshire and the Vicar of Chiswick in the early 1800s, enhancing approaches to Chiswick House and gardens and increasing the size of the Vicar's Glebe allotment.

The parish of Chiswick lies on the north banks of the River Thames where it forms a broad loop between Hammersmith and Kew. The church of St Nicholas, which sits on the loop's south-eastern side, once served fishermen and ferrymen. Other ancient villages in the parish include the riverside Strand-on-the-Green and Turnham Green, to the north. Although by the eighteenth century there were villas and mansions on the parish outskirts and, centrally, the Earl of Burlington's Chiswick House, much of Chiswick's fertile but flood-prone peninsular lands were farmed until the twentieth century.[1] The newly discovered map focuses on parcels of land between St Nicholas's Church and Turnham Green, the ancient Chiswick Common Field south of the Brentford to London road. These were lands allotted to the Duke of Devonshire and Vicar of Chiswick in the Enclosure Acts. The map is a copy of part of the original, drawn up in 1867 when the Vicar's allotment was about to be leased for a housing development: the Glebe Estate. Driving into London today, the map area forms the hinterland surrounding the A3 and A4 as they meet at the Hogarth roundabout before merging onwards to Hammersmith and central London.

The trail leading to this discovery started in February 2013 when residents of the Glebe Estate began researching its history. They wished to know the exact size, shape and ownership of the original Glebe Field.[2] The nineteenth-century Chiswick Enclosure Map would provide the answers, if it could be found, but records showed it had been missing since at least 1958 and one leading expert suggests it may never have existed.[3] Then came the discovery, in August 2013, of a pristine copy of part of the enclosure map. In the file next to it was an extract from the Chiswick Enclosure Award, dated 13 August 1840. The mapping and surveying process had taken twenty-six years to complete and publish. This discovery proved the Enclosure Award and Map did exist after all (Fig. 1).

The Chiswick Enclosure Acts of 1806 and 1814 extinguished all common grazing rights on around 140 acres of Chiswick lands south of the road from Brentford to London and north of the looping River Thames. The Acts also enabled the 6th Duke of Devonshire to block off and privatise former public

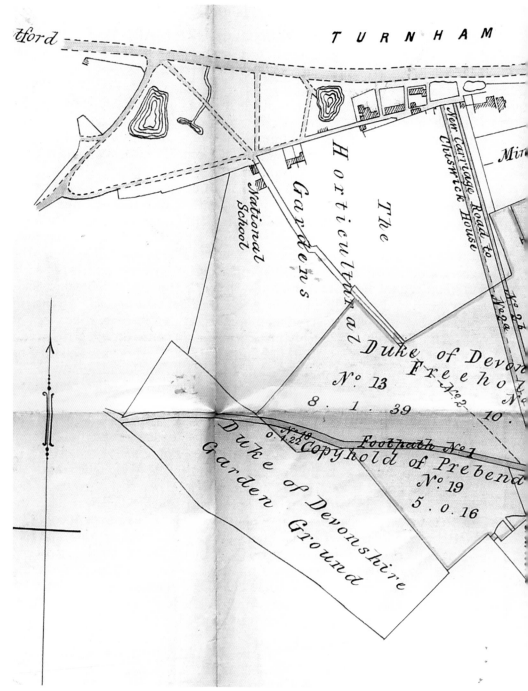

Fig. 1.   Fragment of the lost Chiswick Enclosure Map of 1840:
newly discovered copy dated 14 January 1867.
© *Church of England Record Centre.*

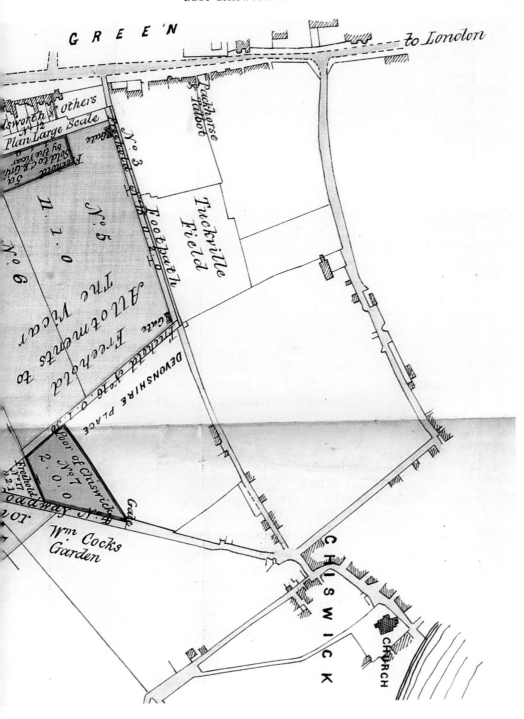

rights of way in Chiswick and to build entirely new private access roads and footpaths, for example to his Chiswick House. Ultimately, this created fertile ground for property speculation later in the nineteenth century, sowing the seeds of suburban development long before the arrival of the railways.

The transformation began in 1806 with an Act of Parliament that extinguished Rights of Common over 100 acres owned by the 5th Duke of Devonshire, and also:

> 'some portion of ... land in Chiswick Field' to which the Vicar of Chiswick 'claims to be entitled' and 'it is alleged that some other Portion of the Land ... belongs to the Poor of Chiswick'.[4]

These were Lammas Lands, so called because commoners were entitled to graze livestock on them for six months each year after Lammas Day (12 August) 'between the time the crop is carried off ... until the same are sown again'. A final forty acres were enclosed by the 1814 Act so that 'intermixed lands' on Chiswick Common Field could be fenced off and redistributed for the benefit of the Duke of Devonshire's Estate and the Vicar of Chiswick.[5] It was this Act which produced the detail on the newly discovered portion of the Chiswick Enclosure Map.

The 1814 Enclosure Act set in stone a land exchange between Duke and Vicar which had probably already happened. This was a common reason for enclosures, establishing in law local informal arrangements. The Act granted lands to William Spencer, 6th Duke of Devonshire which he used to enhance the front and rear approaches to his sumptuous neo-Palladian villa and gardens at Chiswick House. And it gave the Vicar a large and more manageable agricultural plot. The land exchange made the front approach to Chiswick House grander and hid it from the view of passing traffic on Burlington Lane. The deal was as follows: if the Vicar would give the Duke a plot of Glebe land in front of Chiswick House, then the Vicar would get an extra-large chunk of Chiswick Common Field abutting another Glebe allotment.[6] These are the words of the Enclosure Award (Fig. 2):

> And we do hearby further Allot and Award unto ... Thomas Frere Bowerbank ... Vicar and his successors ... All that Allotment piece or parcel of Land No. 6 on the said plan and containing by estimation 8 acres and 2 Roods situate and being in Chiswick Common Field ... in lieu of and as compensation for a certain piece or parcel of Meadow Ground being the North part of the Avenue Meadow fronting Chiswick House containing 4 acres 1 rood 24 perches (in the said recited Act stated to contain 4 acres 2 roods 25 perches) ... being part of the Glebe Land belonging to the ... Vicarage and directed by the said Act to be Awarded to ... William Spencer Duke of Devonshire the ... Allotment No. 6 exceeding by one fourth part in value the ... Meadow Ground as required by the ... Act.[7]

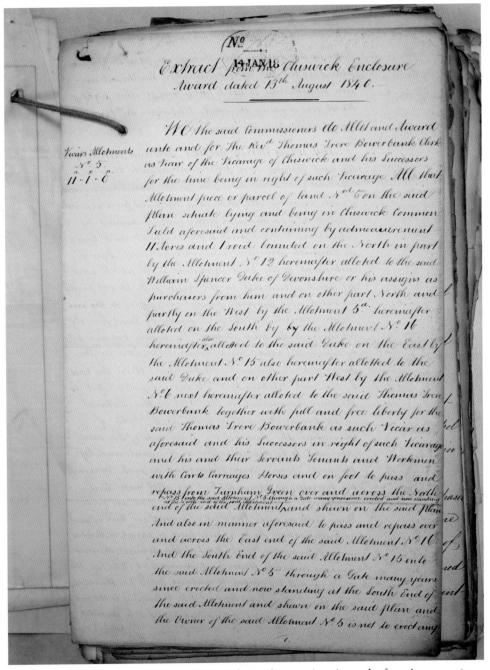

Fig. 2. Extract from the lost Chiswick Enclosure Act Award of 13 August 1840 details land swap between the Duke of Devonshire and the Vicar of Chiswick. © *Church of England Record Centre.*

That this land exchange was already well underway or had even been completed before the 1814 Act was passed is clear from an 1818 survey of the Duke of Devonshire's Chiswick Estate by his surveyor, Peter Potter of Kentish Town. It shows Burlington Lane newly bulging to the south of Chiswick House and the gardens re-landscaped accordingly.[8] Some mystery surrounds the origins of freehold allotment to the Vicar, No. 5 on the map, an 11¼-acre parcel of land acquired by the Vicar in the Enclosure Award, land previously part of Chiswick Common Field. There is no 11-acre field listed in a 1769 list of Chiswick Glebe Lands.[9] Was Plot No. 5 given to the Vicar in exchange for other Glebe plots? Ultimately, the Enclosures gave the Vicar a new, 21-acre field of fertile land conveniently close to the church.

Two independent surveyors, or 'Commissioners for the Execution of the [Enclosure] Act', were appointed to fairly 'value, divide, set out and allot' lands belonging to the Duke of Devonshire, the Vicar of Chiswick and 'other Persons'.

The commissioners named in the Act were John Willock of Golden Square, Middlesex (now London's Soho) and John Burcham of Conisby in Lincoln. However, John Willock died in post, and in 1826 a new commissioner, probably Edward Driver of Richmond Terrace in London, was appointed in his place.[10]

The portion of the Enclosure Map discovered in 2013 focuses mainly on the Vicar's allotments in Chiswick Common Field. But also most intriguing are the new and changed roads and footpaths both around the Glebe Field and across the Duke of Devonshire's freehold lands there.[11] Although less detailed and without explanatory notes, these are of great interest as they show initial plans for what is today known as Duke's Avenue.

The 47 × 36 cm map is a tracing in ink on butter (thick tracing) paper, largely black and white with coloured and patterned features characteristic of the surveyor, Edward Driver's, other enclosure maps.[12] It is stamped '14 JAN 1867'. The crowded area in the centre of the map, near the top, shows 'No. 12 See Plan Large Scale' (newly allotted to the Duke of Devonshire[13]) above C. E. Griffiths' single freehold allotment No. 5a. A rough calculation suggests the scale of this map is one inch to six chains (1:4608), perhaps one-third the original size.[14]

Freehold land is shown in colour: the Duke of Devonshire's plot Nos. 13, 14, 17, 18, 19, and 20 are yellow; plot Nos. 15 and 16 (very thin strips of land adjacent to the eastern and southern boundaries of the Vicar's field) look sepia, not yellow, but they too belonged to the Duke, allotted to him in the Enclosure Award. The Vicar's plot Nos. 5 and 6 are pink; plot No. 5a, owned by Mr C. E. Griffiths, is green and plot No. 7, belonging to the Poor of Chiswick is grey. Buildings are shaded in diagonal black lines with St Nicholas Church, next to the River Thames, cross-hatched in black. Driver's water features are indicated by blue line-work and not by the more common blue shading. Field boundary ownership is indicated by 'T' symbols at right-angles to the boundary. These can be seen along the eastern boundaries of the Vicar's Allotment and the Duke of Devonshire's Freehold, as well as on the western boundary of plot No. 7, marked Poor of Chiswick. The head of the 'T' falls in the field of the owner responsible for upkeep of the fence.[15] Gates to the Glebe Field are fully drawn, though elsewhere are shown by a simple line across a road or footpath. The numbered parts of this map are the most reliable. Spelling and perhaps other errors occur elsewhere. 'Tuckville Field', for example, is probably Tuckwell Field,[16] and the large plot marked 'Mintum' is more likely 'Minton' after Samuel Minton, who owned a large house and land there.[17]

As with many enclosure maps, sepia is the colour of choice for public roads and footpaths, for example along the Brentford to London Road. Private rights of way are here mostly coloured blue. Footpath No. 1 and Roadway No. 4 (a single sepia-shaded 'Public Footpath' in the Potter Map) is blue and labelled 'Copyhold of Prebend Manor'. Also blue are two new private rights of way, plots 2a and 2b, along the Duke's 'New Carriage Road to Chiswick House'. Footpath No. 3, to the east of the Vicar's Allotment, has changed from sepia on the Potter Map to blue here, showing it now to be an enclosed, private, right of way.[18] Finally, a diagonal broken black line marked 'No. 2', across the Duke of Devonshire's Freehold land, follows the route of a former public footpath across Turnham Green shown in the Potter Map. Although lost to the public the 6th 'Bachelor' Duke of Devonshire (sponsor of the 1814 Act) retained this path as a link between his Chiswick House gardens and those of the Horticultural Society, in which he took a keen interest.[19] The juxtaposition of Footpath No. 1 and Roadway No. 4 seem strange at first glance, especially since Roadway No. 4 is very short and gated at both its eastern end (above the words 'Wm. Cocks Garden') and at the west, just above the M in the yellow plot marked 'Manor No. 20'. An 1836 map describes the combined Footpath No. 1 and Roadway No. 4 as 'Bridle Road to Sutton',[20] and a map of 1847 shows this stretch, by then called Hogarth Lane, still gated to the east but with what appears to be a landscaped traffic island at its intersection with 'Duke's Road' (now Duke's Avenue), the Duke's gated estate and a much narrower route to the west.[21]

Today Footpath No. 1 and Roadway No. 4 have been subsumed into the A4's six-lane dual carriageway, a busy gateway from London to the west of England and Wales. In the 'Bachelor' Duke's day, this appears to have been a private thoroughfare. The eastern access gate to Roadway No. 4 may have served as tradesmen's entrance to Chiswick House and gardens, though the author has been unable to locate other documentary evidence for this. However, Roadway No. 4 would not have offered the sort of grand approach to the Duke of Devonshire's lands that his New Carriage Road to Chiswick House provided (plot Nos. 2a and 2b). Although not drawn on this map, that eastern 'Gate' to Roadway No. 4 would, in 1840, have been immediately overlooked by the extremely poor inhabitants of the newly built Chiswick New Town.[22]

Today pedestrians can walk (via the Hogarth Roundabout's ghastly underpass) from Chiswick High Road to St Nicholas's Church and the River Thames. Following the Chiswick enclosures this route, along the 'Chiswick Field Lane', was barred to all but the Vicar and his representatives who had limited north and south access to the Glebe Field. Here were the rules as set out by the Enclosure Commissioners:

> full and free liberty for ... Thomas Frere Bowerbank as such Vicar ... and his Successors in right of such Vicarage and his and their servants tenants and Workmen with carts carriages horses and on foot to pass and repass from Turnham Green over and across the North End of ... Allotment No.15 into ... Allotment No. 5 through a gate many years since erected and now standing at the north end of the said Allotment and shown on the said Plan. And also in manner aforesaid to pass and repass over and across the East end of ... Allotment No.16 and the south end of ... Allotment No. 15 into ... Allotment No. 5.[23]

It was not until 1869 that Chiswick Field Lane, today's Devonshire Road, once again opened to the public.[24]

The answers to those original questions posed by Glebe Estate residents in 2013 have been provided by the discovery of this portion of the Chiswick Enclosure Map. The Glebe field which, after the Enclosures, measured 19 acres and 3 roods, was formed by combining a plot of 11 acres and 1 rood with another measuring 8 acres and 2 roods. It was leased for development in 1868 for a term of 999 years.[25] The details published here now prove the existence of a once doubted Chiswick Enclosure Map and Award dated 13 August 1840. Their loss to modern historians is not so surprising, considering that even in 1844 Tithe Commissioners were told there was no map of Chiswick Parish.[26] The complete and original Enclosure Map and Award have been recorded as missing since 1958.[27] The author would welcome any information or suggestions as to their whereabouts.

Acknowledgements

The author wishes to thank Dr Sally Jeffery for her expert guidance and encouragement in this research. Also, the staff of Chiswick Library's Local Studies Collection, the British Library's map experts Peter Barber and Tom Harper, and Enclosure Acts authority Professor Roger Kain, Dean of the University of London's School of Advanced Study, for their assistance and many helpful pointers.

1. T. F. T. Baker and C. R. Elrington (eds), *Chiswick Growth*, Victoria County History of Middlesex vol. 7: Acton, Chiswick, Ealing and Brentford, West Twyford, Willesden (1982), pp. 54–68, available at British History Online, http://www.british-history.ac.uk/report.aspx?compid=22559&strquery=chiswick%20Growth (accessed 9 February 2014).

2. Chiswick's Glebe Estate consists of the following: Glebe, Dale and Fraser Streets, Reckitt, Quick and Binns Roads, Devonshire Road (west side) and Duke Road, south of Glebe Street.

3. W. E. Tate and M. E. Turner, *A Domesday of English Enclosure Acts and Awards* (Reading: The Library, University of Reading, 1978), p. 174.

4. London Metropolitan Archives (LMA), MS ACC/1437/1, 46 Geo III c.111: 'An Act for extinguishing all Right of Common over certain Parcels of Land in the Parish of *Chiswick*, in the County of Middlesex. [3d July 1806]', p. 2225.

5. LMA, MS ACC/1437/2 54 Geo III c.69: 'An Act for inclosing certain Lands in the Parish of *Chiswick*, in the County of *Middlesex*, over which Right of Common hath been extinguished. [18th *May* 1814]', pp. 1197–8, also p. 1202 (power to stop roads), p. 1203 (allotment to the Vicar in Chiswick to be taken from the share of the Duke of Devonshire), p. 1204 (fencing the Vicar's allotments).

6. Peter Hammond, *Moving Burlington Lane*, Brentford & Chiswick Local History Journal, 21 (London: Carfax Cards Ltd, 2012), p. 22.

7. Church of England Records Centre (CERC), MS ECE-7-1-36597, 'Extract from the Chiswick Enclosure Award dated 13th August, 1840', pp. 2–3.

8. Chatsworth Archive, 'A Plan of the Mansion and Estate of Chiswick in the County of Middlesex Belonging to The Most Noble William Spencer Duke of Devonshire, Surveyed by Peter Potter, Kentish Town, 1818'.

9. Chatsworth Archive, MS L/21/24 'Glebe Lands of Chiswick ... from a Book in the Church Chest by the Vicar in 1769 ... from Mr Driver 27 Nov 1807'.

10. Chatsworth Archive, MS L21/18 'Chiswick Inclosure. Consents to inclosure 1840'. Duke of Devonshire seeks appointment of a new Enclosure Commissioner Grateful following the death of John Willock. Also, *The Morning Chronicle*, Saturday 1 August 1840. 'Chiswick Inclosure' advertises the imminent execution of the 'Inclosure Award' in the presence of John Burchem and Edward River (*sic*), the (enclosure) Commissioners. I am indebted to Peter and Carolyn Hammond for these references.

11. By comparison with Peter Potter map of 1818, op. cit.

12. Roger J. P. Kain, John Chapman and Richard R. Oliver, *The Enclosure Maps of England and Wales 1595–1918* (Cambridge: The Press Syndicate of the University of Cambridge, 2004), p. 230. Also accompanying electronic catalogue and database hosted by: History Data Service of the UK Data Archive, http://hds.essex.ac.uk/em/index.html, search catalogue under *Sellinge, East Malling and Teston in Kent* (accessed 13 January 2014).

13. CERC, op. cit., 'Extract from the Chiswick Enclosure Award ...', p. 1.

14. Kain et al., op. cit., 'a majority (of enclosure maps) are in the range of one inch to 2 chains (1:1584)', p. 170.

15. Kain et al., op. cit., p. 189.

16. Peter Potter's 1818 map, op. cit., has Tuckwell.

17. Assessment no. 364, 'Chiswick Parish Poor Rate Book', 1839, p. 20.

18. Chiswick Library Local Studies Centre, Minutes of the Chiswick Improvement Commissioners, 26 April 1865. Letter from William Currey, Duke of Devonshire's Solicitor, states: 'I find that the late Duke promised Mr Brand of Turnham Green that during his (Mr Brand's) life the road should not be opened'.

19. Gillian Clegg, *Chiswick House and Gardens: A History* (London: McHugh Publications,

2011), p. 58: A private gate (the small gate within the wall from the car park to the Walled Gardens') was installed to allow the Duke (who was made president of the Society in 1838) to enter the gardens whenever he pleased.

20. W. S. Leonard, 'Plan of Sutton Court Boundary', op. cit.

21. LMA, MS D2/D/M/116, 'Plan of the Parish of Chiswick in the County of Middlesex 1847. Dedicated (by permission) To His Grace The Most Noble William Spencer, Duke of Devonshire, By his Grace's most obliged and obedient Servant, John Pyne. Surveyor, Warwick Square, Kensington'.

22. William P. Roe, 'Homes for the workers: Chiswick New Town', *Brentford and Chiswick Local History Journal*, 6 (1997), http://brentfordandchiswicklhs.org.uk/local-history/housing/homes-for-the-workers-chiswick-new-town/ (accessed 23 December 2014).

23. CERC, op. cit., 'Extract from the Chiswick Enclosure Award ...', pp. 1–2.

24. CERC, op. cit., No. 717, Letter from William Binns Smith to Ecclesiastical Commissioners, 13 January 1869: ... the Duke of Devonshire has consented to sell my clients both all of Chiswick Field Lane and the plantation to the south of the Glebe.

25. Church of England Records Centre (CERC), MS ECE-7-1-36597, 'Attested Copy of Memorandum' (lease), 20 November 1868.

26. TNA, MS IR18/5467, 'Chiswick Tithe Files', Minutes of Chiswick Tithe Award meeting of 17 August 1844.

27. W. E. Tate, op. cit., LMA, Ordering List for the Middlesex Enclosure Acts (MR/DE/A) Courts Folder 104, pp. 1814–15. Also private correspondence with Parliamentary Archives, Chatsworth Archives, British Library, and Chiswick Library Local Studies Service shows the Chiswick Enclosure Map to be missing.

XI. WILLAN'S FARM — IN MEMORIAM

By ANN SAUNDERS

THESE two drawings of farmyard tools (Figs 1 and 2) were purchased by me at a small exhibition of London drawings, held about 1967 at Burgh House, Hampstead.[1] One represents an unidentified implement with heavy shafts (Fig. 1), the other a distinctive narrow but lofty farm cart (Fig. 2); the drawing of the complete cow (Fig. 3), affably chewing the cud, was only discovered when the drawings were taken from their frames to be photographed. A second cow, bisected horizontally, is above the complete animal.

Willan's Farm occupied the eastern and northern parts of what is now Regent's Park. In the right-hand corner of the drawing of the complete cow is the date 1814; above it, below the hoof of the now bisected cow, a faint signature can be read with the aid of a powerful magnifying glass – 'Young'. Examination of Algernon Graves, *Exhibitors at the Royal Academy* – suggests that the signature is that of a proficient artist and drawing master, Tobias Young, visiting London, possibly from the Isle of Wight.

James Ward's painting of Marylebone Park (1807) now in the Tate Gallery (NO1175_10), is reproduced here (Fig. 4) from A. J. Skrimshire's engraving (1907) in the Ashbridge Collection at City of Westminster Archives. A similar cart appears on the right-hand side of a watercolour by William Sherlock (Fig. 5), also in the Ashbridge Collection.

1. For the early history of Marylebone (formerly the Manor of Tyburn), see Ann Saunders, *Regent's Park from 1086 to the Present*, 2nd edn (Bedford College, 1981).

Fig. 1   Drawn by Tobias Young (private collection)

Fig. 2   High-sided cart drawn by Tobias Young (private collection)

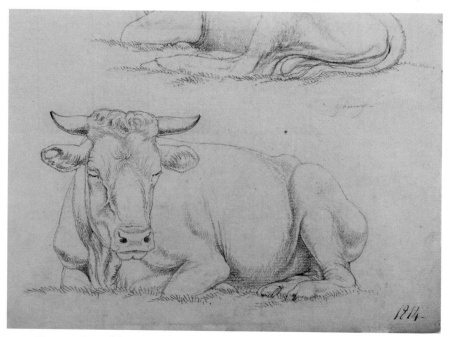

Fig. 3   Amiable cow drawn by Tobias Young (private collection)

Fig. 4.   Engraving of Regent's Park by A. J. Skrimshire (1907).
© *City of Westminster Archives*.

Fig. 5   Willan's Farm, watercolour by William Sherlock, *c.* 1800.
© *City of Westminster Archives*.

XII.   35 PATERNOSTER ROW

By SHEILA O'CONNELL

IN the winter of 1712/13 the young Samuel Molyneux frequented the famous bookshop of Christopher Bateman at the sign of the Bible and Crown at the corner of Paternoster Row and Warwick Lane. In a letter to his uncle William Molyneux written on 15 April 1713, he enthused:

> … when I mention the Opulency of Shops I must not forget my good Friend Mr. Bateman who I believe is the best Bookseller for choice Editions and old Librarys in the whole world and has accordingly vast Loads of Books in his Shop at all times.[1]

Paternoster Row, together with St Paul's Churchyard, had been a centre of the publishing trade from the early days of printing. For a time in the seventeenth century it became known for shops of mercers and lacemen, but they did not return after the Great Fire, and by 1700 the Row was again synonymous with the book trade. Bateman ran his shop from 1689 to 1730. The premises were large, with a frontage of 26 feet 4 inches to the Row and 22 feet to Warwick Lane. By the 1730s it was divided between several booksellers including Charles Davis and Thomas King, and from 1751 to 1788 John Hopkins and his successors were trading from the corner shop as pharmacists.[2] In 1844, ten years before Thomas Hosmer Shepherd made his watercolour for Frederick Crace, the building, by then numbered 35 Paternoster Row, and its neighbour, number 36, had been taken over by the publishers Thomas Nelson. Nelson's replaced the domestic scale building shown here with an imposing stone-faced edifice appropriate for the London offices of an international business. It was that building that was destroyed, along with the rest of the Row, in the bombing raid of 29 December 1940. The site was rebuilt in the 1960s according to designs by William Holford and at the turn of the millennium to designs by William Whitfield.

1. P. Holden, *The London Letters of Samuel Molyneux, 1712–13*, LTS Publication No. 172 (2011), p. 130.
2. J. Raven, 'Location, Size, and Succession: the Bookshops of Paternoster Row before 1800', in R. Myers, M. Harris and G. Mandelbrote, *The London Book Trade: Topographies of Print in the Metropolis from the Sixteenth Century* (Oak Knoll Press & The British Library, 2003), pp. 89–126.

Fig. 1.   Thomas Hosmer Shepherd (1793–1864), *Paternoster Row,
from the corner of Warwick Lane*. Watercolour.
© *British Museum 1880, 1113/4243.*

XIII.   REMEMBERING THE FATHER OF REFORM: THE CARTWRIGHT MEMORIAL AT ST MARY-AT-FINCHLEY

By ROGER BOWDLER

IN 1835, a limestone obelisk was erected over the burial vault of Major John Cartwright (1740–1824), 'the father of reform' (Fig. 1). Currently in a forlorn and dismantled state in one of Middlesex's most interesting graveyards, it is one of those memorials which reminds the visitor of the riches of the English churchyard, and makes an immediate connection with a key figure in the history of English radicalism.[1]

Cartwright was born in 1740 at Marnham, Nottinghamshire, the son of William Cartwright and his wife Anne, née Cartwright.[2] His brother Edward is celebrated as the inventor of the power loom. He entered the Royal Navy in 1758, but over-exertion and exposure while serving on the Newfoundland station forced him to return to England in 1770. In later years he was known as Major Cartwright, having entered the Nottinghamshire militia in 1775 when he felt unable to resume active

Fig. 1.   The Cartwright obelisk, 1835, St Mary-at-Finchley churchyard, London Borough of Barnet in 1995. *Historic England Archive.*

service on grounds of political conscience across the Atlantic. His unease over the governance of the American colonies led to his first published polemic: *American Independence: The Glory and Interest of Great Britain* (1774). Cartwright is therefore a figure of considerable interest to Americans as an early supporter of the republic. His growing interest in constitutional matters led next to a wider attack on parliamentary government in *Take Your Choice* (1776), an early plea for universal male suffrage. He 'formulated the specific demands for manhood suffrage which were to be the basis of a hundred years of agitation', wrote E. P. Thompson.[3] His political programme revolved around a return to imagined Anglo-Saxon political rights, and direct political participation: his own agenda included calls for annual elections, secret ballots, fairly divided electoral districts, paid MPs and the removal of a property qualification for them. Later on, his admiration for this fabled Anglo-Saxon past led him to call for the resurrection of a popular militia based on the *fyrd* during the French invasion scare of 1804–5.

Having attended a celebration of the second anniversary of the fall of the Bastille, in 1791, Cartwright was eventually deprived of his militia commission in the following year and his campaigning career intensified. A champion of various progressive causes (such as the anti-slavery movement and of Greek independence), Cartwright was a tireless promoter of constitutional reform. Among his associates were numbered Francis Place, Sir Francis Burdett, William Cobbett and Thomas Wooler (the printer-publisher of the radical organ *The Black Dwarf*). Together with Thomas Northmore, Cartwright played a leading role in the founding of Hampden Clubs across the country from 1812 onwards, which were dedicated to the promotion through publications and discussion groups of the cause of reform. Some of Cartwright's significance lies in the nature of his political activism: in the eyes of some historians, it was in no small measure thanks to his social conservatism that British radicalism adhered in the main to legal forms of protest. Far from being a demagogue, the Major was a radical campaigner of an eminently respectable cut. The presence of a memorial to his memory in a Middlesex churchyard is testimony enough to this.

No less a figure than Thomas Jefferson, third President of the United States, wrote to him in 1824 to salute his last work, *The English Constitution Produced and Illustrated* (1823). In thanking the Major, Jefferson expressed his eagerness at meeting his fellow octogenarian in the world to come:

> Your age of eighty-four, and mine of eighty-one years, ensure us of a speedy meeting. We may then commune at leisure, and more fully, on the good and evil, which in the course of our long lives, we have both witnessed; and in the meantime, I pray you to accept assurances of my high veneration and esteem for your person and character.[4]

Major Cartwright died later that year, a move to Hampstead having proved insufficient to restore his frail health. He was buried at St Mary-at-Finchley on 30 September 1824, a week after his death on 23 September, just before his eighty-fourth birthday. Not long after, a tablet (Fig. 2) was erected in his memory by his widow in the north aisle of the church.[5]

Cartwright was duly memorialized elsewhere. He had moved from Lincolnshire to Enfield in 1805, and in 1810 moved into town; from 1819 he lived at No. 37 Burton Crescent, Bloomsbury.[6] It is a tribute to his one-time standing that this street was in 1908 re-named as Cartwright Gardens, the name having become distasteful owing to several grisly murders having taken place there.[7] In the centre of its enclosed garden is a seated statue (Fig. 3) of the reformer, designed by the emerging Belfast-born sculptor Patrick Macdowell (1799–1870), who showed a design for the statue at the 1826 Royal Academy. The statue, erected in the end by a different sculptor, was duly unveiled on 20 July 1831. It remains an enigmatic late Georgian public memorial. Vivid and characterful, it depicts the Major as a man of contemplation and of stoic fortitude, Voltaire-like in his aged wisdom. This form of seated public statue in bronze was only just beginning to appear: Sir Richard Westmacott's *all'antica* Charles James Fox statue had been erected in Bloomsbury Square in 1819, and the Cartwright statue shows how the form could be adapted for more modest memorials.

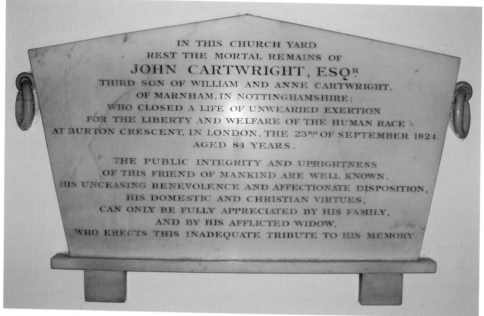

IN THIS CHURCH YARD
REST THE MORTAL REMAINS OF
JOHN CARTWRIGHT, ESQ[R]
THIRD SON OF WILLIAM AND ANNE CARTWRIGHT,
OF MARNHAM, IN NOTTINGHAMSHIRE;
WHO CLOSED A LIFE OF UNWEARIED EXERTION
FOR THE LIBERTY AND WELFARE OF THE HUMAN RACE
AT BURTON CRESCENT, IN LONDON, THE 23RD OF SEPTEMBER 1824.
AGED 84 YEARS.

THE PUBLIC INTEGRITY AND UPRIGHTNESS
OF THIS FRIEND OF MANKIND ARE WELL KNOWN.
HIS UNCEASING BENEVOLENCE AND AFFECTIONATE DISPOSITION,
HIS DOMESTIC AND CHRISTIAN VIRTUES,
CAN ONLY BE FULLY APPRECIATED BY HIS FAMILY,
AND BY HIS AFFLICTED WIDOW,
WHO ERECTS THIS INADEQUATE TRIBUTE TO HIS MEMORY.

Fig. 2.   Memorial tablet to Major Cartwright (d. 1834), St Mary-at-Finchley.
Author.

Fig. 3. Patrick Macdowell (designer), George Clarke (sculptor): Major Cartwright statue, 1831, Cartwright Gardens, London Borough of Camden. *Author.*

Macdowell's design had formed the frontispiece of the second volume of Cartwright's biography, written by his niece and published in 1826. This included an account of the public meeting held in June 1825 at the Crown and Anchor Tavern, chaired by Sir Francis Burdett, which sought to raise money

> to perpetuate the remembrance of one, whose long and laborious life had been devoted to those great principles upon which liberty depends ... I cannot, by any stretch of the imagination, conceive of any Greek or Roman virtue surpassing the public and private worth of my deceased friend.[8]

Burdett went on to outline an emerging commemorative plan:

> a sum, not exceeding £2000 should be raised, in order to perpetuate, by a single monument, the great public worth and private virtues of Major Cartwright. It appeared that £500 had already been subscribed, and the present meeting was called pursuant to resolutions of the Committee, assembled on the 1st inst. at the house of Peter Moore, Esq. MP, with whom, and other friends of the deceased, the idea had originated.[9]

Macdowell may have designed the statue and been its intended author, but in the end it was executed by Birmingham sculptor George Clarke (1796–1842), who offered to execute it for the actual amount raised by the public subscription. This was an offer too far: having undertaken the work, Clarke went bankrupt in 1832, the ambitious fund-raising target initiated by Burdett having not been met; Macdowell noted this come-down with some satisfaction.[10]

The obelisk at Finchley, the third memorial to Cartwright after the memorial tablet and the statue, was erected in 1835, shortly after his wife's death. This date is known from a brief notice in *The Mirror of Literature, Amusement and Instruction* for 19 December 1835:

> *The late Major Cartwright.* — The monument erected in Finchley churchyard, over the remains of Major Cartwright, has recently been pulled down, and a much more splendid one substituted. It bears the following inscription:- 'In this place are deposited the remains of John Cartwright, the son of William and Ann Cartwright, Commander in the Royal Navy, and many years Major in the Nottingham Militia. He was the author of various works on legislation; the earliest, most strenuous, and disinterested Reformer of his time; the intrepid advocate of liberty, whose labours for the public good terminated only with his life, on the 23rd of September, 1834; aged 84. Also the remains of his beloved wife, Anne Catherine Cartwright, who died on the 21st of December, 1834'.[11]

The Mirror did not, however, cite all the inscriptions on the pedestal.[12] These explain that Cartwright was buried at Finchley because his sister Elizabeth had been. The vault had been built by their step-father, George Fothergill (d. 1741), a London barrister, and in due course Cartwright's wife would join him in the grave at Finchley as well. Cartwright, who did not have any children, did not harbour grandiose hopes for his own burial: he asked for the simplest of funerals,[13] and in the event was accompanied to the grave by relatives and 'between 30 and 40 of his personal and political friends, some of whom came from great distance, and showed by their sorrow the sense they had of his worth and values'.[14]

The Cartwright obelisk at Finchley (currently dismantled, and hopefully awaiting conservation) (Fig. 4) consists of a limestone pedestal on a moulded base with a tall frieze, on the front of which is a worn armorial shield, beneath a deeply projecting coping. The sides of the pedestal sport marble inscription panels, including the one cited above; it is now seriously weathered. The upper section of the monument consists of an obelisk, executed in two blocks of stone (the lower block is badly eroded below the joint). On the front of the obelisk are two reliefs: below, executed within a circular field cut into the face of the block is a badly eroded profile portrait of Major Cartwright (Fig. 5). Above this is a second, smaller, circular relief which is so eroded as to be near-undecipherable. It appears to show two interlocked fish. In 1935 these were described as 'a hideous engraving of a head with the legend "Defend the fold". Likewise a coat of arms (with his

Fig. 4.   The dismantled Cartwright obelisk in 2010.
Author.

wife's) and crest'.[15] The armorial presence on the obelisk is a further reminder that this was a memorial to a very respectable variety of radical: 'His whole appearance and manner bore the stamp of an English gentleman of the old school', observed his obituary in *The Gentleman's Magazine*.[16]

Who erected the obelisk is not known: nor is the mason known, either. One other sculptor besides Macdowell and Clarke with known connections with Cartwright is John Ternouth (1796–1848), who exhibited drawings for the Cartwright statue at the Exhibition Society of British Artists in 1826.[17] The modeller John Henning the elder (1771–1851) executed a profile portrait of Cartwright, probably a preparatory study for a medallion:[18] this would provide a helpful source for re-carving, should the replacement of the disfigured relief carving on the monument be an option in the future (as it surely should). The most likely source, however, is probably the engraved profile portrait, undated, by Adam Buck (Fig. 6) which shows the sitter in a Grecian wig. The half-obliterated memorial portrait seems to show this look as well, whereas other representations show the Major as shaven-headed, in the earnest Roman republican manner.

Fig. 5.   The Cartwright obelisk, detail   Fig. 6.   Adam Buck, *Major Cartwright*.
of the portrait medallion in 1995.   Engraving, undated but *c.* 1816.
Historic England Archive.   *Felix Moore.*

Obelisks were not common in Georgian churchyards: more often they
were to be found as wayside memorials, such as the 1740 obelisk erected at
Monken Hadley to mark the putative site of the Battle of Barnet (1471), or
the 1750 obelisk erected at Stanmore Common, Harrow, to remember the
battle against Caesar fought by the Catuvellauni tribe.[19] Others were
essentially decorative embellishments to the street scene, such as George
Dance's St George's Circus obelisk of 1771. The Cartwright memorial,
erected in 1835, is an early example of an obelisk dedicated to the memory
of reformers. Just before, in 1833, the former linen-draper, City of London
Sheriff and MP, Robert Waithman (*c.* 1764–1833), was honoured with a
granite obelisk in Salisbury Court, designed by James Elmes, removed from
Ludgate Circus; Waithman (or 'Linen-draper Bob') was well known to
Cartwright through regular meetings at radical meetings at the Crown and
Anchor tavern and elsewhere.[20] This City obelisk is perhaps the closest
comparison to the Cartwright obelisk in political tone, but occupies a very
different location and was originally without any explicit references to his
radical sympathies. Other such obelisk tributes followed soon thereafter. In

1843, at Chalgrove Field in Oxfordshire, just such a memorial was erected in memory of John Hampden MP who was killed in a skirmish there two hundred years before. In 1851, the Martyr's Memorial was erected in Nunhead Cemetery[21] in emulation of a similar tribute to Scottish radicals of the 1790s, erected on Edinburgh's Calton Hill in 1837; it was funded by a fund-raising drive similar to that which had funded the Cartwright statue in Bloomsbury: the driving force behind both obelisks was the Radical MP Joseph Hume. Cartwright's churchyard memorial would soon be emulated by legions of obelisks in garden cemeteries.

Major Cartwright's name is also included in the roster of radicals on the Reformers' Memorial at Kensal Green Cemetery, erected in 1885. With the rise of the Gothic Revival, obelisks inevitably became more of a feature associated with Nonconformity, radicalism and progressive causes. To make such claims for the Major's obelisk would be going too far, however. Cartwright's obelisk is an interesting transitional memorial, marking the progression from Georgian churchyard tombs to Victorian cemetery monuments, and demonstrating how a private graveyard monument could include aspects more readily associated with public testimonial statues.

It is clear that the obelisk has been in a forlorn state for some time: the oolitic limestone in particular has suffered from decay. Arthur Latimer's *The Illustrated Story of Finchley* (1935) includes this wan account of descendant neglect:

> I was told recently by the verger that some of the descendants of the Major paid a recent visit to the burial place of their distinguished ancestor, and discussed the possibility of repairs to the memorial, of which it is very badly in need, but as their visit was not likely to be repeated, they decided that such a very considerable expense could scarcely be justified.[22]

The decaying obelisk, not teetering on the brink of collapse owing to vault subsidence was dismantled in 2008 in advance of further conservation works, which are still awaited.[23] This has been a protracted issue of local concern: listed Grade II in 1996, it has been on the English Heritage at Risk Register for some time.

Cartwright was an intriguing figure in his time: he is not forgotten, but his former standing as the Father of Reform is diminished. An outspoken commentator on constitutional matters during one of the most remarkable epochs in English political history, he deserves to be better remembered. The conservation of his remarkable obelisk, including the reinstatement of a worthy profile portrait, would be a fitting way of achieving this. At the time of writing, however, there are no current plans to undertake this.[24] All in all, the decline of the Cartwright memorial at Finchley must rank among the saddest episodes in the annals of London's churchyards. Let us hope that the situation will have improved by the time of the 200th anniversary of the Major's death, in 2024.[25]

1. This brief essay is dedicated to Dr Ann Saunders FSA, in admiration of her zealous championing of all that is best about London.

2. See his entry in the *Oxford DNB* by Rory T. Cornish, and John W. Osborne, *John Cartwright* (Cambridge, 1972). Cartwright's niece and adopted daughter, Frances, published *The Life and Correspondence of Major Cartwright*, 2 vols. (1826).

3. E. P. Thompson, *The Making of the English Working Class*, rev. edn. (1968), p. 102.

4. Quoted in Osborne, p. 152.

5. 'In this churchyard rest the mortal remains of John Cartwright Esq., third son of William and Anne Cartwright of Marnham in Nottinghamshire; who closed a life of unwearied exertion for the liberty and welfare of the human race at Burton Crescent, in London, the 23rd of September 1824, aged 84 years. The public integrity and uprightness of this friend of mankind are well-known. His unceasing benevolence and affectionate disposition, his domestic and Christian virtues, can only be fully appreciated by his family and by his afflicted widow who erects this inadequate tribute to his memory.'

6. Osborne, pp. 74 and 104.

7. John Blackwood, *London's Immortals. The Complete Outdoor Commemorative Statues* (1989), p. 177.

8. *Life and Correspondence*, vol. II, pp. 201–2.

9. Idem., pp. 204–5.

10. Ingrid Roscoe et al., *A Biographical Dictionary of Sculptors in Britain 1660–1851* (2009), p. 278.

11. Loc. cit., no. 754, p. 432.

12. See Frank Marcham, 'Monuments in Finchley Church and Churchyard', *Barnet Press and Finchley Borough News*, 23 and 30 March 1935; Peggy Wells, *Monumental Inscriptions with Index Recorded in the Church and Churchyard of St Mary at Finchley, Middlesex* (North Middlesex Family History Society, *c.* 1968).

13. Osborne, op. cit., p. 151.

14. *The Gentleman's Magazine*, XCIV, part 2 (1824), p. 468.

15. Marcham, op. cit.

16. Loc. cit. in n. 14 above.

17. Roscoe, op. cit., p. 1231.

18. Copy in the National Portrait Gallery Archive: the drawing was sold at Christie's, 4 March 1975, lot 2, and at Sotheby's, 15 March 1984, lot 25.

19. For a survey of British obelisks, see Richard Barnes, *The Obelisk. A Monumental Feature in Britain* (Kirstead, 2004).

20. Philip Ward-Jackson, *Public Sculpture of the City of London* (Liverpool, 2003), pp. 389–90.

21. Wally Macfarlane, *The Scottish Martyrs: Their Memorial in Nunhead Cemetery* (1983).

22. Op. cit., n.p.

23. For a note on the dismantling and construction, see the Hendon and District Archaeological Society website, http://newsletters.hadas.org.uk/volume-8-2005-2009/newsletter-460-july-2009 (accessed 29 November 2014).

24. Re. Jonathan Hardy, Conservation Officer at the London Borough of Barnet, 3 December 2014, pers. comm. The churchyard is in the guardianship of the local authority.

25. Any interested readers are asked to make contact with the author at rhbowdler@gmail.com.

XIV. HERMIONE HOBHOUSE

2 February 1934–17 October 2014

THE indomitable Hermione Hobhouse, outstanding historian of London's architecture and tireless campaigner for Victorian buildings, has died aged eighty. Graduating in Modern History from Lady Margaret Hall, Oxford, she honed her communication skills working in television on both sides of the Atlantic. Her publication of *Thomas Cubitt Master Builder* in 1971 — awarded the Hitchcock Medal of the Society of Architectural Historians — was a revelatory turning point in nineteenth-century urban and architectural studies and hugely influential. Then, in 1972, her powerful polemical publication, *Lost London*, vividly exposed the appalling post-war destruction of London's architectural heritage, and established her pre-eminent place in the front line of the emerging Conservation Movement.

Hermione published, broadcast, organized exhibitions and lectured extensively in the United Kingdom, Europe, the United States of America and South Africa on town planning and urban history, Victorian architecture, and on Prince Albert. She was a ferocious and fearless campaigner, using her eloquence, wit and intellect from a succession of platforms: tutor in Architectural History at the Architectural Association School 1973–8; Secretary of the Victorian Society 1976–82; and as General Editor of and contributor to the Survey of London from 1983–94. On her appointment to the Survey, she strategically redirected its research to reach areas under imminent threat of radical redevelopment.

Appointed MBE in 1981, she was a member of the Council of the National Trust, a Commissioner of the Royal Commission for the Exhibition of 1851, an Honorary Vice-President of the Council of the Royal Albert Hall, an Honorary Fellow of the research department of the Victoria and Albert Museum, and a Fellow of the Society of Antiquaries of London. Consulted on the twentieth-century restorations of all major Victorian buildings —

including, in London, the Albert Hall, the Albert Memorial, the Victoria and Albert Museum, the Houses of Parliament, the Foreign Office, Spencer House, the St Pancras Hotel, Kings Cross Station and the Reform Club (of which she was among the first lady members elected in 1980). Hermione's London legacy lives on in these and many other Victorian buildings her scholarship illumined and her campaigns saved.

Her books included:

Thomas Cubitt Master Builder (1971)

The Ward of Cheap in the City of London (1959)

Lost London (1972)

History of Regent Street (1975)

Prince Albert: his Life and Work (1983)

Good and Proper Materials, the Fabric of London since the Great Fire, conference papers edited with Ann Saunders (1989)

London Survey'd: the Work of the Survey of London 1894–1994 (1994)

The Crystal Palace and the Great Exhibition Art, Science and Productive Industry: the History of the Royal Commission for the Great Exhibition of 1851 (2002).

GILL CHANNER

XV. ANTHONY MOSS

1932–2012

Tony Moss, who died in December 2012, was a tall, distinguished figure with impeccable manners who appeared regularly at LTS AGMs. Jointly with his wife, Jennifer, he wrote an illustrated article for the Newsletter (November 2002) about the Corporation of London Cemetery. Moss's interest in London, its history and buildings was evident to anyone visiting his office in Ely Place, Holborn; he was only too pleased to point out the eighteenth-century houses and divulge the secrets of St Etheldreda's church.

Tony Moss read law at Jesus College, Cambridge, and worked for the Metal Box Company as the prelude to a long career as a trust and probate lawyer with a solicitors' firm in Ely Place. He was Master of the Ironmongers' Company 1987–8, taking a special interest in the Company's residential care homes and its school at Landrake, Cornwall. Elected to the Common Council of the City in 1989, Tony was Lay Sheriff in 1992–3 and a Governor of Christ's Hospital and the Museum of London.

PENELOPE HUNTING

LONDON TOPOGRAPHICAL SOCIETY

The London Topographical Society, founded as the Topographical Society of London in 1880, is mainly a publishing society and is registered as a charity (no. 271590). Its purpose is to make available facsimiles of maps, plans and views illustrating the history and topography of London, and to publish research.

Over the years, the Society has produced facsimiles of most of the important large-scale maps of London, as well as plans of many individual parishes and buildings. Reproductions of views include panoramas by Wyngaerde, Visscher, Hollar, Kip and Barker, the Rhinebeck Panorama, and sets of drawings by E W Cooke, William Capon, Philip Norman and Sir George Scharf.

The Society has published thirty-one volumes of its journal, the *London Topographical Record*, which contains articles relating to London topography. There are also seven volumes in *The A–Z of London* series, covering *Elizabethan, Restoration, Charles II, Georgian, Regency, Victorian* and *Edwardian London*. Other books include major works on *The Mercers' Hall, Royal Exchange, Somerset House, John Tallis's London Street Views, Pleasures of London* and *London Bomb Damage Maps*.

The annual subscription, currently £20 in the UK and £30 abroad (reduced to £18 and £28 respectively for members paying by standing order), entitles members to receive one or more publications for the year. Members can obtain earlier publications at a preferential rate. A newsletter is issued twice a year.

Further information about the Society, its Council and its publications can be found on the internet at www. topsoc.org.

LONDON TOPOGRAPHICAL SOCIETY

Officers and Members of the Council, 31 December 2014

RULES

I.   The London Topographical Society is a publishing Society: its purpose is to assist the study and appreciation of London's history and topography by making available facsimiles of maps, plans and views and by publishing research.

II.   The affairs of the Society shall be conducted by a Council, consisting of a Chairman, Hon. Treasurer, Hon. Secretary, and not more than twenty-one elected Members of the Society.

III.   The Subscription shall be not less than one guinea, payable in advance on the 1st January.

IV.   The names of those wishing to become Members shall be submitted to the Council for approval.

V.   There shall be each year a General Meeting of the Society, at which the Council elected for the preceding year shall report upon the work of the Society during that year.

VI.   At each Annual Meeting all the members of the Council shall retire from office, and shall be eligible for re-election.

VII.   No Member whose Subscription for the preceding year remains unpaid shall be eligible for election to the Council.

VIII.   A certified Cash Statement shall be issued to all Members with the Annual Report of the Council.

IX.   The Council shall have power to fill up occasional vacancies in their number during the year, and to elect any Member of the Society to serve on any Committee or Sub-Committee of the Council.

X.   A publication of the Society shall be issued each year to all members whose subscriptions have been paid. No Member whose subscription is in arrears shall be entitled to receive such publication. Occasional additional publications may be issued at a reduced rate to paid-up Members.

XI.   No alteration shall be made in these Rules except at an Annual General Meeting, or at a Special General Meeting called upon the requisition of at least five Members. One month's previous notice of the change to be proposed shall be given in writing to the Secretary, and the alteration proposed must be approved by at least three-fourths of the Members present at such Meeting.

London Topographical Society

REPORT FOR THE YEARS 2010–2014

The Council's annual reports were carried in the May *Newsletter* each year: the *Newsletter* continued to be published twice yearly in May and November. Over the period of this Report the Society issued seven publications:

2010. LTS No. 169. *London Topographical Record, XXX*, ed. Ann Saunders: hardback, 268 pp.

2010. LTS No. 170. *London Displayed – Headpieces from the Stationers' Company Almanacks*, by Ralph Hyde: large-format hardback, 80 pp.

2011. LTS No. 171. *The Palace of Westminster – Surveyed on the Eve of Conflagration, 1834*, by H.M. Port: set of seven sheets with accompanying booklet, in folder.

2011. LTS No. 172. *The London Letters of Samuel Molyneux, 1712–13*, with an Introduction and Commentary by Paul Holden, ed. Ann Saunders: hardback, 168 pp.

2012. LTS No. 173. *London – A History in Maps*, by Peter Barber with notes on the engravers by Laurence Worms, ed. Roger Cline and Ann Saunders, published in association with the British Library, hardback, 380 pp.

2013. LTS No. 174. *The A to Z of Charles II's London, 1682*, with introductory notes by Peter Barber and Ralph Hyde; an index compiled by Robert Thompson, ed. Ann Saunders: hardback, 152 pp.

2014. LTS No. 175. *The Singularities of London, 1578 by L. Grenade*, (Biblioteca Apostolica Vaticana MS Reg. Lat. 672), ed. Derek Keene and Ian Archer: hardback, 288 pp.

In 2011, thanks to the inspiration of Mireille Galinou, the Society established a website (www.topsoc.org) containing a wide range of information about the work of the Society and, in particular, providing an on-line ordering facility for the Society's publications, as well as for membership applications and subscription renewals. The Society's *Newsletter* is now published on the website six months after the paper version is sent out to members.

On 31 December 2014 there were 1221 paid-up and five honorary members – a sizeable increase over 31 December 2009 when membership numbers were 1122 paid-up and four honorary members. The Society's annual subscription remained at £20 for UK members (reduced to £18 for members paying by standing order) – unchanged since 1992.

Finances continued to be healthy over the period of the Report with the Society generally recording a surplus of income over expenditure in each year.

Annual General Meetings were held at Wesley's Chapel, City Road (2010), the Liberal Jewish Synagogue in St John's Wood (2011), St Botolph's Church, Bishopsgate (2012), St Clement Danes Church, Strand (2013) and the Mansion House (2014). The latter venue was special in that the Society's inaugural meeting was held there in 1880 and this was the first time the Society had returned since then. AGM attendance continued to be strong, annually attracting around 300 members and their guests.

There were several changes on the Council during the period of the *Record*. Patrick Frazer became the Hon. Membership Secretary in 2011 being succeeded as Hon. Secretary by Mireille Galinou. Mireille stood down from the Council in 2012 and was succeeded by Mike Wicksteed as the Hon. Secretary. In 2013 Patrick Frazer stood down from the Council and was succeeded as the Hon. Membership Secretary by John Bowman.

LIST OF PUBLICATIONS

Dimensions are given in inches to the nearest eighth of an inch, with centimetres in brackets to the nearest half-centimetre; height precedes width. In the case of items in several sheets dimensions may be approximate only. Borders, original titles, and other wording are included in the dimensions but added titles are excluded.

Dates in brackets are those of publication and do not necessarily coincide with the year for which the publication was issued.

1. Van den Wyngaerde's View of London, *c.* 1550 (Topographical Society of London), 1881–2: 20¾ × 116¼ in. (52.5 × 295.5 cm), on 7 sheets 31½ × 23⅜ in. (80 × 59.5 cm), with sheet of text. (See 151.)

2. Plan of London, *c.* 1560, attributed to Hoefnagel (T.S.L 1882–3): from Braun and Hogenberg's *Civitates Orbis Terrarum*, second state showing Royal Exchange, 13¼ × 19⅜ in. (35.5 × 49 cm), on sheet 22¼ × 29¼ in. (56.6 × 74.5 cm).

3. *Illustrated Topographical Record of London*, first series (1898) drawings by J. P. Emslie of changes and demolitions, 1880–7: 11½ × 8⅞ in. (29 × 22.5 cm), sewn, paper wrapper.

4. Visscher's View of London, 1616 (T.S.L. 1883–5): 16⅝ × 85⅛ in. (42 × 216.5 cm), on 4 sheets 23¼ × 31¾ in. (59 × 78 cm). (See 'Notes on Visscher's View of London, 1616' by T. F. Ordish, *L.T.R.* VI, 39.)

5. Porter's 'Newest and Exactest Mapp of London and Westminster', *c.* 1660 (1898): 11¼ × 30¼ in. (28.5 × 77 cm), on 2 sheets 22¼ × 29¼ in. (56.5 × 74.5 cm).

6. *Illustrated Topographical Record of London*, second series (1899), drawings by J. P. Emslie of changes and demolitions, 1886–7: 11½ × 8⅞ in. (29 × 22.5 cm), sewn, paper wrapper.

7. Norden's Maps of London and Westminster, 1593, from the *Speculum Britanniae* (1899): 6¾ × 9⅝ in. (17 × 24.5 cm) and 6⅛ × 9⅞ in. (15.5 × 25 cm), on one sheet 29¼ × 22⅛ in. (74.5 × 56 cm). (See 'Notes on Norden and his Map of London', by H. B. Wheatley, *L.T.R.* II, 42.)

8. Kensington Turnpike Trust Plans, 1811, by Salway, of the road from Hyde Park Corner to Counter's Bridge (1899–1903): 20⅝ in. × 56 ft 1⅝ in. (52.5 × 1711 cm), in colour, 30 sheets and title–page 24 × 27 in. (61 × 69 cm). (See 'Notes on Salway's Plan', by W. F. Prideaux, *L.T.R.* III, 21, and V, 138.)

9. *Illustrated Topographical Record of London*, third series (1900), drawings by J. P. Emslie of changes and demolitions, 1888–90: 11½ × 8⅞ in. (29 × 22.5 cm), sewn, paper wrapper.

10. Comparative Plan of Whitehall, 1680/1896: modern ground plan superimposed on Fisher's plan of 1680 as engraved by Vertue (1900): one sheet 26⅜ × 22 in. (67.5 × 56 cm).

11. *Annual Record* I, ed. T F. Ordish (1901): 8¾ × 5⅞ in. (22.5 × 15 cm), quarter cloth; continued as *London Topographical Record*.

12. Hollar's West-Central London, *c.* 1658, a bird's eye-view (1902): 13⅛ × 17¼ in. (33.5 × 44 cm) on 17 × 23¼ in. (43 × 59 cm). (See 'Hollar's Map', by W. R. Lethaby and R. Jenkins, *L.T.R.* II, 109.)

13. *London Topographical Record,* II, ed. T. R. Ordish (1903); 9 × 5⅞ in. (23 × 15 cm), quarter cloth.

14. Kip's View of London, Westminster and St James's Park, 1710 (1903): *c.* 53 × 82 in. (134 × 208 cm) on 12 sheets 22⅛ × 24 in. (56 × 61 cm). (See No. 161.)

15. Morden and Lea's Plan of London, 1682, also known as Ogilby and Morgan's Plan (1904): 300 ft to 1 in., 59¼ × 93¾ in. (150.5 × 238 cm) on 9 sheets 22 × 30⅛ in. (56 × 76.5 cm) and 3 sheets 22 × 15⅛ in. (56 × 38.5 cm). (See 'Morden and Lea's Plan of London', by W. L. Spiers, *L.T.R.* V, 117.)

16. *London Topographical Record,* III, ed. T. F. Ordish (1906): 9 × 5⅞ in. (23 × 15 cm), quarter cloth.

17. Map of Elizabethan London, formerly attributed to Ralph Agas (1905): 28⅛ × 72 in. (71.5 × 183 cm) on 8 sheets 23½ × 17¼ in. (59.5 × 44 cm).

18. Faithorne and Newcourt's Map of London, 1658 (1905): map *c.* 32½ × 71 in. (82.5 × 180.5 cm) on 6 sheets 20 × 25¼ in. (51 × 64 cm) and 2 sheets 20 × 12½ in. (51 × 31.5 cm), and title on 4 pieces.

19. Hollar's Long View of London, 1647 (1906–7): 18 × 92 in. (46 × 233.5 cm) in 7 pieces on 6 sheets 25⅜ × 19 in. (64.5 × 48.5 cm).

20. *London Topographical Record,* IV (1907): 9 × 5⅞ in. (23 × 15 cm), quarter cloth.

21. Wren's Drawings of Old St Paul's (1908): (i) plan of old cathedral before the Great Fire, 18⅞ × 14½ in. (48 × 37 cm); (ii) section of Wren's Scheme for rebuilding, 18½ × 12 in. (47 × 30.5 cm); on 2 sheets 29⅜ × 22½ in. (74.5 × 57 cm). (See 'Wren's Drawings of Old St Paul's ...', by W. R. Lethaby, *L.T.R.* V, 136.)

22 and 26. Hollar's 'Exact Surveigh', 1667 (1908, 1909): 21⅜ × 32½ in. (54.5 × 82.5 cm) on 2 sheets 25⅜ × 19 in. (64.5 × 48.5 cm).

23. *London Topographical Record,* V (1908): 9 × 5⅞ in. (23 × 15 cm), quarter cloth.

24. The Palace of Whitehall, View from the River, 1683 (1909): 14 × 24½ in. (35.5 × 62.5 cm) on sheet 24 × 35 in. (61 × 89 cm). (See 'View of the Palace of Whitehall', by W. L. Spiers, *L.T.R.* VII, 26.)

25. *London Topographical Record,* VI (1909): 9 × 5⅞ in. (23 × 15 cm), quarter cloth.

26. See 22.

27. Seven London Views by Deceased Artists (1910): 14 × 11 in. (35.5 × 28 cm). (See 'Notes on London Views', by P. Norman, *L.T.R.* VIII, 94.)

28. *London Topographical Record,* VII, ed. H. G. Head (1912): 9 × 5⅞ in. (23 × 15 cm), quarter cloth.

29. Seven More London Views by Deceased Artists (1911): 14 × 11 in. (35.5 × 28 cm). (See 'Notes on London Views', by P. Norman, *L.T.R.* VIII, 94.)

30. Roads out of London, from Ogilby's *Britannia,* 1675, with descriptive letterpress (1911): 15⅛ × 11⅜ in. (38.5 × 29 cm), sewn, paper wrapper.

31. Jonas Moore's Map of the River Thames from Westminster to the Sea, 1662 (1912): part only, 20⅞ × 23⅝ in. (53 × 60 cm) on one sheet 23¼ × 33 in. (59 × 84 cm). (See 'A Seventeenth Century Map of London and the Thames', by M. Holmes, *L.T.R.* XX, 26.)

32. *London Topographical Record*, VIII, ed. H. G. Head (1913): 9 × 5⅞ in. (23 × 15 cm), quarter cloth.

33. Seven Drawings of London Bridge by E. W. Cooke (1913): 14 × 11 in. (35.5 × 28 cm). (See 'Drawings of Old and New London Bridge by E. W. Cooke', by P. Norman, *L.T.R.* IX, 1; see also publication no. 113.)

34, 36, 37, 41, 42, 43 and 44. Rocque's Plan of London, 1746 (1913–19): 6 ft 8 in. × 12 ft 8½ in. (203 × 387.5 cm), with key, on 49 sheets 17 × 22½ in. (43 × 57 cm). (See 'Rocque's Plan of London', by H. B. Wheatley, *L.T.R.* IX, 15.)

35. *London Topographical Record*, IX, ed. H. G. Head (1914): 9 × 5⅞ in. (23 × 15 cm), quarter cloth.

36. See 34.

37. See 34.

38. *London Topographical Record*, X, ed. H. G. Head (1916): 9 × 5⅞ in. (23 × 15 cm), quarter cloth.

39. A Plan of Ebury Manor, *c.* 1663–70 (1915): in colour, one sheet 30⅛ × 19⅞ in. (76.5 × 50.5 cm), and sheet of text.

40. *London Topographical Record*, XI, ed. H. G. Head (1917): 9 × 5⅞ in. (23 × 15 cm), quarter cloth.

41. See 34.

42. See 34.

43. See 34.

44. See 34.

45. A View of London Bridge by John Norden, 1597 (1919): 15¼ × 20⅛ in. (38.5 × 51 cm) on one sheet 18⅞ × 25¼ in. (48 × 64 cm).

46. *London Topographical Record*, XII, ed. H. G. Head (1920): 9 × 5⅞ in. (23 × 15 cm), quarter cloth.

47. A View of London Bridge from both sides, by Sutton Nicholls, *c.* 1710 (1921): 11 × 17¼ in. (28 × 44 cm) on sheet 14⅞ × 22 in. (37.5 × 56 cm).

48. Tallis's Plan of Bond Street (1921): 12 pages 5¾ × 9 in. (14.5 × 23 cm). (See 'Tallis's Street Views of London', by E. B. Chancellor, *L.T.R.* XII, 67; see also publication 110.)

49. Matthew Merian's View of London, 1638 (1922): 8¾ × 27½ in. (22 × 70 cm) on sheet 13½ × 31½ in. (34.5 × 80 cm), folded.

50. Seven Unpublished Drawings by Hollar: from the Pepysian Library, Cambridge (1922): 4 sheets 14 × 11 in. (35.5 × 28 cm).

51. *London Topographical Record*, XIII, ed. H. G. Head (1923): 8⅞ × 5⅞ in. (22.5 × 15 cm), quarter cloth.

52 and 53. Views of Westminster, 1801–1815, by William Capon, with Capon's descriptions annotated by P. Norman (1923–4): 16 views, 1 in colour, and map, 5 sewn sections 14 × 11 in. (35.5 × 28 cm).

53. See 52.

54. A London Plan of 1585 (1925): 22½ × 31 in. (57 × 98 cm) on sheet
    25⅛ × 35⅞ in. (63.5 × 91 cm), folded. (See 55.)
55. *The Early History of Piccadilly, Leicester Square, Soho and their
    Neighbourhood,* by C. L. Kingsford (1925): written to explain the map of
    1585 (see 54,) 8⅞ × 5⅞ in. (22.5 × 15 cm), quarter cloth, uniform with
    the *Record.*
56. Drawings of Buildings in the Area described in *The Early History of Piccadilly ...*
    (1926): 11 drawings on 7 sheets 14 × 11 in. (35.5 × 28 cm), and plan of West
    London, *c.* 1710, on double sheet folded. (See 55.)
57. *London Topographical Record,* XIV, ed. W. H. Godfrey (1928): 8⅞ × 5⅞ in.
    (22.5 × 15 cm), quarter cloth.
58. Plan of Nevill's Alley, Fetter Lane, 1670 (1928): 20¼ × 25 in.
    (51.5 × 63.5 cm). (See 'Nevill's Court, Fetter Lane', by W. G. Bell, *L.T.R.*
    XV, 87.)
59. Seven Views of the Inns of Court and Chancery, with notes by J. B.
    Williamson (1928): 14 × 11 in. (35.5 × 28 cm), 2 sewn sections.
60. *London Topographical Record,* XV, ed. W. H. Godfrey (1931): 8⅞ × 5⅞ in.
    (22.5 × 15 cm), quarter cloth.
61. Area east of St Katherine's Dock, *c.* 1550, from a tracing by M. B.
    Honeybourne of a plan in the Public Record Office (1929):
    27¼ × 21¼ in. (69 × 54 cm) on sheet 29¼ × 23⅜ *in.* (74 × 59.5 cm),
    folded.
62. *London Topographical Record,* XVI, ed. W. H. Godfrey (1932):
    8⅞ × 5⅞ in. (22.5 × 15 cm), quarter cloth.
63. Hollar's View of Greenwich, 1637 (1930): 5¾ × 33 in. (14.5 × 84 cm) on
    sheet 7¾ × 35¾ in. (19.5 × 90.5 cm), folded.
64. A Plan in the Public Record Office of property on the south-east side of
    Charing Cross, 1610 (1930): 19 × 26 in. (48 × 66 cm) on sheet
    22⅝ × 29⅛ in. (57.5 × 74 cm).
65. Plan of the Manor of Walworth and Parish of Newington, Surrey, 1681
    (1932): two–thirds scale, 13¾ × 18 in. (35 × 45.5 cm) on sheet
    18⅛ × 23 in. (46 × 58 cm). (See 'Thomas Hill's Maps ...' by I. Darlington,
    L.T.R. XXI, 37.)
66. Plan of the Duke of Bedford's Estates, 1795 (1933), from Bloomsbury to the
    river: 23⅛ × 40⅞ in. (59 × 103.5 cm) on sheet 28⅜ × 43⅛ in.
    (72 × 109.5 cm), folded. (See 'Duke of Bedford's Estate Map, 1795' by
    E. Jeffries Davis, *L.T.R.* XVIII, 134.)
67. Plan of the Parish of St Mary, Kensington, 1822 (1934): 28 × 34⅝ in.
    (71 × 88 cm) on sheet 31⅝ × 37¼ in. (81.5 × 94.5 cm), folded, with
    sheet of notes.
68. Eight Views of Kensington, from originals in Kensington Public Library
    (1934): 8 sheets 11 × 14 in. (28 × 35.5 cm).
69. *London Topographical Record,* XVII, ed. W. H. Godfrey (1936):
    8⅞ × 5⅞ in. (22.5 × 15 cm), quarter cloth.
70. Four drawings by Philip Norman (1936): (i) Vine Tavern, Mile End;
    (ii) nos 5 and 7, Aldgate; (iii) nos 10 and 11, Austin Friars; (iv) St

Magnus' Church, London Bridge: 4 sheets 14 × 11 in. (35.5 × 28 cm), in folder.

71. A further four drawings by Philip Norman (1937): (v) no. 13, Leather Lane; (vi) Staircase in the Old Bell Inn, Holborn; (vii) Old houses, Chelsea; (viii) Backs of old houses, Cheyne Walk: 4 sheets 14 × 11 in. (35.5 × 28 cm), in folder with 70.

72. Clothworkers' Company, Survey of Properties in 1612 and 1728 (1938): (i) Clothworkers' Hall, 1612; (ii) St James's in the Wall, 1612; (iii) St James's in the Wall, 1728: 3 sheets 22½ × 17½ in. (57 × 44.5 cm) in folder. (See 'The Clothworkers' Company: Book of Plans. . .' by W. H. Godfrey, *L.T.R.* XVIII, 51.)

73. Clothworkers' Survey (1939): (iv) Neighbourhood of the Fleet Prison, 1612: (v) Neighbourhood of the Fleet Prison, 1728, 2 sheets 22½ × 17½ in. (57 × 44.5 cm), in folder.

74. Clothworkers' Survey (1940): (vi) Richard Fishburne's House, Throgmorton Street, 1612: 22½ × 35 in. (57 × 89 cm), folded; (vii) Fox Court, Nicholas Lane, 1612: 22½ × 17½ in. (57 × 44.5 cm), in folder.

75. Clothworkers' Survey (1941): (viii) Sir Edward Darcy's House, Billiter Street, 1612: 22½ × 34⅞ in. (57 × 88.5 cm), folded; (ix) Fox Court, Nicholas Lane, 1728: 22½ × 17½ in. (57 × 44.5 cm), in folder.

76. *London Topographical Record*, XVIII, ed. W. H. Godfrey (1942): 8⅞ × 5⅞ in. (22.5 × 15 cm), quarter cloth.

77. Van den Wyngaerde's View of the City of London between Fleet River and London Bridge, *c.* 1550 (1944): 5⅛ × 50⅛ in. (13 × 127.5 cm) in 3 sections on 1 sheet 23⅛ × 18⅝ in. (58.5 × 47 cm).

78. View of London from Southwark, attributed to Thomas Wyck (1616–77), at Chatsworth House (1945): original size 20¼ × 30½ in. (51.5 × 87.5 cm), reproduced 15⅛ × 22¾ in. (38.5 × 57.5 cm) on sheet 20 × 30 in. (51 × 76.5 cm).

79. *Survey of Building Sites in the City of London after the Great Fire of 1666* by Mills and Oliver, vol. 1: (i.e. part i of Mills 1) (1946, extra publication): reduced facsimile, 8⅞ × 5⅝ in. (22.5 × 14.5 cm), quarter cloth, uniform with the *Record*.

80. *London Topographical Record*, XIX, ed. W. H. Godfrey (1947): 8⅞ × 5⅞ in. (22.5 × 15 cm), quarter cloth.

81. Whitehall Palace, a seventeenth–century painting at Kensington Palace (1948): original size 16 × 37 in. (40.5 × 94 cm) reproduced 9½ × 22¼ in. (24 × 56.5 cm) on sheet 20 × 30 in. (51 × 76.5 cm).

82. A Prospect of the City of London from the South-east, 1945, by Cecil Brown (1949): original size 9 ft × 6 ft 6 in. (274.5 × 183 *cm*) reproduced 14⅞ × 20⅞ in. (37.5 × 53 cm) on sheet 16⅝ × 23 in. (42 × 58.5 cm). (See 142.)

83. *Le Guide de Londres*, 1693, by F. Colsoni, edited by W. H. Godfrey (1951): 8⅞ × 5⅞ in. (22.5 × 15 cm), quarter cloth, uniform with the *Record*.

84. Seventeenth–century Plans of the Properties belonging to St Bartholomew's Hospital (1950–1): (i) The Grey Friars, *c.* 1617 (see 'The Precinct of the

Greyfriars' by M. B. Honeybourne, *L.T.R.* XVI, 9); (ii) Properties adjoining Hosier Lane; (iii) St Nicholas Flesh Shambles: on 2 sheets 19½ × 29 in. (49.5 × 74 cm) folded, in folder.

85. *London Topographical Record*, XX, ed. W. H. Godfrey (1952): 8⅞ × 5⅞ in. (22.5 × 15 cm), quarter cloth.

86. *Berkeley Square to Bond Street, The Early History of the Neighbourhood*, by B. H. Johnson (1952): 8⅞ × 5⅞ in. (22.5 × 15 cm), full cloth, published by John Murray in association with the London Topographical Society.

87. Seventeenth-century Plans of Properties belonging to St Bartholomew's Hospital (1953–4): (iv) south-west portion of the hospital adjoining the City Wall Ditch; (v) north portion adjoining Smithfield from Duck Lane to the Hospital Church; (vi) south portion adjoining Little Britain and the City Wall and Ditch; (vii) property north of Chick Lane: on 2 sheets 19½ × 29 in. (49.5 × 74 cm), folded in folder with 84.

88. Plan of the precinct of St Bartholomew's Hospital, *c.* 1617 (1955): in colour, 15⅞ × 10¼ in. (40.5 × 26 cm) on sheet 19½ × 14½ in. (49.5 × 37 cm), in folder with 84. (See 'The Fire of London and St Bartholomew's Hospital' by G. Whitteridge, *L.T.R.* XX, 47.)

89. *Survey of Building Sites in the City of London after the Great Fire of 1666*, by Mills and Oliver, vol. II (i.e. part ii of Mills I) (1956, extra publication): reduced facsimile, 8⅞ × 5⅞ in. (22.5 × 14.5 cm), quarter cloth, uniform with the *Record*.

90. Plan of the precinct (eastern part) of the Hospital of St Katherine by the Tower, 1685, part of a survey by John Ogilby (1957): 1 sheet 28 × 25 in. (71.5 × 63.5 cm).

91. *London Topographical Record*, XXI, ed. W. H. Godfrey (1958): 8⅞ × 5⅞ in. (22.5 × 15 cm), quarter cloth.

92. The City of London, showing Parish Boundaries prior to the Union of Parishes Act, 1907, on the 1:2500 Ordnance Survey Map, 1st edition, 1876 (1959): in colour, 24¾ × 44⅛ in. (63 × 112 cm) on sheet 27 × 46 in. (68.5 × 117 cm).

93. A Map of London under Richard II, from original sources, by M. B. Honeybourne (1960): 27⅜ × 41 in. (69.5 × 104 cm) on sheet 31⅞ × 45 in. (81 × 114.5 cm).

94. A View of London, 1600, by John Norden, from the engraving in the de la Gardie Collection in the Royal Library, Stockholm (1961): 18⅛ × 47⅞ in. (46 × 121.5 cm) on sheet 24⅛ × 50 in. (61 × 127 cm).

95 and 96. A Survey of the Parliamentary Borough of St Marylebone, including Paddington and St Pancras, 1834, engraved by B. R. Davis (1962–3): slightly reduced scale, 40½ × 34⅛ in. (103 × 86.5 cm) on 2 sheets 22 × 36½ in. (50.5 × 92.5 cm).

96. See 95.

97, 98 and 99. *Survey of Building Sites in the City of London after the Great Fire of 1666*, by Mills and Oliver, vols. III, IV and V (i.e. Mills II and Oliver I and II) (1963, extra publication): reduced facsimile, 9½ × 6⅛ in. (24 × 15.5 cm), quarter cloth.

98. See 97.

99. See 97.

100. *The Map of Mid-sixteenth Century London, An investigation into the relationship between a copper-engraved map and its derivatives*, by S. P. Marks (1964): 11½ × 8⅞ in. (29 × 22.5 cm), quarter cloth.

101. *Survey of Building Sites in the City of London after the Great Fire of 1666*, by Mills and Oliver, vol. II (i.e. Mills I) (1965, extra publication): reduced facsimile, 9½ × 6⅛ in. (24 × 15.5 cm), quarter cloth, uniform with 97, 98 and 99: a new edition of 79 and 89.

102. *London Topographical Record*, XXII, ed. M. B. Honeybourne (1965): 8⅞ × 5⅞ in. (22.5 × 15 cm), quarter cloth.

103. *Survey of Building Sites in the City of London after the Great Fire of 1666*, by Mills and Oliver, Vol. I, Introduction and Indexes (1967, extra publication): 9½ × 6¼ in. (24 × 16 cm), quarter cloth, uniform with 97, 98, 99 and 101.

104. Hollar's 'Exact Surveigh', 1667 (1966, extra publication): 21½ × 32½ in. (54.5 × 82.5 cm) on sheet 25 × 34¾ in. (63.5 × 88 cm), replacing 22 and 26.

105. Grand Architectural Panorama of London, Regent Street to Westminster, by R. Sandeman, 1849 (1966): 4¾ in. × 22 ft 6 in. long (12 × 686 cm) in a small case 6 × 7⅛ in. (15 × 18 cm).

106. Horwood's Plan of London, 1792–9 (1966, extra publication, a memorial to the work of the London Survey Committee): 7 ft 3 in. × 13 ft 4 in. (221 × 406 cm), iv + 32 sheets 24½ × 23 in. (62.5 × 58.5 cm); includes variant plates from sheets A1 and B1.

107. The Banqueting House with the Whitehall and Holbein Gates, by Inigo Jones, for a masque by Ben Jonson performed in 1623 (1967): 14 × 24¼ in. (37 × 61.5 cm) on sheet 19 × 26⅞ in. (48 × 68 cm); with 'A Prospect of Whitehall by Inigo Jones' by J. Harris, offprint from *The Burlington Magazine*, February 1967.

108. *Index to Rocque's Plan of the Cities of London and Westminster and the Borough of Southwark*, 1747 (1968, extra publication): facsimile, 11½ × 8⅞ in. (29 × 22.5 cm), full cloth, uniform with 100.

109. *The London Panoramas of Robert Barker and Thomas Girtin, c. 1800*, by H. J. Pragnell (1968): 11½ × 8⅞ in. (29 × 22.5 cm), quarter cloth, uniform with 100. (See 139.)

110. *John Tallis's London Street Views, 1838–1840 and 1847*, with introduction by Peter Jackson (1969, extra publication): 8 × 11¼ in. (20 × 28.5 cm), full cloth; published by Nattali and Maurice in association with the London Topographical Society. (See Nos. 48 and 60.)

111. Map of Chelsea by F. P. Thompson, 1836 (1969): 27¾ × 41⅝ in. (70.5 × 104.5 cm), on 2 sheets 29⅞ × 22½ in. (76 × 57.5 cm).

112. Hollar's Long View of London from Bankside, 1647 (1970, extra publication): 18½ × 93 in. (47 × 236.5 cm) on 7 sheets 25 × 19 in. (63.5 × 48 cm), replacing 19.

113. A Selection of Drawings of Old and New London Bridge, c. 1830, by E. W. Cooke (1970): 14 × 11 in. (35.5 × 28 cm) in folder.

114. Langley and Belch's 'New Map of London', 1812 (1971): in colour, 20¾ × 30¾ in. (52.5 × 78 cm) on sheet 25 × 35 in. (63.5 × 89 cm).

115. *London Topographical Record*, XXIII, ed. M. B. Honeybourne (1972): 8¾ × 5¾ in. (22 × 14.5 cm), quarter cloth.

116. Map of the Railways proposed by the Bills of the Session of 1863 in the Metropolis and its vicinity (1973): 24¼ × 23⅞ in. (61.5 × 60.5 cm) on sheet 28 × 24⅞ in. (71 × 63 cm). (See 'Parliament and the Railways', by David J. Johnson, *L.T.R.* XXIV, 147.)

117. *The Public Markets of the City of London surveyed by William Leybourne in 1677*, by Betty R. Masters (1974): 11½ × 8⅞ in. (29 × 22.5 cm), quarter cloth.

118 and 119. Thomas Milne's Lane Use Map of London and Environs in 1800, with an introduction by Dr G. B. G. Bull (1975–6): north and south sections each 20⅛ × 40½ in. (51 × 103 cm) on 3 sheets, iii + 6 sheets 24 × 16½ in. (61 × 42 cm) in folder, available in colour and in black and white.

119. See 118.

120. *The Artillery Ground and Fields in Finsbury*, two maps of 1641 and 1703 reproduced with a commentary by James R. Sewell (1977): 14¾ × 11⅜ in. (37.5 × 29 cm), sewn in card wrapper.

121. *The Park Town Estate and the Battersea Tangle, A peculiar piece of Victorian London property development and its background*, by Priscilla Metcalf (1978): 11⅛ × 9 in. (28 × 22.5 cm), Linson.

122. *The A to Z of Elizabethan London*, compiled by Adrian Prockter and Robert Taylor with introductory notes by John Fisher (1979): 12⅛ × 8⅝ in. (31 × 22 cm), Linson, published concurrently by the Society and by Harry Margary in association with Guildhall Library.

123. *London Topographical Record*, XXIV, ed. Ann Saunders (1980, centenary volume): 8¾ × 5¾ in. (22 × 14.5 cm), quarter cloth.

124. London from the North, by J. Swertner, 1789 (1980, extra centenary publication): 19 × 31½ in. (48.5 × 80 cm) on sheet 23 × 32¾ in. (58.5 × 83 cm).

125. The 'Rhinebeck' Panorama of London, c. 1810, with an introduction by Ralph Hyde and keys by Peter Jackson (1981): in colour, reduced, 18¾ × 107¼ in. (47.5 × 272.5 cm) on iii + 4 sheets 24⅝ × 18¾ in. (62.5 × 47.5 cm) in folder. (See 'A London Panorama, c. 1800 Resurrected', by Ralph Hyde, *L.T.R.* XXIV, 211.)

126. *The A to Z of Georgian London*, with introductory notes by Ralph Hyde (1982): 12 × 8⅝ in. (30.5 × 22 cm), Linson, uniform with 122, published concurrently by the Society and by Harry Margary in association with Guildhall Library.

127. Robert Baker of Piccadilly Hall and his Heirs, by Francis Sheppard (1982, extra publication): 11⅛ × 8¾ in. (28 × 22 cm), Linson, uniform with 121.

128. A Survey of Hatton Garden by Abraham Arlidge 1694 (1983): in colour, 31¼ × 26 in. (79.5 × 66 cm) on sheet 36⅜ × 27¾ in. (92.5 × 70.5 cm)

with sheet of text. (See 'The Survey of Hatton Garden in 1694 by Abraham Arlidge', by Dr Penelope Hunting, *L.T.R.* XXV, 83.)

129. A Plan of the Tower of London in 1682 (1983): in colour, 25¾ × 25¾ in. (63 × 63 cm) on sheet 30 × 27½ in. (76 × 70 cm) with sheet of text. (See 'Five Seventeenth-Century Plans of the Tower of London', by Geoffrey Parnell, *L.T.R.* XXV, 63.)

130. Charles Booth's Descriptive Map of London Poverty 1889, with an introduction by Dr David A. Reeder (1984): in colour, 36½ × 46¼ in. (93 × 117.5 cm) on ii + 4 sheets averaging 20 × 25 in. (51 × 64 cm) in folder.

131. *The A to Z of Regency London*, with introduction by Paul Laxton and index by Joseph Wisdom (1985, extra publication): 12 × 8⅝ in. (30.5 × 22 cm), Linson, uniform with 122, published concurrently by the Society and by Harry Margary in association with Guildhall Library.

132. *London Topographical Record*, XXV, ed. Ann Saunders (1985): 8¾ × 5¾ in. (22 × 14.5 cm), quarter cloth.

133. The Kentish Town Panorama, by James Frederick King *c.* 1850, with explanatory booklet by John Richardson (1986): 6 in. × 39 ft 8 in. (15.5 × 1209 cm) on 26 sheets 9⅜ × 23½ in. (24 × 59.5 cm) in folder.

134. Satellite View of London, taken by Landsat on 21 October 1984 (1986, extra publication): in colour, 20¼ × 23½ *in.* (51.5 × 59.9 cm) on sheet.

135. *The London Surveys of Ralph Treswell*, ed. by John Schofield, illustrated with all of Treswell's London plans, several in colour (1987): 11⅛ × 9 in. (28 × 23 cm).

136. *The A to Z of Victorian London*, with notes by Ralph Hyde (1987, extra publication): 12⅛ × 8¾ in. (31 × 22 cm), Linson, uniform with 122, published concurrently by the Society and Harry Margary in association with Guildhall Library.

137. *Hugh Alley's Caveat - The Markets of London in 1598*, eds. Ian Archer, Caroline Barron and Vanessa Harding (1988): 9½ × 10¼ in. (24 × 26 cm).

138. Hollar's Prospect of London and Westminster taken from Lambeth in 2 versions *c.* 1665 and *c.* 1707 (1988, extra publication): 12¾ in. × 10 ft 6½ in. (32.5 × 322.4 cm) on 8 sheets 14 in. × 11 ft (35.6 × 336 cm) in folder. (See 'Some Notes on Hollar's *Prospect* . . .' by Peter Jackson, *L.T.R.* XXVI, 134.)

139. Barker's Panorama of London from the Roof of the Albion Mills, 1792, with an introduction by Ralph Hyde and keys by Peter Jackson (1988, extra publication): in colour, 16¾ × 130½ in. (42.5 × 343 cm) on iii + 6 sheets 19¼ × 23½ in. (49 × 59.5 cm) in folder, published concurrently by the Society and Guildhall Library. (See 109.)

140. *Good and Proper Materials, the Fabric of London since the Great Fire*, papers given at a conference organised by the Survey of London, ed. Hermione Hobhouse and Ann Saunders (1989): paperback, 70 pp., 10¾ × 8¾ in. (27.5 × 22 cm).

141. *London Topographical Record*, XXVI, ed. Ann Saunders (1990): 8¾ × 5¾ in. (22 × 14.5 cm), quarter cloth.

142. Devastated London (The Bombed City 1945), drawn by Cecil Brown, with notes by Ralph Hyde (1990): on sheet 33⅛ × 46½ in. (84 × 188 cm), available flat or folded. (See 82.)

143. *The Mercers' Hall*, by Jean Imray, with an introduction by Derek Keene (1991, extra publication): 11⅛ × 9⅛ in. (28 × 23 cm).

144. Facsimile of the Ordnance Surveyors' Drawings of the London Area 1799–1808, with an introduction by Yolande Hodson (1991): in colour, on iii + 6 sheets 35 × 25⅛ in. (89 × 64 cm) in folder.

145. *The A to Z of Restoration London (The City of London, 1676)*, with introductory notes by Ralph Hyde and index by John Fisher and Roger Cline (1992): 12 × 8⅝ in. (30.5 × 22 cm), Linson, uniform with 122, published concurrently by the Society and Harry Margary in association with Guildhall Library.

146. Map of the Geology and Contours of London and its Environs, by R. W. Mylne (1856), with an introduction by Eric Robinson and topographical notes by Simon Morris (1993): in colour, on vi + 4 sheets 23¼ × 17¼ in. (59 × 44 cm) in folder.

147. *Drawings of Westminster* by Sir George Scharf (1859–74), with text by Peter Jackson (1994): 11⅛ × 9 in. (28.5 × 23 cm).

148. *Topography of London*, facsimile of John Lockie's *Gazetteer* (2nd edition, 1813) with introduction by David Webb (1994): 7⅛ × 4½ in. (18 × 11.5 cm).

149. *London Topographical Record*, XXVII, ed. Ann Saunders (1995): 8¾ × 5¾ in. (22 × 14.5 cm), quarter cloth.

150. *Joel Gascoyne's Engraved Maps of Stepney, 1702–04*, with an introduction by W. Ravenhill and D. Johnson (1995); eight sheets 21½ × 24½ in. (54.5 × 62.5 cm) in folder + with an explanatory booklet.

151. *The Panorama of London circa 1544*, by Anthonis van den Wyngaerde, ed. Howard Colvin and Susan Foister (1996): 13⅜ × 19¼ in. (34 x 48.5 cm).

152. *The Royal Exchange*, ed. Ann Saunders (1997): hardback, 444 pp., 11¼ × 8⅞ in. (28.5 × 22.5 cm).

153. *The Whitehall Palace Plan of 1670*, by Simon Thurley (1998): hardback, 55 pp., 12⅛ × 9 in. (31 × 23 cm).

154. *Ward Maps of the City of London*, by Ralph Hyde (1999): 12 × 9⅞ in. (30.5 × 25 cm).

155. A Map of the Ecclesiastical Divisions within the County of London 1903, with introductory notes by Simon Morris (1999): on sheet 26½ × 39 in. (67 × 99 cm), folded.

156. Two thousand years of London, by Andrew Ingamells (2000): screenprint in colour 15¾ × 25 in. (40 × 63.5 cm) on sheet 21½ × 29¾ in. (54 x 75.5 cm).

157. *London Topographical Record*, XXVIII, ed. Ann Saunders (2001): 8¾ × 5¾ in. (22 × 14.5 cm), quarter cloth.

158. *The Elizabethan Tower of London: the Haiward and Gascoyne Plan of 1597*, by Anna Keay (2001): 11⅞ × 8⅝ in. (30 × 22 cm).

159. *Tudor London - a Map and a View*, ed. Ann Saunders and John Schofield (2001): paperback, 57 pp., 11⅞ × 8⅝ in. (30 × 22 cm).

160. *John Tallis's London Street Views 1838–1840*, with the revised and enlarged views of 1847. Introduction and biographical essay by Peter Jackson (2002): hardback, 305 pp., 8 × 11½ in. (20 × 29 cm). (See Nos 48 and 110.)

161. Jan Kip's View of London, Westminster and St James's Park 1720, with an introduction by Ralph Hyde and keys by Peter Jackson (2003): 51⅝ × 75½ in. (131 × 192 cm) on 12 map sheets each *c.* 20 × 27 in. (51 × 69 cm). (See No. 14.)

162. Charles Robert Cockerell's Tribute to Sir Christopher Wren, with an introduction by John Schofield and key by Tracy Wellman (2003): 19½ × 22¼ in. (50 × 57 cm).

163. *'Old St Paul's': The Society of Antiquaries' Diptych, 1616*, by Pamela Tudor-Craig with Christopher Whittick, published in association with The Society of Antiquaries (2004): 67 pp., 11⅞ × 8¾ in. (30 × 22 cm).

164. *The London County Council Bomb Damage Maps 1939–1945*, with an introduction by Robin Woolven, ed. Ann Saunders, published in association with London Metropolitan Archives (2005): 215 pp., 14⅝ × 10¾ in. (37 × 27 cm).

165. *London Topographical Record*, XXIX, ed. Ann Saunders (2006): 236 pp., 10 × 7 in. (25.5 × 18 cm)

166. *The A to Z of Edwardian London*, with an introduction by M H Port, ed. Ann Saunders (2007): in colour, hardback, 169pp., 14¼ × 10¾ in. (36 × 27.5 cm)

167. *The Pleasures of London*, by Felix Barker and Peter Jackson (2008): hardback, 249 pp., 11⅞ × 8¾ in. (30 × 22 cm)

168. *Somerset House: The Palace of England's Queens 1551–1692*, by Simon Thurley with contributions by Patricia Croot and Claire Gapper, ed. Ann Saunders and Roger Cline (2009): hardback, 144 pp., 12 × 9 in. (30.5 × 23 cm)

169. *London Topographical Record*, XXX, ed. Ann Saunders (2010): hardback, 276 pp., 10 x 7 in. (25.5 x 18 cm)

170. *London Displayed – Headpieces from the Stationers' Company Almanacks*, by Ralph Hyde (2010): hardback, 88 pp., 11¾ x 9½ in. (30 x 22 cm)

171. *The Palace of Westminster – Surveyed on the Eve of the Conflagration, 1834*, by M. H. Port (2011): set of seven large sheets with accompanying booklet, in folder. 10½ x 7⅝ in. (26.8 x 19.5 cm)

172. *The London Letters of Samuel Molyneux, 1712–13*, with an Introduction and Commentary by Paul Holden, ed. Ann Saunders (2011): hardback, 182 pp., 9¾ x 6⅞ in., (24.7 x 17.6 cm)

173. *London – A History in Maps*, by Peter Barber with notes on the engravers by Laurence Worms, eds Roger Cline and Ann Saunders, published in association with the British Library (2012): hardback, 388 pp. 9½ x 12 in. (24 x 30.6 cm)

174. *The A to Z of Charles II's London, 1682*, with introductory notes by Peter Barber and Ralph Hyde; an index compiled by Robert Thompson, ed. Ann Saunders (2013): hardback, 158 pp., 11¾ x 8⅜ in. (30 x 21.3 cm)

175. *The Singularities of London, 1578* by L. Grenade, (Biblioteca Apostolica Vaticana MS Reg. Lat. 672), eds Derek Keene and Ian Archer (2014): hardback, 296 pp., 9¾ x 6⅞ in. (24.7 x 17.4 cm)

LIST OF MEMBERS 2015
(prepared 1 March 2015)

Institutional members are listed separately

His Royal Highness the Duke of Edinburgh, KG, KT, *Patron*

Adams, Dr R, *MA*   Centre for Editing Lives and Letters, University College London, Gower Street, London WC1E 6BT
Adshead, Mr D J, *MA MLitt FSA*   23A Huntingdon Street, London N1 1BS
Aickin, Dr R M   69 Lauriston Road, London E9 7HA
Ainsworth-Smith, The Revd Canon I M, *MA*   Knutsford Cottage, North Street, Milverton, Somerset TA4 1LG
Aitchison, Mr J S, *BEng*   9a Wilbury Road, Hove, East Sussex BN3 3JJ
Alderman, Mrs M, *LLB*   16 Crescent Road, Sidcup, Kent DA15 7HN
Aldous, Mr A M   12 Eliot Hill, London SE13 7EB
Aldrich, Mr T   16 Chapel House Street, London E14 3AS
Allen, Mr G R   183 Putnoe Street, Bedford MK41 8JR
Allen, Mr M   17 Heather Close, St Leonards, Ringwood, Hants BH24 2QJ
Allen, Professor M E, *PhD*   533 Nova Way, Madison WI 53704 USA
Allen, Mr W J C, *AADipl*   76 Half Moon Lane, London SE24 9JE
Allin, Mr P V, *MSc*   7 Pontymason Rise, Rogerstone, Newport NP10 9GJ
Ambler, Dr R W, *FSA*   7 Heron Close, Grimsby DN32 8PW
Anderson, Mr P   47 Wood Lodge Lane, West Wickham, Kent BR4 9LY
Archer, Dr I W, *MA*   Keble College, Oxford OX1 3PG
Archer, Mr Q D R, *MA LLM*   Postwick Lodge, Postwick, Norwich NR13 5HF
Arthurs, Mr W M, *MA FRSA*   PO Box 635, Amersham HP6 9AH
Ash, Mr H J, *BA(Hons)*   6 Holly Brooke Close, Shanklin, Isle of Wight PO37 7PD
Ash, Miss S   29 Foord Street, Rochester, Kent ME1 2BX
Ashby, Mr A   4 Forsyte Crescent, London SE19 2QN
Ashdown, Mr J H, *FSA*   5 Hall Farm Paddocks, Springhill Road, Begbroke, Kidlington OX5 1FW
Ashley, Mrs M P, *RDSA*   16 Charles Road, Chadwell Heath, Romford, Essex RM6 4NH
Askey, Dr M K, *BA(Hons)*   6 Burch Place, Eyam, Hope Valley S32 5QE
Ault, Mr C J, *FCCA*   114 Queenstown Road, London SW8 3RZ
Avery, Mr P   10 Meadow Bank, Police Station Road, West Malling, Kent ME19 6LF
Axford, Mr M E   33 Langley Way, Watford, Herts WD17 3EH
Aylward, Mr R   85 West Lane, London SE16 4PA
Ayres, Mrs S   39 Savernake Road, London NW3 2JU
Ayton, Mr R   32 Pentney Road, London SW12 0NX
Ayton, Mrs V H, *CertEd*   70 Frithwood Lane, Billericay, Essex CM12 9PW
Backman, Mr P R   6A The Avenue, London N3 2LB
Bacon, Miss S J   16 Slade End, Theydon Bois, Essex CM16 7EP
Bacon, Mr T R   Ramsden Farm, Stone-cum-Ebony, Tenterden, Kent TN30 7JB
Badcock, Mr A J   59 Felsham Road, London SW15 1AZ
Badcock, Mr D   43 Carter Street, London SE17 3EN

Badham, Mr P E   Old School House, Old Radnor, Presteigne, Powys LD8 2RH

Baggaley, Mrs S M, *BA BEd*   Saddlers House, High Street, Farningham,
  Kent DA4 0DT

Bagshaw, Ms Sarah   10 Gastigny House, Lever Street, London EC1V 3SU

Bailey, Dr K   20 Station Gardens, Cornhill on Tweed TD12 4TS

Bailey, Mr S   27 Toot Baldon, Oxford OX44 9NE

Bain, Mr I S *Vice-President*   New Cottage, Newnham, Baldock, Herts SG7 5JX

Baird, Dr B M   Flat 3, 52 Lennox Gardens, London SW1X 0DJ

Baker, Professor J H, *LLD FBA*   St Catharine's College, Cambridge CB2 1RL

Baker, Mr J J, *MA FRGS*   27 Carson Road, London SE21 8HT

Baker, Dr P   2 Maclise House, Marsham Street, London SW1P 4JJ

Baker-Smith, Professor M P D, *MA PhD*   23 Breedons Hill, Pangbourne,
  Berks RG8 7AT

Baldwin, Mr R H, *BSc MSc*   Kester, Cotmans Ash Lane, Kemsing, Sevenoaks,
  Kent TN15 6XD

Bamji, Dr A N, *MB FRCP*   Norman House, West Street, Rye,
  East Sussex TN31 7ES

Bankes, Mr A G K   24 Willifield Way, London NW11 7XT

Bankes, Mrs J M   26 Eardley Road, Sevenoaks, Kent TN13 1XT

Bannister, Mrs J A, *MA MEd MBA*   282 Tubbenden Lane South, Orpington,
  Kent BR6 7DN

Bar, Mr N C   48 Granville Road, London N12 0HJ

Barber, Mr P M, *OBE Member of Council*   16 Tivoli Road, London N8 8RE

Barker, Mr B A   3 South Parade, Penzance, Cornwall TR18 4DJ

Barker, Mrs J, *BA(Hons)*   115 Baizdon Road, London SE3 0UL

Barker, Mr J W   Badgers Brook, School Lane, Abbess Roding, Ongar CM5 0NY

Barker, Mr K   Watermill House, Mill Street, Iden Green, Cranbrook TN17 4HL

Barratt, Mr S, *MA*   Parsonage Farm, Mallows Green Road, Manuden,
  Bishop's Stortford, Herts CM23 1BP

Barrett, Cllr J M, *JP*   Highfield Cottage, Uxbridge Road, Hillingdon UB10 0LT

Barriff, Mr S J   Quackers, 13 Canal Walk, Hungerford, Berks RG17 0EQ

Barron, Dr C   Royal Holloway & Bedford College, Egham Hill, Surrey TW20 0EX

Barter Bailey, Mrs S E, *FSA*   3 Cambridge Mansions, Cambridge Road,
  London SW11 4RU

Bartlett, Mr R K   5 Aldersgrove, East Molesey, Surrey KT8 0AB

Bate, Mr G, *CEng MICE FICD*   Halcyon House, Landing Lane, Newport,
  Brough, East Yorkshire HU15 2RU

Baty, Mr P R   47 Haldon Road, London SW18 1QF

Baxter, Mr A, *CBE*   Alan Baxter Limited, 75 Cowcross Street, London EC1M 6EL

Bayliss, Mr C   Flat 5, Lower Ground Floor, Northwood Hall, Hornsey Lane,
  London N6 5PE

Bayman, Mr R E, *MCIT*   109 Park Road, New Barnet, Barnet EN4 9QR

Bazely, Mr R, *BA MSc*   119 Byrne Road, London SW12 9JA

Beacham, Mr J W   Abbotsford, Elmstead Road, West Byfleet, Surrey KT14 6JB

Beard, Mr A   58 Perry Street, Billericay, Essex CM12 0NA

Beautyman, Dr A C, *PhD CEng*   Upper Maisonette, 200B Hammersmith
  Grove, London W6 7HG

Belcher, Mr V R, *MA*   55 Gore Road, London E9 7HN

Bell, Mr N D J, *BA*   30 Church Crescent, St Albans, Herts AL3 5JE

Bell, Mr P W R   2 The Court, Cascade Avenue, London N10 3PS
Bell, Mr T A P   84b London Road, Redhill RH1 2JP
Bellamy, Mrs J   28 Beach Road, Shoreham-by-Sea, West Sussex BN43 5LJ
Bellenie, Mrs L F G   14 Collard Drive, Willesborough, Ashford,
    Kent TN24 0JR
Bendall, Mr A   128 Elm Park Mansions, Park Walk, London SW10 0AR
Bendall, Dr S, *MA PhD MCLIP*   Emmanuel College, Cambridge CB2 3AP
Bennell, Mr J E G, *MLitt CertEd*   92 Buriton Road, Winchester SO22 6JF
Bennett, Mr H F   9 Howard Road, Dorking RH4 3HR
Bennett, Mrs W   16 Grayshott Laurels, Lindford, Bordon GU35 0QB
Bennett-Richards, Dr P, *MB BS BSc MRCGP*   14 Storers Quay, London E14 3BZ
Benson, Mr S, *BA FIPA*   8 Laurier Road, London NW5 1SG
Bentley, Mr L   Ascot, Randolph Lane, Iden, Rye, East Sussex TN31 7PR
Berkeley, Ms A   28 Tite Street, London SW3 4JA
Berry, Mr I M   61 Longfield Street, London SW18 5RD
Berthoud, Mr P   56A Lascotts Road, London N22 8JN
Bestavachvili, Miss M, *BSc LRAM*   11 Micheldever Road, London SE12 8LX
Bevan, Mr I, *BA*   130 Aylesford Avenue, Beckenham, Kent BR3 3RY
Bill, The Revd A, *BA AKC*   13 Wilmington Close, Newcastle upon Tyne NE3 2SF
Bimson, Miss M, *FSA*   32 Upper Park Road, London NW3 2UT
Bird, Mr P   Flat 911 Point West, 116 Cromwell Road, London SW7 4XL
Birney, Mrs I J   Kelmscott House, 26 Upper Mall, London W6 9TA
Bishop, Mrs J B   1 Falcon Square, Castle Hedingham, Halstead CO9 3BS
Blaber, Mr R G   24 Carisbrooke Road, Harpenden, Herts AL5 5QT
Black, Dr I S, *BA PhD*   12 High Street, Girton, Cambridge CB3 0PU
Blades, Mr D   52 Carlisle Road, Hove, East Sussex BN3 4FS
Blakeman, Mrs H   14 Lambscroft Way, Chalfont St Peter, Gerrards Cross SL9 9AX
Blight, Mr I   129 Epsom Road, Guildford, Surrey GU1 2PP
Bloice, Mr B J   220 Woodmansterne Road, London SW16 5UA
Blunt, Mr I W   6 Ufton Grove, London N1 4HG
Board, Dr C   36 Wakefield Gardens, London SE19 2NR
Bodnar, Mr A   8 Robinson Court, Pickering, North Yorks YO18 8EG
Boon, Mr M C M, *BA MSt FCA FCMI*   Hill House, 5 Addison Road,
    Gorleston, Great Yarmouth NR31 0PA
Booth, Mr P A   4 Ventnor Place, Sheffield S7 1LA
Booth, Mrs S   (address unknown)
Booth, Mr S J, *FRGS*   2b North Road, Stevenage, Herts SG1 4AT
Borchard, Mr J D   Coburg House, 5 Gloucester Road, Teddington,
    Middlesex TW11 0NS
Boris, Mr B   Flat 2, 19 Normanton Road, South Croydon CR2 7JU
Boulton, Professor J   32 Cavendish Road, Jesmond, Newcastle upon Tyne NE2 2NJ
Bovill, Mr P J, *BSc MA MRICS FRGS*   Lemon Tree House, Main Street,
    Wentworth, Ely, Cambridgeshire CB6 3QG
Bowden, Mr R A, *MA DAA*   4 Ascott Avenue, London W5 5QB
Bowers Isaacson, Dr L   62 Breton House, Barbican, London EC2Y 8DQ
Bowley, Mrs J   10 Church Crescent, London N10 3ND
Bowlt, Mrs E M, *BA*   7 Croft Gardens, Ruislip, Middlesex HA4 8EY
Bowman, Dr J H, *JP MA PhD MCLIP FSA Honorary Membership Secretary*
    17 Park Road, London W7 1EN

Bowsher, Mr D, *MA FSA*   Museum of London Archaeology, Mortimer
  Wheeler House, 46 Eagle Wharf Road, London NI 7ED
Boyce, Mrs M   137 West Grove, Woodford Green IG8 7NW
Boylan, Mr H   30 Scott Farm Close, Thames Ditton, Surrey KT7 OAN
Bradley, Mr G   Moorside, White Cross Road, Woodbury Salterton, Devon
  EX5 IPT
Bradley, Mr P   110A Haverstock Hill, London NW3 2BD
Brady, Mr D   Flat 28, 7 Elm Park Gardens, London SW10 9QG
Braham, Mrs M F   9 Chestnut Avenue, Tunbridge Wells, Kent TN4 OBS
Brandy, Mr C P   5 Sulina Road, London SW2 4EJ
Brill, Mr M J   Well Cottage, Abbess Roding, Ongar, Essex CM5 OPB
Bristowe, Mr S J   35 Sedgewick Avenue, Uxbridge UB10 9DF
Britten, Mr N W, *FCA*   19 College Gardens, London SE21 7BE
Brodie, Mrs L, *BA(Hons)*   Penthouse E, St John's Wood Court, St John's
  Wood Road, London NW8 8QT
Brook, Mr C A   27 Ormsby Lodge, The Avenue, London W4 1HS
Brooker, Mr P H, *FRICS LLB(Hons)*   137 Goddard Way, Saffron Walden,
  Essex CB10 2ED
Brooks, Miss M M, *MA DipTexCons*   51 Westwood Terrace, South Bank,
  York YO23 1HJ
Brothers, Ms H A   86 Breton House, Barbican, London EC2Y 8PQ
Brown, Mr C   The Coach House, 10A Eliot Place, London SE3 OQL
Brown, Mr D G   44 King Henry's Road, London NW3 3RP
Brown, Mr J W   316 Green Lane, London SW16 3AS
Brown, Miss K M   20 Oakcroft Road, London SE13 7ED
Brown, Mrs M   54 Mentmore Road, Linslade, Leighton Buzzard,
  Bedfordshire LU7 2NZ
Brown, Dr N   Flat 2, 2 Dalebury Road, London SW17 7HH
Brown, Mr P   47 Wharfedale Gardens, Thornton Heath CR7 6LE
Brown, Mr P A P, *BA MBA*   72 The Avenue, Richmond, Surrey TW9 2AH
Brown, Mr R E   21 Fir Tree Close, Hemel Hempstead HP3 8NG
Brown, Mr S   8 Loxton Road, London SE23 2ET
Brown, Mr S   Stuart Brown Partnership LLP, 3rd Floor, Cutlers Court, 115
  Houndsditch, London EC3A 7BR
Brown, Miss S F   5 Homecroft Drive, Packington, Ashby de la Zouch,
  Leics LE65 1WG
Bruce, Mr J A   37 Augustus Close, Brentford, Middlesex TW8 8QE
Brushfield, Mr J M, *MCAM*   Old Highgate House, Rye Road, Hawkhurst,
  Kent TN18 4EY
Bryars, Mr T   7 Cecil Court, London WC2N 4HE
Budworth, Dr D W, *MBE BSc PhD*   10 Sydney House, Woodstock Road,
  London W4 1DP
Bundock, Mr M   33 Upper Park Road, Kingston, Surrey KT2 5LB
Burgess, Mr M S   Stoke Cottage, Stoke St Mary, Taunton, Somerset TA3 5BZ
Burgess, Mr V   224 Priests Lane, Shenfield, Essex CM15 8LG
Burke, Ms M   228 Main Street, Groton MA 01450 USA
Burley, Mr P R   180 Waller Road, London SE14 5LU
Burrell, Mr A B   14 Leybourne Road, London NW9 9QE
Burt, Mr H C   12A Coinagehall Street, Helston, Cornwall TR13 8EB

Burton, Mrs C W   10 Marechal Niel Avenue, Sidcup, Kent DA15 7PD
Burton, Mr N H, *BA FSA*   18 Gower Mews, London WC1E 6HP
Bussey, Mr J C   96 Haven Lane, London W5 2HY
Butcher, Mr D C, *BSc(Hons)*   Vine Cottage, 23 Hollybush Hill,
    London E11 1PP
Buxton, Mr E B, *MA*   26 Dodson Vale, Kesgrave, Ipswich, Suffolk IP5 2GT
Bye, Mr P   c/o The Keep, Woollards Way, Brighton BN1 9BP
Byrne, Mr R   6 Copperways, 80 Palatine Road, Manchester M20 3JZ
Caistor, Ms M E, *MA*   13 Studd Street, London N1 0QJ
Canepa, Ms B   Prints & Drawings Department, British Museum,
    Great Russell Street, London WC1B 3DG
Caplin, Miss E T, *MA*   15 Edward Bond House, Cromer Street,
    London WC1H 8DT
Carey, Mr P   56A Woodville Road, New Barnet, Herts. EN5 5NG
Carlin, Dr M   History Department, PO Box 413, University of Wisconsin,
    Milwaukee WI 53201 USA
Carnaby, Mr J J, *EngTech MIP*   3 Lakeside Crescent, Barnet EN4 8QH
Carter, Mr N R W, *FRICS DipTP*   40 Westwood Park, London SE23 3QH
Carvagal, Mr F P   14 Brading Terrace, London W12 8ES
Catford, Mr K E   17 The Looms, Parkgate, Neston, Cheshire CH64 6RE
Caulfield, Mrs A   11 Hambledon Road, London SW18 5UD
Causer, Mr J C   9 Oakcroft Road, London SE13 7ED
Cerasano, Professor S P   15 Madison Street, Hamilton NY 13346 USA
Chafer, Mr P   26 Milton Abbas, Blandford Forum, Dorset DT11 0BL
Chaffin, Mr D E   11 Abercromby Place, Stirling FK8 2QP
Chandler, Miss J   92 Morden Hall Road, Morden, Surrey SM4 5JG
Chapple, Mrs E   63 Gloucester Road, Kew, Richmond, Surrey TW9 3BT
Charlish, Mrs D M   132 Park Lane, Carshalton, Surrey SM5 3DT
Charlton, Miss J M, *BA(Hons)*   Room 21 Whitgift House, 76 Brighton Road,
    South Croydon CR2 6AB
Charlton, Mr S A   Flat 1, 7 Riverdale Road, Twickenham TW1 2BT
Chartres, The Rt Revd & Rt Hon R J C   The Old Deanery, Dean's Court,
    London EC4V 5AA
Cherry, Mrs B K, *OBE FSA Newsletter Editor*   Bitterley House, Cleestanton
    Road, Bitterley, Ludlow, Shropshire SY8 3HJ
Christmas, Mr C A   33 The Drive, London E4 7AJ
Chweidan, Dr C D, *BA BDS*   92 Brim Hill, London N2 0EY
Clark, Miss J E, *BA MCLIP*   Flat 8, 2 Trinity Church Square, London SE1 4HU
Clark, Mr R J, *MA*   53 Bedford Gardens, London W8 7EF
Clarke, Mr P D   36 Eldred Drive, Orpington, Kent BR5 4PF
Clarke, Ms S   29 Longfield Road, Tring, Herts HP23 4DG
Claxton-Stevens, Mr C P   24 Shandon Road, London SW4 9HR
Claydon, Mr K   9 Hawthorn Road, Ripley, Surrey GU23 6LH
Cleaver, Mr H *Honorary Auditor*   91 Malford Grove, London E18 2DH
Clifton, Dr G C, *BA PhD*   55 The Ridgeway, Sutton, Surrey SM2 5JX
Cline, Mr R L, *MA LLB FSA Honorary Treasurer*   Flat 13, 13 Tavistock
    Place, London WC1H 9SH
Clute, Mrs J L   221 Camden High Street, London NW1 7BU
Cockings, Mr J H, *BA MSc*   8 Ardilaun Road, London N5 2QR

Coggin, Mr R   Appleton, Clay Lane, Fishbourne, Chichester,
West Sussex PO19 3PX
Cohen, Mr M A, *LLB*   3 Grays Inn Square, Grays Inn, London WC1R 5HP
Coldwells, Mr C A   15 Roxburgh Road, London SE27 0LB
Collier, Mr L H   Greenlands, Park Road, Barnham, Bognor Regis, West
Sussex PO22 0AQ
Collins, Dr M, *MSc PhD*   15 Talacre Road, London NW5 3PH
Collins, Mr P H, *BA*   39 Queens Crescent, London NW5 3QD
Conlin, Mr S W, *MA*   5 Ridgewood, Knoll Hill, Bristol BS9 1QZ
Cook, Dr A S   Woodmoor, 4 West Road, Newport-on-Tay, Fife DD6 8HG
Cook, Mr D   56 Clerkenwell Road, London EC1M 5PX
Cook, Mr S G   20 Cautley Close, Quainton, Aylesbury, Bucks HP22 4BN
Cookson, Mr B D, *BA*   26 Fitzjames Avenue, Croydon, Surrey CR0 5DH
Coombes, Mr A J   12 Westfield Gardens, Dorking, Surrey RH4 3DX
Coombes, Mr M   Flat 29 Cathedral Lodge, 110–115 Aldersgate Street,
London EC1A 4JE
Cooper, Mr R M   120 Wheelers Lane, Kings Heath, Birmingham B13 0SG
Cooper-Smith, Mr M   The Coach House, Tokens Green Lane, Kidmore End,
Reading RG4 9EE
Coote, Mr N A   20A New Quebec Street, London W1H 7RZ
Cope, Mr P F, *BSc*   Cameley, 17 Broadwater Rise, Tunbridge Wells, Kent TN2 5UE
Corlett, Ms H P, *MA*   Elm Tree Cottage, Sutton Mandeville, Salisbury SP3 5LY
Cornes, Mr C N   80 Coombe Road, Croydon, Surrey CR0 5RA
Cornish, Mr S M, *MA BSc*   16 Gatehill Road, Northwood, Middlesex HA6 3QD
Cornwell, Mr C E   5 John Fielden House, Canrobert Street, London E2 0BJ
Cosh, Miss M   10 Albion Villas, Thornhill Road, London N1 1HW
Costin, Mr R C   Kilronan, Polmorla, Wadebridge, Cornwall PL27 7JU
Coughlin, Mr P M, *BSc*   Chapel Cottage, Chiddingstone Heath, Edenbridge,
Kent TN8 7BT
Coupe, Mr M J, *BSc MRICS*   48 Rosendale Road, London SE21 8DP
Cousins, Mr B T   Wagtails, Hillborough Avenue, Sevenoaks, Kent TN13 3SG
Cowe, Mrs M, *MA*   12 Nettlecroft, Boxmoor, Hemel Hempstead HP1 1PQ
Cowley, Mrs C A   52 Beaumont Road, Purley, Surrey CR8 2EG
Cox-Johnson, Mr N   8 Blenkarne Road, London SW11 6JD
Craig, Mr J F   60 Headley Chase, Warley, Brentwood, Essex CM14 5DH
Crane, Mr P   Meadowbank, Old Mill Road, Denham UB9 5AW
Craven, Mrs A-M   19 Albany Street, London NW1 4DX
Crawford, Mr D L   22 The Avenue, Bickley, Kent BR1 2BT
Crawshay Jones, Mr N   2 Cossor Road, Pewsey, Wiltshire SN9 5HX
Croad, Mr S J, *MBE BA FSA*   16 Hammet's Wharf, Bridge Street,
Taunton TA1 1JY
Croft, Mr R J   3 Westbourne Road, London SE26 5NJ
Crook, Mr A J   2 Tan Cottages, Ashford Hill Road, Headley, Thatcham,
Berks RG19 8AP
Crouch, Mr D   5 Helen Road, Oxford OX2 0DF
Crowe, Mr N G, *BSc ARICS*   11 Stanley Terrace, Douglas, Isle of Man IM2 4EP
Crutchlow, Miss S B, *BSc CEng*   29 Ellerby Road, London SW6 6EX
Cudby, Mr B E   Homefield, White Hill, Pitton SP5 1DU
Cufflin, Mrs M   28 Lamorbey Close, Sidcup, Kent DA15 8BA

Cumming, Mr & Mrs D L *Honorary Members*   Sunrise of Purley,
Russell Hill Road, Purley, Surrey CR8 2LF
Cumming, Mr G, *MA MSc*   21 Friars Lane, Braintree, Essex CM7 9BL
Cumming, Mr J, *BA MSc FCIPD*   7 Frere Street, London SW11 2JA
Cundy, Dr P J, *MBBS FRACS*   Memorial Hospital, 1 Kermode Street, North
Adelaide 5006 South Australia
Curling, Mr M   Cherokee, Lower Wokingham Road, Crowthorne RG45 6DB
Currell, Mrs J   Stowfield, Station Road, Bosham, Chichester,
West Sussex PO18 8NG
Cutbill, Mr C D, *LLB(Hons)*   4 Lower Barn Road, Purley, Surrey CR8 1HQ
Cuthbert, Mr John, *MBE*   94 Blackborough Road, Reigate, Surrey RH2 7DF
Da Costa, Mr C I, *BA*   19 Green Road, Reading RG6 2BS
Dack, Mr E G   70 Palace View, Shirley, Croydon CR0 8QN
Daley, Mr P, *BSc MSc*   37 Aylesbury Road, Bromley, Kent BR2 0QP
Dalton, Mrs C   7 Park Hill, Wheatley, Oxfordshire OX33 1NE
Daniels, Mr P J   35 Benthal Road, London N16 7AR
Davidge, Mr I   64 Alexandra Road, Great Wakering, Essex SS3 0HW
Davie, Mr R J, *BA FCA*   196 Princess Park Manor, Royal Drive, London N11 3FR
Davis, Dr M I M, *BA MB BChir*   10 Church Avenue, Sidcup DA14 6BV
Day, Mr N C   6 Rose Cottages, Uppertown Lane, Bonsall, Matlock,
Derbyshire DE4 2AW
de Mare, Mr S, *MA*   6 Oakfield Street, London SW10 9JB
De'Ath, Mr D A   32 Queensway, Caversham Park Village, Reading RG4 6SQ
Dean, Mr C, *MA*   3 St Hilda's Road, London SW13 9JG
Degg, Mr R   27 Gainsborough House, Erasmus Street, London SW1P 4HX
del Rosario, Ms N   14 Garfield Mews, London SW11 5GZ
Dell, Mr D J   66 Vallance Road, London N22 7UB
Denning, Mr I, *BA(Hons)*   3 Wilmington Square, London WC1X 0ES
Dennison, Mr P R   4 Betula Close, Kenley, Surrey CR8 5ET
Densem, Mr R G   The Dell, 210 Hertfordingbury Road, off Old Thieves
Lane, Hertford SG14 2LA
Deschamps, Mrs J A   35 Medusa Road, London SE6 4JW
Dickson, Mr M E, *BA(Hons) BArch*   6 Fletcher House, 122 Nuttall Street,
London N1 5LL
Dimen, Mr S T   10 West 16 Street, Apartment 1NS, New York NY 10011 USA
Dixon, Mr P J, *BSc*   33 Tredegar Square, London E3 5AE
Dobby, Mr S   39 Chester Road, Winsford, Cheshire CW7 2NG
Dodd, Dr A   53 Radley Road, Abingdon OX14 3PN
Dolan, Dr P, *BSc PhD*   33 Montpelier Row, Twickenham TW1 2NQ
Doolittle, Dr I G, *MA DPhil*   Trantlebeg, 1 Derby Road, Haslemere,
Surrey GU27 1BS
Dore, Ms S   31 Longfield Road, Bristol BS7 9AG
Dowley, Dr T E, *PhD BA(Hons)*   44 Carson Road, London SE21 8HU
Doyle, Mr P J   61 Green Lane, Farnham, Surrey GU9 8QE
Doyle, Mr R   219 Sternhold Avenue, London SW2 4PG
Drake, Mr A D G, *BA MA PGCE*   3/6 Bedford Avenue, Bexhill on Sea,
East Sussex TN40 1NE
Drew, Miss A M, *BA*   2 Branstone Road, Kew Gardens, Richmond,
Surrey TW9 3LB

Drewett, Mrs J   13 Lincoln Road, Worcester Park, Surrey KT4 8AN
Drummond, Mr P, *MA FRSA*   25b Miranda Road, London N19 3RA
Duggan, Mr S J   34 Wantage Road, Reading RG30 2SF
Duncan, Dr A I M   19 Boileau Road, London SW13 9BJ
Duncan, Mr C   Flat 4, 17 Coldharbour, London E14 9NS
Duncan, Mr D H S   116 Fairlawn Drive, Berkeley CA 94708-2108 USA
Dunmore, Mr T L   19 Cornwallis Grove, London N9 0JR
Dunn, Mr M J, *BA FCII*   Flat 32, 129 Park Street, London W1K 7JB
Dunning, Mr R   3 Waveney Avenue, London SE15 3UF
Durne, Mr M E, *BA*   Fir Bank Cottage, Warren Lane, Cross in Hand,
   Heathfield, East Sussex TN21 0TE
Durne, Mrs V M, *BA(Hons)*   Fir Bank Cottage, Warren Lane, Cross in Hand,
   Heathfield, East Sussex TN21 0TE
Duthie, Mr R   5 Levyne Court, Pine Street, London EC1R 0JQ
Earl, Mr J   60 Balcaskie Road, London SE9 1HQ
Eastment, Mr M J   301 Woodstock Road, Oxford OX2 7NY
Easton, Mr R J   19 Bradford Drive, Ewell, Surrey KT19 0AQ
Edinburgh, HRH The Duke of *Patron*   (Private Secretary), Buckingham
   Palace, London SW1A 1AA
Edwards, Mr H G   34 Capstan Square, London E14 9EU
Edwards, Mr R   12 Blacklands Drive, Hayes End, Middlesex UB4 8EU
Elam, Mr R A   31 Loxley Road, London SW18 3LL
Elbourne, Miss J M   98 Russell Court, Woburn Place, London WC1H 0LP
Eley, Ms J   100 Parkway, London NW1 7AN
Eliot, Professor S J   2 Widcombe Terrace, Bath BA2 6AJ
Ellis, Mr R, *BSc MSc*   50 Shakespeare Drive, Upper Caldecote,
   Biggleswade SG18 9DD
Elliston, Mr M F, *BSc CEng*   96 Sparrows Herne, Basildon, Essex SS16 5EX
Epstein, Mr J A   72 Stanhope Avenue, London N3 3NA
Evans, Mr J   10 Mount Vernon Close, Woking, Surrey GU22 7TU
Evans, Mr M   47 Holmes Road, Twickenham, Middlesex TW1 4RF
Everett, Mr C   56 Inchmery Road, London SE6 2NE
Everitt, Mr D   16 Great Calcroft, Pershore, Worcs WR10 1QS
Everitt, Mr K D, *BSc RIBA*   4 St Albans Crescent, Woodford Green IG8 9EH
Everson, Mr T F J, *MA MPhil DipLib*   40 Woodlands Avenue, New Malden,
   Surrey KT3 3UQ
Eyton, Mr L   72 Hatherley Road, London E17 6SB
Fearnley, Mrs Y   10 Leyburne Gardens, Chinnor, Oxon OX39 4EL
Feltham, Mr I, *MA CEng MICE*   5 Fergus Road, London N5 1JS
Fenwick, Mr P H   78 Herald Walk, Knight's Manor, Temple Hill, Dartford,
   Kent DA1 5SS
Fernandez, Sra N H   205 Abbott Road, Poplar, London E14 0NE
Ferris, Mr S R   51 Cedar Drive, Kingsclere, Newbury, Berks RG20 5TE
Field, Mr E F   165 Raeburn Avenue, Surbiton, Surrey KT5 9DG
Fielding, Mr A   27 Forton Road, Newport, Shropshire TF10 7JR
Figueiredo, Mr P   25A Lebanon Gardens, London SW18 1RQ
Firshman, Mr B   Flat H, 9–11 London Lane, London E8 3PR
Fitzgerald, Mr K P   New Cabin, Church Road, Sea Palling, Norfolk NR12 0UB
Flaxman, Mr R H   10 Sandgate Lane, London SW18 3JP

Fleming, Mr W B, *MA BCL*   268 Latymer Court, Hammersmith Road, London W6 7LB

Ford, Ms B   9 Welbeck Road, London E6 3ET

Ford, Mr T T, *ARAM ARSCM HonRCO*   151 Mount View Road, Stroud Green, London N4 4JT

Forrest, Mr J A   13 Worcester Drive, Southfield Road, London W4 1AB

Forrester, Mr R G, *LLM*   84 Litchfield Road, London E3 5AL

Forrestier Smith, Mr P A   64 Gordon Road, Carshalton Beeches, Surrey SM5 3RE

Fosdal, Mr M   Groom's Cottage, 1 Dyers Hill, Charlbury, Oxon OX7 3QD

Foster, Dr B   4 St Mary's Court High Street, Little Addington, Kettering, Northants NN14 4BF

Foster, Mrs H   16 Pellor Fields, Breage, Helston, Cornwall TR13 9UL

Fowler, Mr J A   6 George Street, Bridlington, East Yorkshire YO15 3PG

Fowler, Mr S   254A Kew Road, Richmond, Surrey TW9 3EG

Fox, Mr H, *MA FCA*   3 Shakespeare Gardens, London N2 9LJ

Foxell, Mr S M, *BA*   23 Beacon Hill, London N7 9LY

Foxwell, Miss H J   135 Topsham Road, London SW17 8SW

Frankland, Mr C J, *FCA*   29 Montalt Road, Woodford Green, Essex IG8 9RS

Frazer, Dr P A T, *MA MSc PhD*   6 The Avenue, Richmond, North Yorkshire DL10 7AZ

Freestone, Ms T M   Flat C, 33 Windsor Road, London W5 3UL

French, Mrs A   Keepers Cottage, 5 Langton Road, Great Bowden LE16 7EZ

French, Mrs J, *BA*   11 Montague Road, Berkhamsted, Herts HP4 3DS

Frost, Mr A   17 Hazelwood Avenue, Eastbourne, East Sussex BN22 0SB

Frost, Ms E   Flat 2, 161 Clapham Road, London SW9 0PU

Frost, Mr P M, *BDS*   178 Peckham Rye, London SE22 9QA

Fuller, Mr G W   30 Lonsdale Square, London N1 1EW

Fulwell, Miss S   26 Avenue Road, Leigh-on-Sea, Essex SS9 1AX

Gale, Mr L T   9404 S E 54th Street, Mercer Island WA 98040 USA

Galer, Mr B R, *RIBA*   37 Victoria Park Road, Malvern, Worcs WR14 2JK

Galer, Mr D W, *BPharm*   507 Hurst Road, Bexley, Kent DA5 3JX

Galinou, Miss M   8 Green Court, 27 Beckenham Grove, Bromley, Kent BR2 0XS

Gamble, Mr T H   Flat G02, Ivan Hampshire Place, 231 Main Road, Newlands 7700 South Africa

Gan, Mr R L, *BA BSc MEd*   The Beeches, Sands Lane, Carlton-le-Moorland, Lincoln LN5 9HJ

Gapper, Dr C, *BA PhD FSA*   12 Officers' Terrace, The Historic Dockyard, Chatham, Kent ME4 3LJ

Gardner, Mr S   11 Mount Road, Barnet EN4 9RL

Garrett, Mrs E A S   25 Abbeville Close, Exeter, Devon EX2 4SJ

Gatford, Mr K   The Ridge House, 2c Kemerton Road, Beckenham, Kent BR3 6NJ

Gaylard, Mr D, *FRGS FBCS*   7 Woodland Drive, St Albans, Herts AL4 0EL

Gentles, Dr I J   Department of History, Glendon College, 2225 Bayview Avenue, Toronto, Ontario M4N 3M6 Canada

Gerhold, Mr D J, *MA*   19 Montserrat Rd, London SW15 2LD

Gestetner, Mr J   7 Oakhill Avenue, London NW3 7RD

Gibbons, Mr S J   83 Hewitt Avenue, St Helens, Lancs WA10 4EF

Gibbs, Mr P M E, *BA*   75 Arlington Road, London NW1 7ES

Gidley-Kitchen, Mr G C B   Wybournes, Kemsing, Sevenoaks, Kent TN15 6NE

Gilbody, Mr J P, *BA(Hons)*   43 Serpentine Road, Sevenoaks, Kent TN13 3XS
Giles, Mrs K D, *BA*   77 Kingswood Road, Tadworth, Surrey KT20 5EF
Gilmore, Mr D   44 Strand Building, 29 Urswick Road, London E9 6DW
Glennie, Mr D   Winter's Grace, Tonbridge Road, Ightham, Kent TN15 9AN
Glews, Mr D   90 Cleveland Gardens, London SW13 0AH
Glithero, Mrs B J, *BA(Hons)*   15 Chestnut Close, Witney, Oxon OX28 1PD
Glover, Mr G E   228 Malpas Road, Brockley, London SE4 1DH
Glover, Mrs J J   48 Hermitage Lane, London NW2 2HG
Gloyn, Mr W J   33 Dale View Crescent, London E4 6PH
Goddard, Mr R A, *BA ACA*   Mockbridge Cottage, Brighton Road,
    Shermanbury, Horsham, West Sussex RH13 8HD
Gold, Mr R M F   Lawrence Fine Art, South Street, Crewkerne,
    Somerset TA18 8AB
Goldfinch, Mr J   63 The Quadrant, London SW20 8SW
Goodison, Mrs K   37 Stepney Green, London E1 3JX
Gordon-Smith, Mr B   36 Munster Road, Teddington, Middlesex TW11 9LL
Gotlop, Mr P F, *MA MRTPI*   32 Walmington Fold, London N12 7LR
Gough, Mr D   Ainsdale House, Maesbrook, Oswestry, Shropshire SY10 8QP
Grabham, Mr C   84a Kingston Road, Luton LU2 7SA
Graham, Mr D A M, *FRICS*   May Cottage, Fragnall Lane,
    Winchmore Hill HP7 0PG
Grange, Mrs E K C, *BA(Hons)*   9 Peacemarsh Farm Close, Gillingham,
    Dorset SP8 4XQ
Gray, Mr C   23 Windsor Road, Beaconsfield HP9 2JJ
Green, Mr C, *BA MBA*   Noddyshall, Rockshaw Road, Merstham,
    Surrey RH1 3DB
Green, Dr D R, *BA PhD*   Department of Geography, King's College, Strand,
    London WC2R 2LS
Greggains, Mr A   24 Nightingale Road, Carshalton, Surrey SM5 2EL
Greggains, Miss R   23 Avenue Road, Wallington SM6 9QF
Grice, Mr R I   198 Sandbed Lane, Belper, Derbyshire DE56 0SN
Griffiths, Mrs F A   3 Holyoake Walk, London N2 0JX
Grindlay, Mr S J S   48 Thorpewood Avenue, London SE26 4BX
Groom, Ms S   15 High Park Road, Kew, Richmond, Surrey TW9 4BL
Grynberg, Mr W   36 Denham Drive, Gants Hill IG2 6QU
Guillery, Mr P   13 Swallowfield Road, Charlton, London SE7 7NS
Hadley, Mrs S J   43 Elmhurst Drive, South Woodford, London E18 1BP
Hagger, Mr A H D   (address unknown)
Hahn, Ms S   17 Highbury Hill, London N5 1SU
Hall, Mr D A, *DipCart*   Coombe House, Chapel Street, Axmouth, Seaton,
    Devon EX12 4AU
Hall, Mr G   24 Avenue Road, London N12 8PY
Hall, Mr J M   8 Woodside Road, Woodford Green IG8 0TR
Hall, Mrs J M   10 Elsworthy, Thames Ditton, Surrey KT7 0YP
Hall, Mr P J   178 Albert Road, London E10 6PD
Hallett, Mrs A M H, *BA MA*   6 George Lane, Lichfield, Staffs WS13 6DX
Hallett, Dr D, *BSc PhD FGS*   13 York House, Courtlands, Sheen Road,
    Richmond, Surrey TW10 5BD
Halligan, Mr J   36 Hayes Garden, Bromley, Kent BR2 7DG

Halpin, Dr D M G, *MA DPhil*   Dept of Respiratory Medicine, Royal Devon Exeter Hospital, Barrack Road, Exeter EX2 5DW

Halson, Mrs P   12 Bentinck Mansions, 12–16 Bentinck Street, London W1U 2ER

Hamilton, Mr A P, *BA*   Meadowmist, Church Hill, Chacewater, Cornwall TR4 8PZ

Hamilton, Mr H R B   2 Wild Hatch, London NW11 7LD

Hammill, Mr L P   115 Eleanor Road, London E8 1DN

Hammond, Mrs L   17 Chemin de Hajau, 32170 Mielan France

Hammond, Mr P W   Flat 4, 9 Devonshire Place, Heathfield Terrace, London W4 4JB

Hampshire, Dr E C G   (address unknown)

Hansell, Mr B P   43 Graham Road, London N15 3NH

Hanson, Dr K W   24 Straightsmouth, London SE10 9LB

Harding, Mr J J, *MBE MA*   29 Aylward Road, Merton Park, London SW20 9AJ

Harding, Mr P G   30 Avondale Court, Churchfields, London E18 2RD

Harding, Dr V A   202 Muswell Hill Broadway, London N10 3SA

Hardy, Dr P J   Curator of Paintings, Prints & Drawings, Museum of London, 150 London Wall, London EC2Y 5HN

Hardy, Ms S   32 Whiteadder Way, London E14 9UR

Harper, Mr J C, *QC*   Landmark Chambers, 180 Fleet Street, London EC4A 2HG

Harper, Mr T   Flat 7, 1 Harry Day Mews, Chestnut Road, London SE27 9AR

Harris, Ms C, *BA MA*   70 Engadine Street, London SW18 5DA

Harris, Mr M R A   135 Anson Road, London NW2 4AH

Harrod, Mrs J, *BA*   15 Berry Close, Hornchurch RM12 6UB

Harry, Mr C D   54 Oakmere Lane, Potters Bar, Herts EN6 5LT

Hart, Ms V   19 Norman Road, East Ham, London E6 6HN

Harte, Mrs C   Greenham Farm, Wadhurst, Kent TN5 6LE

Harte, Mr N B, *BSc FRHistS FSA*   Department of History, UCL, Gower Street, London WC1E 6BT

Harvey, Mr R M   55 Ammonite House, 12 Flint Close, London E15 4QR

Harward, Mr C, *BA MifA*   103 Summer Street, Stroud, Glos GL5 1PQ

Hasenfratz, Dr R   8 Willard Street, Willimantic CT 06226 USA

Hathway, Mr N   30 Shirlock Road, London NW3 3HS

Hawgood, Mr D, *MA FBCS FSG*   26 Cloister Road, London W3 0DE

Hayes, Mrs A B   7 Speed House, Barbican, London EC2Y 8AT

Haynes, Mr D   Flat F, 44–48 Shepherdess Walk, London N1 7JP

Hayward, Dr M A, *BA MA*   32 Clatford Manor, Upper Clatford, Andover, Hants SP11 7PZ

Hazeldine, Mrs R   52 Jacksons Lane, London N6 5SX

Heather, Mr W R F   23 Pandora Road, London NW6 1TS

Hebbert, Mr C   85 Windus Road, London N16 6UR

Hedgecock, Ms D   1 Addington Road, Stroud Green, London N4 4RP

Heller, Mr B, *MPhil*   22 St Mary's Road, Weybridge, Surrey KT13 9PT

Helyer, Mr J   2 Chestnut Place, Epsom, Surrey KT17 3BL

Hemsley, Miss C M   18 Hawthorn Way, Shepperton TW17 8QH

Henderson, Dr P, *MA PhD FSA*   The Old Mill, Upper Swell, Cheltenham, Glos GL54 1EW

Hendy, Mr J, *LLB DipLL LLM*   75 Hillway, London N6 6AB

Henry, Mr J, *BA DipITC FGS FRGS*   71A Oxford Gardens, London w10 5uj
Hepher, Mr R A, *BA MTP FRICS*   76 Castle Road, Bedford mk40 3ps
Herbert, Mr F, *HonFRGS*   46 Chilcombe House, Fontley Way, London sw15 4nb
Herron, Mr J J   34 Alacross Road, London w5 4ht
Hewett, Mr D, *MRICS*   44 Heathhurst Road, South Croydon cr2 0ba
Hewett, Mr P G, *MA*   White Cottage, Church Road, Milford, Surrey gu8 5jd
Hewitt, Dr L E   School of Social and Political Sciences, University of
    Glasgow, 25–29 Bute Gardens, Glasgow g12 8rs
Heyking, Baroness G   2c Alleyn Road, London se21 8al
Heyworth, Mr L   Office 370, 19–21 Crawford Street, London w1h 1pj
Hibberdine, Mr S, *BSc FRICS*   38 Alleyn Road, London se21 8al
Hidson, Mr R, *DipArch FCLIP*   117 St Thomas's Road, London n4 2qj
Higgott, Dr G   17 Windermere Avenue, London nw6 6lp
Higgs, Ms G, *RIBA*   53 Balcombe Street, London nw1 6hd
Higham, Mr G A   32 East Saint Helen Street, Abingdon, Oxon ox14 5eb
Hillier, The Revd J F   70 Royal Way, Trumpington, Cambridge cb2 9ax
Hillier, Mr M J S   71 Haydon Park Road, London sw19 8jh
Hilling, Dr D, *MSc PhD*   4 Torrington Road, Berkhamsted hp4 3dd
Hills, Mrs C M   Tile House, 36 Wansunt Road, Bexley, Kent da5 2dq
Hilson, Dr A J W, *MA MB BChir MSc FRCP*   62 Ossulton Way, London n2 0lb
Hina, Mr R P J   6a Park Road, Ashford, Middlesex tw15 1ey
Hinchliffe, Mrs C L   221 Tring Road, Aylesbury hp20 1jh
Hinks, Dr J   52 Fairefield Crescent, Glenfield, Leicester le3 8eh
Hinshelwood, Mr J   9 Umfreville Road, London n4 1ry
Hird, Mr R L   25 Rozel Road, London sw4 0ey
Hitchcock, Dr T, *DPhil*   19A Cecil Road, London n10 2bu
Hoare, Mr P, *MA FSA*   80 St Ann Street, Salisbury sp1 2dx
Hobson, Mrs A M R   77 Onslow Road, Richmond, Surrey tw10 6qa
Hodgson, Mr G M T   32 The Playing Close, Charlbury, Oxon ox7 3rj
Hodgson, Ms L, *BA(Hons) MA*   30A Marsh Lane, Oxford ox3 0ng
Holder, Mr N   25 Monmouth Street, Topsham, Exeter ex3 0aj
Hollamby, Mr K, *BSc FSA(Scot) FRGS FEI*   2 Queensway, Lincoln ln2 4ah
Holland, Mr T E, *BSIM MBA*   315 South Royal Street, Alexandria va 22314 USA
Holloway, Professor R G, *MA PhD*   Gonville & Caius College,
    Cambridge cb2 1ta
Holness, Mrs A   18 Elm Close, Bowerhill, Melksham, Wiltshire sn12 6sd
Honour, Mr D J   9 Windermere Road, Bacup ol13 9dn
Hook, Mr A   54 Egerton Road, Bristol bs7 8hl
Hooker, Mr A H   40 Shirley Gardens, Rusthall, Tunbridge Wells, Kent tn4 8th
Hornby, Mr J R   The Croft, Lyndon Road, Manton, Oakham le15 8sr
Horne, Mr M A C   175 Exeter Road, South Harrow, Middlesex ha2 9pg
Horsfall Turner, Dr O   63 Calvert Road, London se10 0dg
Horton, Mrs J A F   26 The Crescent, Slough, Berks sl1 2lq
Houghton, Mr S J   2 The Maltings, Orpington, Kent br6 0dh
Howard, Mr M   10 Earlston Grove, London e9 7ne
Howcutt, Mr F   22 Thurlestone Road, London se27 0pd
Howel, Ms S M   21 Wyatt Park Road, London sw2 3tn
Howell, Mr J, *BSc*   Valley Cottage, Laxfield, Woodbridge, Suffolk ip13 8hn
Howse, Ms D, *BSc MSc FRES*   34 Rounton Road, Waltham Abbey en9 3ar

Hughes, Mr E W, *FCIS*   Killigarth, Morant Road, Ringwood,
   Hampshire BH24 IJX
Hughes, Mr K J   Worcester Lodge, 35 Forty Hill, Enfield, Middlesex EN2 9EQ
Humm, Ms D   385 Russell Court, Woburn Place, London WCIH ONH
Humphries, Mrs S   8 Rydens Grove, Hersham, Surrey KT12 5RX
Hunt, Mr B R   26 Joiners Road, Linton, Cambridge CB21 4NP
Hunting, Dr P S, *PhD Chairman*   40 Smith Street, London SW3 4EP
Hurdley, Mr J R   Jones Farm, Hollington Lane, Highclere, Newbury RG15 9XX
Hurst, Mr B L   The Spinney, 2 Richfield Road, Bushey Heath, Herts WD2 3LQ
Hurst, Mr M G   57 Uphill Road, London NW7 4PR
Hutchings, Mr G F   Spruce Wood, Warren Cutting, Kingston-on-Thames,
   Surrey KT2 7HS
Hutchings, Mrs V   Lesters, Maperton Road, Charlton Horethorne,
   Sherborne, Dorset DT9 4NT
Hutchinson, Mr A   West Hurstgate, Hook Heath Road, Woking,
   Surrey GU22 ODT
Hyde, Mr M R   Villa Farm, Rushmere St Andrew, Ipswich, Suffolk IP5 7DT
Hyde, Mr R N, *FCLIP FSA Member of Council*   5 Streetfield Mews,
   London SE3 OER
Insall, Sir Donald W   73 Kew Green, Richmond, Surrey TW9 3AH
Irving, Mr J   27 Brockenhurst Road, Croydon CRO 7DR
Israel, Mr N B, *FSA*   14 Ryfold Road, London SW19 8BZ
Jackman, Mr D   332 Shakespeare Tower, Barbican, London EC2Y 8NJ
Jackson, Mr B T, *MS FRCS*   Mapledene, 7 St Matthew's Avenue, Surbiton,
   Surrey KT6 6JJ
Jackson, Mr D S   65 Longley Road, Harrow, Middlesex HA1 4TQ
Jackson, Mr P   White House, Noon's Folly, Newmarket Road, Royston SG8 7NG
Jackson-Harris, Mrs V   PO Box 327, Northwood, Middlesex HA6 9ES
Jacob, Mr R E   c/o RGC Jenkins & Co., 26 Caxton Street, London SWIH ORJ
Jago, Mr M F   60 Cromwell Road, Ribbleton, Preston PR2 6YF
Javes, Mr G A, *MA*   45 Rushdene Avenue, Barnet EN4 8EN
Jay, Mr P   40 Rocks Lane, London SW13 OOA
Jeal, Mr R   48 Malden Green Avenue, Worcester Park, Surrey KT4 7SQ
Jefferson Smith, Mr P   22 Iveley Road, London SW4 OEW
Jeffery, Dr B   46 Parliament Hill, London NW3 2TL
Jeffery, Dr S   67 Devonshire Road, London W4 2HU
Jeffryes, Mr A   (address unknown)
Jelley, Mrs S   Little Oak, 1 Vennings Copse, Budleigh Salterton, Devon EX9 6AX
Jenk, Mr T   4 Hunt Club Lane, Malvern PA 19355-3406 USA
Jenkin, Mr D   157 Arlington Road, London NW1 7ET
Jenkins, Sir Brian   Vine Cottage, 4 Park Gate, London SE3 9XE
Jenkins, Mr D K   2 Moody Street, London E1 4BY
Jennings, Mr V, *BA*   24B Kylemore Road, London NW6 2PT
Jeremiah, Mr M G, *CB JP FRSA*   110 Ashley Gardens, Thirleby Road,
   London SWIP IHJ
Johnson, Mr I, *BA*   Slydersgate, 11 Church Hill, Loughton, Essex IG10 IQP
Johnson, Mr I A   Green Tiles, Mill Lane, Chalfont St Giles, Bucks HP8 4NR
Johnson, Mr K E, *MA CEng*   19 Clarence Road, Redhill, Surrey RH1 6NG
Johnson, Mr P C   32 Ivere Drive, Barnet EN5 IAS

Johnson, Mr T, *BSc*   14 Penn Road, London N7 9RD

Johnston, Mr J S, *MA BSc*   46 Main Street, Strathkinness, St Andrews KY16 9SB

Jollye, Mr S H   Bramble Down Nursing Home, Woodland Road, Denbury,
   Newton Abbot, Devon TQ12 6DY

Jones, Mr D, *BSc MA*   12 The Beechams, Mursley, Milton Keynes MK17 0RX

Jones, Mrs E   Reay Garth, 39 Woodcroft Road, Wylam,
   Northumberland NE41 8DH

Jones, Ms L, *BA*   The Lodge, Snaresbrook House, Woodford Road,
   London E18 2UB

Jones, Mr M J K   49 Boscombe Road, London SW17 9JL

Jones, Mr S   450b Lea Bridge Road, London E10 7DY

Jones, Mr S   17 Cross Road, Tadworth, Surrey KT20 5ST

Kariya, Mr M   62a Trinity Church Square, London SE1 4HT

Karran, Mr D   Flat 26, 1 Bywell Place, London E16 1JW

Kastl, Mr G   18 Wat Tyler House, Boyton Road, London N8 7AU

Kauder, Ms A   54 Aberdeen Road, London N5 2XB

Kaupe, Mr J W   40 Chauncy Court, Blue Coats Avenue, Hertford SG14 1DU

Kaye, Mr I F, *CEng BSc MICE*   103 Hassall Street, Corinda, Brisbane
   QUEENSLAND 4075 Australia

Keates, Mr J B, *MA FRSL FSA*   5 Houblon Road, Richmond, Surrey TW10 6DB

Keay, Ms A, *BA(Hons)*   Clifton House, 17 Queen Street, King's Lynn,
   Norfolk PE30 1HT

Keegan, Mr V   174 Ashley Gardens, London SW1P 1PD

Kehaya, Mr C A, *BSc CEng MICE*   6 Holne Cross, Ashburton, Devon TQ13 7QU

Kellas, Mrs S H   243 Cromwell Tower, Barbican, London EC2Y 8DD

Kelly, Miss A A, *MA*   Flat 8, 34 Phillimore Gardens, London W8 7QF

Kelsall, Mr A F   4 Woodlands Avenue, London N3 2NR

Kendall, Ms D   115 Howards Road, London E13 8AZ

Kendall, Mr P   20 Ramsbury Road, St Albans AL1 1SW

Kennedy, Mrs J L, *JP*   6 Great Spilmans, London SE22 8SZ

Kenny, Mr M G C   3/82 Hailesland Park, Edinburgh EH14 2PG

Kent, Ms E J   103 Friern Road, London SE22 0AZ

Kent, Mrs P E   16 Newmans Way, Hadley Wood, Barnet EN4 0LR

Kermath, Ms V   92 Hill Road, Pinner, Middlesex HA5 1LE

Kerry, Mr A   7 Bermans Way, London NW10 1SD

Kewley, Mr J, *MA*   Flat G, 2 Calthorpe Street, London WC1X 0JS

Keynes, Mr R H, *MA*   31 Baalbec Road, London N5 1QN

Kidd, Mrs F M   3 St Helens Crescent, Sandhurst GU47 9AX

King, Mr B D   17 Wellington House, Eton Road, London NW3 4SY

King, Mr J P   64 Alric Avenue, New Malden, Surrey KT3 4JW

King, Mr T T   Flat 44 Gun Wharf, 130 Wapping High Street, London E1W 2NH

Kinney, Mr L W   9 Old Park Lane, Farnham, Surrey GU9 0AJ

Kirby, Mr J D   10 Harkerside Close, Manchester M21 8XQ

Kirby, Mr M   7 Uplands, Beckenham, Kent BR3 3NB

Klopke, Mrs J K D   8 Kennet Court, Wokingham, Berkshire RG41 3DB

Knight, Mr L A   19 Howcroft Crescent, London N3 1PA

Knight, Mr P   62 Effingham Road, London SE12 8NU

Knight, Mr R J   Stoneleigh, Dean Lane, Stoke Orchard, Cheltenham,
   Glos GL52 7RX

Lambert, Mr M J   7 Coniston Gardens, Hedge End SO30 0LP
Lane, Mr R J   9 Mill View Gardens, Croydon CR0 5HW
Lang, Mrs D M   10 Abbeymead Court, The Old School Place, Sherborne,
    Dorset DT9 3AU
Large, Mrs L   36 Louisville Road, London SW17 8RW
Larkham, Professor P, BA PhD   172 Cole Valley Road, Hall Green,
    Birmingham B28 0DQ
Latey, Mr W N   27 Hospital Bridge Road, Twickenham TW2 5UL
Lathaen, Ms A, BSc   9 Boston Road, Henley-on-Thames, Oxon RG9 1DY
Laurie, Mr R, BA(Hons) DipLib   201 Alberta Avenue, East Kilbride,
    Glasgow G75 8HU
Laxton, Mr P, BA   79 Wellington Road, New Brighton, Merseyside CH45 2NE
Layton-Jones, Dr K   79 Churchill Road, London NW2 5EG
le Pavoux, Mrs B M   78 Copers Cope Road, Beckenham, Kent BR3 1RJ
Lea, Mrs A S, BA(Hons) DMS   12 Morell Close, New Barnet EN5 5JU
Leal, Mr D J   56 Micheldever Road, London SE12 8LU
Lear, Mr M   20 Oakland Place, Buckhurst Hill IG9 5JZ
Leary, Mr R   18 Downton View, Ludlow, Salop SY8 1JF
Leaver, Miss E P, FRCS FRCDG   147 Wistaston Green Road, Crewe CW2 8RA
Lee, Mr C L   107 Queens Road, Hertford SG13 8BJ
Lee, Mrs C M   51 Lawford Road, London N1 5BJ
Lee, Professor J M   The Courtyard Cottage, 1 Cross Deep, Twickenham TW1 4QJ
Lee, Mr S, BSc   16 Dickens Way, Romford RM1 4GQ
Lefroy-Brooks, Mr S R, MSc LBH   Wembley Geotechnical and
    Environmental, 12 Little Balmer, Buckingham Industrial Park MK18 1TF
Leith, Mr I   127 Wood Lane, Chippenham, Wiltshire SN15 3EA
Lelliott, Mr V J T, MSc   47 Debden Road, Saffron Walden, Essex CB11 4AD
Leon, Mr R   Sanchez de Ortega 18, Aracena 21200 HUELVA Spain
Lester, Ms M C   43 Beversbrook Road, London E15 4EP
Letherby, Mrs J E, DipArch RIBA   101 Clonmell Road, London N17 6JT
Leverton & Sons Ltd (for Andrew Leverton)   212 Eversholt Street,
    London NW1 1BD
Levey, Dr B   29 Beatrice Road, Cardiff CF14 1DT
Levy, Mr P L   52 Springfield Road, London NW8 0QN
Lewin, Mrs H B   48 Methley Street, London SE11 4AJ
Lewsey, Mrs C   50 Cambridge Road, Impington, Cambridge CB24 9NU
Liffen, Mr J   71 Burleigh Road, Enfield EN1 1NU
Lillystone, Mr S   24 Fairfield Road, Crouch End, London N8 9HG
Lindsay, Mr J A   13 Stoneyfield Road, Old Coulsdon, Surrey CR5 2HP
Linnell, Mr R F H, MA FRICS   85 Ennerdale Road, Kew, Richmond,
    Surrey TW9 2DN
Linthicum, Mr J   (address unknown)
Lipton, Sir Stuart   44 Acacia Road, London NW8 6HH
Livingstone, Dr H J, BSc   Orchard Cottage, Wineham Lane, Wineham, West
    Sussex BN5 9AY
Lloyd, His Honour Judge H J, QC   1 Atkin Building, Grays Inn,
    London WC1R 1AT
Lloyd, Dr S, DPhil   146 Howard Street, Oxford OX4 3BG
Lobel, Mrs C   5 Bryanston Mews East, London W1H 2DB

Lock, Mr G   Nathaniel Lichfield & Partners, 14 Regent's Wharf, All Saints Street, London N1 9RL

Lock, Mr J F   111 Capel Road, London E7 0JS

Lockhart, Mr D A, *MA LLB*   Evergreen Lodge, Back Lane, Canonstown, Hayle, Cornwall TR27 6NF

Logan, Dr R I   6 Woodnutt Close, Bembridge, Isle of Wight PO35 5YF

Long, Mr NJ   58 Crescent Lane, London SW4 9PU

Long, Mr T, *BA DipLib MCLIP*   44 Gabriel House, Odessa Street, London SE16 7HQ

Loost, Mr M J, *BA LLD*   36 Upper Addison Gardens, London W14 8AJ

Loveland, Mr M J S   1 Maids of Honour Row, Richmond, Surrey TW9 9NY

Lucas, Jr., Mr Harry   327 Congress Avenue, Suite 500, Austin TX 78701-3656 USA

Luckins, Dr A, *BSc PhD*   Schiehallion, Hill o'Blair, Upper Allan Street, Blairgowrie, Perthshire PH10 6HL

Lund, Mr T   151 Silverdale, London SE26 4SQ

Lynch, Ms E K, *MA*   Department of English, PO Box 400121, University of Virginia, Charlottesville VA 22904-4121 USA

Lynch, Mr M J, *MA LLB*   11 Saberton Close, Waterbeach, Cambridge CB25 9QW

Lyon, Mr E, *BA BA MA MA MA*   39A Colyestone Crescent, London E8 2LG

Lyster, Miss B   9 Bainton Road, Oxford OX2 7AF

Macarthur, Ms A   6 Priory Road, Richmond, Surrey TW9 3DF

Macdonald, Mr C A   5 Priory Close, Sunbury, Middlesex TW16 5AB

Mackillop, Mr T C, *LLB*   137 West 67th Street, Apt 2e, New York NY 10023 USA

Maddocks, Dr A C, *BM MRCPath*   The Small House, Willow Grove, Chislehurst, Kent BR7 5BS

Major, Mr C T   71 Bromley Common, Bromley, Kent BR2 9LP

Major, Mr I   40 Greenhill Gardens, Guildford, Surrey GU4 7HH

Major, Mr M   1 Frobisher Gardens, Guildford, Surrey GU1 2NT

Makepeace, Mrs M   Bulbarrow, Milton Avenue, Gerrards Cross, Bucks SL9 8QN

Mandelbrote, Mr G H   Flat 1, 137A Gray's Inn Road, London WC1X 8TU

Mann, Ms E   24 West Street, Harwich CO12 3DB

Mann, Miss S A F   18 Upper Montagu Street, London W1H 2PF

Mannix, Mr P A V, *MA*   The Court House, The Green, Shamley Green, Guildford, Surrey GU5 0UB

Marks, Mr S N P, *MA FSA RIBA Vice-President*   23 Cleveland Walk, Bath BA2 6JW

Marle, Mr W J   1 Kingsmere, 43 Chislehurst Road, Chislehurst, Kent BR7 5LE

Marriner, Miss R   28 Townley Road, Bexleyheath, Kent DA6 7HN

Marsden, Mr P, *BA MA MSc*   Chequers Cottage, Dunsmore, Aylesbury, Bucks HP22 6QH

Marshall, Mr H R   Roughlands Farm, Goudhurst Road, Marden, Kent TN12 9NH

Marshall, Dr J, *MA BEd PhD*   54 Bath Buildings, Montpelier, Bristol BS56 5PU

Marshall, Mrs J A, *BSc*   Wildacre, 27 Cedar Road, Farnborough, Hants GU14 7AU

Marshall, Mr K   219 Fordwych Road, London NW2 3NH

Marshall, Dr K C   76 Ennismore Avenue, Greenford UB6 0JW

Martell, Ms V   22 Plashett Road, London E13 0PU

Marter, Mr J S   3 Williams Way, Blandford Forum, Dorset DT11 7YA

Martin, Mr J   38 Rusthall Avenue, London W4 1BP
Martin, Mr J E   23 The Drive, Sidcup, Kent DA14 4ER
Martin-Ross, Mr C J, *BSc BA MCLIP*   6 Castledown Terrace,
    Hastings TN34 3RQ
Mason, Mr A D   Finches House, Hiham Green, Winchelsea,
    East Sussex TN36 4EG
Massil, Mr S W   138 Middle Lane, London N8 7JP
Mathews, Mr G W, *BA(Hons)*   17 The Spinney, Taunton, Somerset TA1 4RY
Mathieson, Mr G, *BSc FICE*   83 Blackheath Park, London SE3 0EU
Matthams, Miss J K   113 Ninesprings Way, Hitchin, Herts SG4 9NX
Matthews, Mr P J, *BA(Hons)*   20 Wenderholme, 68 South Park Hill Road,
    Croydon CR2 7DW
Maude, Miss A   Dept of Prints & Drawings, British Museum, Gt Russell
    Street, London WC1B 3DG
May, Mr L E   24 Reachview Court, London NW1 0TY
Mayfield, Ms K   First Floor, 29A Daleham Mews, London NW3 5DB
McCarthy, Ms S   45 Sandringham Road, London E10 6HJ
McCartney, Mr A   27 Hill Street, St Albans, Herts AL3 4QS
McDermott, Mrs J, *BA*   109 London Lane, Bromley, Kent BR1 4HF
McEvoy, Mr M   White Cottage, The Street, Lidgate, Newmarket,
    Suffolk CB8 9PP
McGowan, Dr A C, *BA MA PhD*   73 Barnfield Wood Road, Beckenham,
    Kent BR3 6ST
McGrath, Mr M I   11 Regina Drive, Leeds LS7 4LR
McIntosh, Miss F   Oak Farm House, Rue de la Dame, St Saviour, Jersey JE2 7NH
McKellar, Mr T   3 Wellfield Close, Ridgeway, Sheffield S12 3XN
McKitterick, Professor D J, *MA LittD*   Trinity College, Cambridge CB2 1TQ
McMaster, Mr A R   35 Cannington Road, Dagenham RM9 4BE
McMillan, Ms B I   4 Grosvenor Court, London Road, Morden SM4 5HG
McNie, Mr T M   80 Wharncliffe Road, London SE25 6SL
McRory, Mrs C O   11 North Washington St, #240, Rockville MD 20850-4267 USA
McVeagh, Mr T, *BA MA*   Fourways Cottage, 35 The Green, Braunston,
    Northants NN11 7HW
Mead, Mr C W, *FRPSL*   70 Gernons, Basildon, Essex SS16 5TN
Meadway, Dr R J, *MA PhD*   4 Glebe Avenue, Woodford Green, Essex IG8 9HB
Medlock, Mr S D, *BSc*   35 Eastling Close, Gillingham, Kent ME8 6XT
Mendoza, Mr N   28 Ladbroke Square, London W11 3NB
Mercer, Mr I   26A Downs Court Road, Purley, Surrey CR8 1BB
Mernick, Mr P   42 Campbell Road, London E3 4DT
Merrell, Mr H C   6 Cleveland Gardens, London W2 6HA
Merrill, Mr A J S, *MA*   5 Woodhall Road, Colinton, Edinburgh EH13 0DQ
Merryweather, Mrs J   8 Meadow Close, Purley, Surrey CR8 3HN
Mesquitta, Mr B   81 Harewood Road, Isleworth, Middlesex TW7 5HN
Michaelson, Mr R W, *MA FIA Member of Council*   6 Oakwood Court,
    London W14 8JU
Mickleburgh, Mr S P, *BSc MSc*   1 East View Cottages, Merlesford,
    Woodbridge, Suffolk IP13 0AT
Middleton, Mr J C   West Poundgate Manor, Chillies Lane, Crowborough,
    East Sussex TN6 3TB

Miele, Dr C   Montagu Evans LLP, 5 Bolton Street, London W1J 8BA
Miller, Mr D J, *MA*   100 Rosebery Avenue, London EC1R 4TL
Miller, Mr L   102 Brandon Street, London SE17 1AL
Miller, Ms M   95A Fairbridge Road, London N19 3EP
Minchinton, Mr P C   396 Erith Road, Northumberland Heath, Erith,
  Kent DA8 3NJ
Mitchell, Mr A J M   Grey Wings, Sea Road, Fairlight, Hastings TN35 4DR
Mitchell, Mr P   7 Lakeside Crecent, East Barnet EN4 8QH
Moncrieff, Miss J   15a Buxton Road, Chingford, London E4 7DP
Monk, Mr J   50C Crayford Road, London N7 0ND
Moodie, Mr T B   416 Addison House, Grove End Road, London NW8 9EL
Moore, Mr A P, *BA MBA MCIM*   Old Post Cottage, The Shoe, North
  Wraxall, Chippenham, Wilts SN14 8SA
Moore, Mr J R   27 Halliford Road, Sunbury-on-Thames, Middlesex TW16 6DP
Moore, Mr N H   54 Lord Avenue, Clayhall, Essex IG5 0HN
Morgan, Mrs F   First Floor Flat, 84 Tachbrook Street, London SW1V 2NB
Morgan, Mr G   30 Addison Road, Guildford, Surrey GU1 3QG
Morley, Mr G P, *PIFA*   21 Hillside Road, Crabbe, Kent CT17 0JQ
Morris, Mr D B, *MSc CGeol*   21 Haddon Court, Shakespeare Road,
  Harpenden, Herts AL5 5NQ
Morris, Dr S J, *MA PhD Publications Secretary*   7 Barnsbury Terrace,
  London N1 1HJ
Morrison, Mr C   18b Granville Square, London WC1X 9PF
Mottram, Mrs L M M   99 Bethwin Road, London SE5 0YJ
Mullinger, Mr J P A   5 Parsons Gate, Ansford, Castle Cary, Somerset BA7 7JS
Mundell, Mrs T A, *BA(Hons)*   5 Elm Grove, Wivenhoe, Colchester CO7 9AY
Munro, Mr E   Flat 51 Hargrave Mansions, Hargrave Road, London N19 5SR
Murphy, Mrs M, *BA*   7 Grove Park, London E11 2DN
Murray, Mr P, *FRIBA FRSA AoU*   NLA, 26 Store Street, London WC1E 7BT
Myers, Miss R   7 Whiston House, Bingham Court, Halton Road,
  London N1 2DH
Myers, Mr S, *BSc FICE FCIWEM*   Eversholt, Cuckoo Hill, Pinner,
  Middlesex HA5 2HJ
Needham, Mr D J, *BSc MSc*   5 Sussex House, 3 Maidstone Buildings Mews,
  London SE1 1GF
Nenk, Ms B, *MA*   9 Marston Close, London NW6 4EU
Neville, Miss L   18 Malfort Road, London SE5 8DQ
Newens, Mr S   The Leys, Park Hill, Harlow, Essex CM17 0AE
Newman, Mr M   19 Plover Close, Worle, Weston-super-Mare BS22 8XB
Nichol, Ms Sue, *BA MSc PGCE*   355 Lonsdale Road, London SW13 9PY
Nicholls, Mr A   33 Heskett Park, Pembury, Kent TN2 4JF
Nicolson, Mr J M   20 Albert Square, London SW8 1BS
Nixon, Mrs C   30 Ashden Walk, Tonbridge TN10 3RL
Noble, Mrs B   13 Garrett Close, Seaton, Devon EX12 2FE
Noel, Mr C G   2 Church House, Church Lane, Ledbury, Herefs HR8 1DP
Norris, Mr T   60 Lupino Court, 140 Lambeth Walk, London SE11 6EZ
Northcott, Mr B J, *FCA*   Langstone Manor Cottage, Brentnor,
  Tavistock PL19 0NE
Norton, Mr H   35 Somerset Road, Brentford TW8 8BT

Nurse, Mr E B, *MA MCLIP FSA*   18 Ruskin Walk, Herne Hill, London SE24 9LZ
Nurse, Ms M E, *BA(Hons)*   60 Great Brownings, College Road,
    London SE21 7HP
O'Brien, Mr C J   34 Sedgeford Road, London W12 0ND
O'Connell, Ms S *Member of Council*   Print Room, British Museum, Great
    Russell Street, London WC1B 3DG
O'Connor, Mr D   67 Grange Park Avenue, London N21 2LN
O'Connor-Taylor, Mrs D   (address unknown)
Oggins, Dr R S, *PhD FRHS*   Department of History, Binghamton University,
    New York NY 13902-6000 USA
O'Hara, Mr M M, *MA*   66 Tanner Street, London SE1 3DR
Oldham, Mr P E   15 Hermitage Lane, Barming, Maidstone ME16 9NR
Olney, Mrs A C M   1 Art School Yard, Victoria Street, St Albans AL1 3YS
Olutniks, Mr M, *MITG*   15 Jewel Road, London E17 4QU
Orrell, Mr S J M   7 Aylsham Road, Norwich NR3 3EQ
Osborne, Dr I   169 Goodmans Park, Slough SL2 5NR
Oska, Mr T H   28 Adolphus Road, London N4 2AY
Ossowski, Mr M   83 Pimlico Road, London SW1W 8PH
Overy, Mr P   18 Lawn Gardens, London W7 3JN
Owens, Mrs G   187A Brondesbury Park, London NW2 5JN
Owens, Mr P D   5 Hatch Close, Kirtlington, Kidlington, Oxon OX5 3JT
Palmer, Mr C J   23 Hartington Road, Twickenham, Middlesex TW1 3EL
Palmer, Mr R W   19 Newlands Avenue, Thames Ditton, Surrey KT7 0HD
Palmer, Ms S K C, *MA*   Sir John Soane's Museum, 13 Lincoln's Inn Fields,
    London WC2A 3RP
Panes, Mr N   4 Hook Hill, Sanderstead CR2 0LA
Park, Mr S J W   35 Medora Road, Romford RM7 7EP
Parker, Miss G, *BSc(Hons) MA*   Alan Baxter Limited, 75 Cowcross Street,
    London EC1M 6EL
Parker, Mr S M   20 Bramford Court, High Street, London N14 6DH
Parnell, Mr G, *FSA*   2 The Follies, Torrington Road, Winkleigh,
    Devon EX19 8HR
Parrott, Mr B J, *FBEng FIAS MaPS*   95 Chestnut Copse, Hurst Green, Oxted,
    Surrey RH8 0JJ
Parsonson, Mr S L, *MA*   The Cottage, Tithe Barn Lane, Briston,
    Norfolk NR24 2JB
Pascoe, Dr G   Passaustrasse 18, D-84453 Mühldorf am Inn   Germany
Paterson, Mr M G, *BA(Hons)*   141 Windmill Road, Brentford,
    Middlesex TW8 9NH
Paton, Mr J   Valley Cottage, Bagpath, Tetbury, Glos GL8 8YG
Payne, Mr M T W, *BA MA*   Keeper of the Monuments, Westminster Abbey,
    The Chapter Office, 20 Dean's Yard, London SW1P 3PA
Payne, Mr S C, *BSc*   19 Southernhay Avenue, Cliftonwood, Bristol BS8 4TJ
Peach, Mr J C   28 Onslow Gardens, London N21 1DX
Peacock, Mr J H B   Ravenford Farm, Hamsterley, Bishop Auckland, Co.
    Durham DL13 3NH
Pearce, Mr P J   1 Heybridge Road, Ingatestone, Essex CM4 9AG
Pearson, Mr J E   64 Scotts Road, London E10 6LW
Pegg, Mr I   64 Dennis Road, East Molesey, Surrey KT8 9ED

Pembrooke, Mr R E, *BA(Hons)*   223 Cromwell Tower, Barbican,
London EC2Y 8DD

Pepper, Professor S M   21 Warmington Road, London SE24 9LA

Perry, Mr J C, *BSc*   5 Park House, 123/5 Harley Street, London W1N 1HE

Pessell, Mr M   24 Henley Lodge, 2 Willow Walk, London E17 7LB

Petrie, Mr C J   Trundle Mead, Oudle Lane, Much Hadham, Herts SG10 6HS

Peverley, Mr J R, *RIBA*   Whitemill, Marston Lane, Frome, Somerset BA11 4DG

Phillips, Miss A J   11 Middleton Close, London E4 8EA

Phillips, Dr M   5 Greyfriars Place, Edinburgh EH1 2QQ

Philpotts, Mr R A   3 Brook Meadow, Church Stretton, Shropshire SY6 7EH

Pick, Mr C C, *BA MA*   41 Chestnut Road, London SE27 9EZ

Pigott, Mr T D   48 Abinger Road, London W4 1EX

Pillinger, Mr R N, *BA FRES*   58 Gadby Road, Sittingbourne, Kent ME10 1TJ

Pinching, Mr A A   11 Braemar Avenue, London N22 4BY

Pines, Ms Y   Flat 6, 12 Spencer Hill, London SW19 4NY

Piper, Mr R J, *BA*   20 Brakespeare Road South, Ickenham UB10 8HE

Plaskett, Mr R D, *MA*   302 Lauderdale Tower, Barbican, London EC2Y 8NA

Pleace, Mr I   62 Durham Road, Raynes Park, London SW20 0TW

Pollock, Mr C A E, *CBE*   28 Crooms Hill, London SE10 8ER

Port, Professor M H, *MA BLitt Member of Council*   26 Brookfield Park,
London NW5 1ER

Porter, Mr A R   58 Greenwich Park Street, London SE10 9LT

Porter, Mr N G, *BSc CEng MICE*   2 Eastcote View, Pinner, Middlesex HA5 1AT

Porter, Mr S   12 West End Crescent, Stratford on Avon CV37 6DY

Powell, Mr D M   46 Wilson Gardens, West Harrow, Middlesex HA1 4DZ

Powell, Mr K, *MA HonFRIBA*   Flat 1, 78 Nightingale Lane, London SW12 8NR

Powers, Mr G   9a Emu Road, London SW8 3PS

Poynter, Mr D J   17 Neath Abbey, Bedford MK41 0RU

Poynton, Mr T   Flat 10 Greyfriars, Wells Park Road, London SE26 6RJ

Pragnell, Mr H J   12 Meadow Road, Canterbury CT2 8EU

Pratt, Mr P J   15 The Grove, Walton on Thames KT12 2HP

Prebble, Mr T N   56 Mahlon Avenue, South Ruislip, Middlesex HA4 6TE

Prentice, Mrs M   17 Elizabeth Drive, New Mill, Tring HP23 5HL

Pretlove, Mrs V   10 Brunswick Hill, Reading RG1 7YT

Price, Mr A, *MA*   13 Wharfview Court, 12 Blair Street, London E14 0NY

Price, Mr J P   20 Rossmore Court, Park Road, London NW1 6XX

Price, Mr R M, *MA MCLIP*   Flat 2, 5/7 Princedale Road, London W11 4NW

Prince, Mr I P, *MRICS MBEng*   Lavender Cottage, Little Top Lane, Lound,
Retford, Notts DN22 8RH

Prior, Mr C J, *BSc CEng MICE*   18 Boileau Road, London W5 3AH

Prockter, Mr A C   21 Queenswood Road, London SE23 2QR

Pulleyn, Dr S   7 Louisa Street, London E1 4NF

Purcell, Mr T A, *BA(Hons)*   27 West Park Avenue, Kew, Richmond,
Surrey TW9 4AN

Purt, Mr D C, *FCMI FMAAT*   Red Beech Cottage, Polecat Valley, Hindhead,
Surrey GU26 6BE

Quade, Miss A   4 Heathway, Woodford Green, Essex IG8 7RG

Quarme, Mr G, *BA DipArch RIBA FRSA*   41 Cardigan Street, London SE11 5PF

Quinn, Miss H F   38 Lancaster Road, London NW10 1HA

Rabin, Mr N   Flat 3, 11 Rochester Terrace, London NW1 9JN
Rains, Mr J M, *BS MA JD*   14905 Winterwind Drive, Tampa FL 33624 USA
Ramon, Mrs A E, *BA(Hons)*   63 Ancaster Crescent, New Malden,
   Surrey KT3 6BD
Ramsbottom, Mr F   63 Todwick Road, Sheffield S8 0NR
Raphael, Mr H, *FCA*   Kfar Hittim, PO Box 92, Lower Galilee Israel
Rastall, Professor G R, *MA MusB PhD FSA*   5 Albert Grove, Leeds LS6 4DA
Rau, Mrs D C, *BA MSc*   38 Fairfax Road, London NW6 4HA
Raven, Dr J   Fenders, Ferry Road, Fingrinhoe CO5 7BX
Rawcliffe, Mr J W   9 Copley Deane, Bromley, Kent BR1 2PW
Ray, Mr A L, *BA*   83 Barrons Way, Comberton, Cambridge CB23 7DR
Reding, Mr J P, *BA*   18 Winchendon Road, Teddington, Middlesex TW11 0SX
Reed, Miss P H, *MA*   Old Bridge House, 2 Bridge Street, Uffculme,
   Cullompton, Devon EX15 3AX
Reed, Dr T, *BA(Hons)*   4A Burton Street, London WC1H 9AQ
Rees, Mr D J   Flat 1 St Nicholas House, 33 Glamorgan Road, Hampton
   Wick, Surrey KT1 4HS
Reeves, Dr L H D, *BSc(Hons) PhD*   91 Speed House, Barbican,
   London EC2Y 8AV
Reeves, Mr S   288 Kents Hill Road, South Benfleet, Essex SS7 5XS
Reid, Dr A M M, *MA PhD*   38 Tompion House, Percival Street,
   London EC1V 0HU
Reid, Mr D   89 Alfred Road, Kingston upon Thames, Surrey KT1 2TZ
Reid, Dr I, *MA MSc PhD FCIPD*   68 Elizabeth Court, Palgrave Gardens,
   London NW1 6EJ
Relf, Sqn Ldr B R F   6 MacDonnell Gardens, Leavesden, Herts WD25 7AG
Renier, Ms H, *BA(Hons)*   19 Harleyford Road, London SE11 5AX
Reynolds, Mr J S, *BA*   7 Devonshire Road, London E17 8QH
Reynolds, Mrs P M, *MBBS DO*   15 Great Spilmans, London SE22 8SZ
Reynolds, Mr R   19 St Michael's Court, Ruscombe, Reading RG10 9UF
Rhind, Mr N, *MBE*   8 Dunstable Court, 12 St John's Park, London SE3 7TN
Richards, Ms J   59 Sunnyside Gardens, Upminster RM14 3DT
Richardson, Mr G   76 Hadleigh Road, Leigh-on-Sea, Essex SS9 2LZ
Richardson, Dr G J, *BA PhD*   School of Arts & Humanities, St Mary's
   University College, Twickenham TW1 4SX
Richardson, Mr J C   14 Saddleton Road, Whitstable, Kent CT5 4JD
Ridge, Mr T S   7 Shepton Houses, Welwyn Street, London E2 0JN
Ridgway, Mr P W, *FRGS FRIN*   3 The Green, Ketton, Stamford, Lincs PE9 3RA
Rigby, Mr M S, *BSc*   148 Old Bath Road, Cheltenham, Glos GL53 7DP
Roberts, Ms J, *BA*   24 Ley Hey Road, Marple, Stockport SK6 6PQ
Roberts, Mr J R S, *DipTS FRGS*   Bridge House, Wanstrow, Shepton Mallet,
   Somerset BA4 4TE
Roberts, Mr R A   9 Long Down, Petersfield, Hants GU31 4PD
Robinson, Mr D   19 Lansdown Crescent, Bath BA1 5EX
Robinson, Mrs J   2 Willow Green, Worlingworth, Suffolk IP13 7LP
Robinson, Mr P   24 Academy Court, 34 Glengall Road, London NW6 7FB
Robson, Mr A, *BSc RIBA FRSA*   Pouchlands Farmhouse, Mill Lane, South
   Chailey, Lewes, East Sussex BN8 4PY
Robson, Mr M, *MA MPhil*   73 Endwell Road, London SE4 2NF

Rogers, Miss M, *MBE* 145 Hartington Road, London SW8 2EY

Rogers, Mr R W 20 Montague Road, Richmond, Surrey TW10 6QW

Rogers, Mr W R 149 Summerhouse Drive, Dartford DA2 7PD

Rollason, Mr M P 40 St Christians Road, Cheylesmore, Coventry CV3 5GX

Romani, Mrs J E The Beams, Udimore Road, Broad Oak, Rye,
East Sussex TN31 6DG

Rooney, Mr D, *MSc DIC MInstP* 303 Nevada Building, 40 Blackheath Road,
London SE10 8ED

Rose, Mrs L A Mickleton Cottage, Warren Lane, Cross-in-Hand,
Heathfield TN21 0TF

Rose, Mr M T, *MA MPhil* 20 Beeches Close, Saffron Walden, Essex CB11 4BT

Rosenfield, Dr M C Box 395, Mattapoisett MA 02739-0395 USA

Ross, Dr P C, *MA PhD DipLib MCLIP Member of Council* 59 Glenham
Drive, Gants Hill IG2 6SF

Rosser, Dr A G St Catherine's College, Manor Road, Oxford OX1 3UJ

Rowston, Mr G S, *MA DipEd* 6 Kenneth Court, 173 Kennington Road,
London SE11 6SS

Roy, Dr I, *MA DPhil FRHistS* 26 The Lane, London SE3 9SL

Rubin, Professor P C, *MA DM FRCP* Flat 6 Alec Court, 47 Catherine Place,
London SW1E 6DY

Ruge, Ms Y M 133 Friern Barnet Lane, London N20 0XZ

Ruge-Cope, Mrs C 21 Chace Avenue, Potters Bar EN6 5LX

Rumble, Mr R 19 Parr Crescent, Hemel Hempstead, Herts HP2 7LJ

Russell, Mr T F, *BA PGCE* 94 Hamilton Avenue, Ilford IG6 1AD

Russell, Mr W 50 Finland Road, London SE4 2JH

Russell-Duff, Mrs J, *JP* Watch Lane Farm, Moston, Sandbach,
Cheshire CW11 9QS

Ruston, Mr A R 41 Hampermill Lane, Oxhey, Herts WD19 4NS

Ryan, Miss C 22 Stansfield Place, Headington, Oxford OX3 8QH

Sage, Mr D Flat 1, 10 George Street, Stroud GL5 3DX

Sandison, Mr J S, *FCA FRSA* 33 Montagu Road, Highcliffe, Christchurch,
Dorset BH23 5JT

Saul, Mr G M 20 West Way, Rickmansworth, Herts WD3 7EN

Saunders, Mrs A L, *MBE PhD FSA Honorary Editor* 3 Meadway Gate,
London NW11 7LA

Saunders, Mr M Spectacle, Unit 25, 99–109 Lavender Hill, London SW11 5QL

Saunders, Mr R L F 46 Church Lane, Mill End, Rickmansworth WD3 8HD

Sawczenko, Dr A, *BM MRCP MRCPCH* 169 Victoria Road, London N22 7XH

Schneider, Mr W 188 Windermere Avenue, Wembley HA9 8QT

Schofield, Mr A, *BSc MRICS* 12 Kenwood Avenue, London N14 4SR

Schofield, Mr J 2 Carthew Villas, London W6 0BS

Scott, Mr F 4 Bayer House, Golden Lane Estate, London EC1Y 0RN

Scott, Dr M 22 Little London, Chichester, West Sussex PO19 1PB

Seaborn, Mr H R, *FRICS* 41 Geraldine Road, London SW18 2NR

Seekings-Foster, Mrs S P 53 Boeing Way, Mildenhall, Suffolk IP28 7RJ

Seeley, Dr J S, *PhD MInstPhys* 1 Churchill Crescent, Sonning Common,
Reading RG4 9RU

Selby, Dr J, *MA MSc PhD* 50 Medway Crescent, Leigh-on-Sea, Essex SS9 2UY

Service, Mr M R, *BA* 4 Fleur Gates, Princes Way, London SW19 6QQ

Sewell, Mr J R, *OBE MA FSA*   120 Addiscombe Road, Croydon CR0 5PQ
Shalit, Mr D M   8 Staverdale Lodge, Melbury Road, London W14 8LW
Shenton, Dr C, *DPhil FSA FRHistS*   Angels Cottage, Market Street, Charlbury, Oxon OX7 3PJ
Shepherd, Dr A, *PhD*   3 Outwoods Drive, Loughborough, Leics LE11 3LR
Shepherd, Mr L   13 Brockwell Park Gardens, London SE24 9BL
Sheppard, Dr F H W, *MA PhD Honorary Member*   10 Albion Place, West Street, Henley-on-Thames RG9 2DT
Sheppard, Mr M L   102 Gloucester Avenue, London NW1 8HX
Sherwood, Mr K R   72a Sedgewick Street, Cambridge CB1 3AL
Shipley, Dr M E, *MA MD FRCP*   21b Brownlow Mews, London WC1N 2LA
Shute, Dr J D, *MA MLitt PhD*   70 Bevan Avenue, Ryhope, Sunderland SR2 0JJ
Shuter, Mr P D   30 Portland Road, Oxford OX2 7EY
Silverman, Dr L, *PhD*   10 Adams Way, Earley, Reading RG6 5UT
Silvester-Carr, Miss D *Member of Council*   1 The Firs, 162 Longlands Road, Sidcup, Kent DA15 7LG
Simmonds, Mrs C   122 Birch Crescent, Hornchurch RM11 2NJ
Simmons, Dr P D, *MB FRCP*   96 Thomas More House, Barbican, London EC2Y 8BU
Simms, Mr D J   10 Woodland Crescent, Bracknell, Berks RG12 2LH
Simpson, Mr E   176 Hadleigh Road, Leigh-on-Sea, Essex SS9 2LP
Simpson, Mr R   12a Manley Street, London NW1 8LT
Skeet, Mr M, *BA(Hons)*   2 St Lukes Mews, London W11 1DF
Skilton, Mr A J, *ARIBA*   30 Park Crescent, Enfield EN2 6HS
Skrzpczyk, Mr A   39 Addiscombe Road, Croydon CR0 6SA
Slater, Canon Dr T R, *BA PhD FRGS*   School of Geography, Earth & Environmental Sciences, University of Birmingham, Birmingham B15 2TT
Sleap, Miss S E, *BA DipLib MCLIP*   12 Vernon Avenue, Woodford Green, Essex IG8 0AU
Slorah, Miss J E   5 The Pleasance, Rockdale Road, Sevenoaks, Kent TN13 1JU
Smith, Mr A   6 Owen Gardens, Gwynne Park, Woodford Green, Essex IG8 8DJ
Smith, Mr A C   3 Greenwich South Street, London SE10 8NW
Smith, Mr A N   1 Church Stretton Road, Hounslow TW3 2QP
Smith, Mr B D   227 Ashley Gardens, London SW1P 1PA
Smith, Dr C S, *BSc MA*   61 Cedar Road, Romford RM7 7JS
Smith, Mr D C   3 Bowgrave Copse, Abingdon, Oxon OX14 2NL
Smith, Mr E G   37 High Street, West Malling, Kent ME19 6QH
Smith, Ms J E, *MA BA(Hons)*   9 Grange Road, Grays, Essex RM17 6RE
Smith, Mr M P   2 Mill Terrace, Thorpe Thewles, Stockton-on-Tees TS21 3JS
Smith, Mr P G   2 Wilton Grove, London SW19 3QX
Smith, Mr R   7 Prospect Road, St Albans, Herts AL1 2AT
Smith, Mr R G, *BA MSc*   29 Berrymede Road, London W4 5JE
Smith, Mr T L   51 Dunwich Road, Bexleyheath DA7 5EN
Smythe, Mr D   88 Wren Road, Sidcup DA14 4NF
Solomon, Dr D   Foundry Farm, Kiln Lane, Redlynch, Salisbury SP5 2HT
Speer, Mr P   8 Prideaux Court, Prideaux Road, Eastbourne BN21 2NN
Spence, Mr C G, *BSc MA MIFA*   7 Ridgeway, Nettleham, Lincoln LN2 2TL
Spence, Mr R, *BSc*   81 The Hall, Foxes Dale, London SE3 9BG
Spencer, Mr H J   10 Park Gate, Somerhill Road, Hove, East Sussex BN3 1RL

Stacey, Miss A 20b Grove Hill, London E18 2JG
Stacpoole, Mr J, *MRICS* 1 Queen's Road, London W5 2SA
Stamp, Mr G 15 Belle Vue Court, 122d Devonshire Road, London SE23 3SY
Stanford, Mr A Walsh Associates, 32 Lafone Street, London SE1 2LX
Starkey, Mrs B M 3 Roderick Road, London NW3 2NN
Starkey, Dr D R, *MA PhD* 49 Hamilton Park West, London N5 1AE
Starling, Miss K M Museum of London, London Wall, London EC2Y 5HN
Stater, Mrs J S, *BA(Hons)* 124 Langton Way, London SE3 7JS
Steer, Mr M, *BEng MA* Flat 25, 8 Muscovy House, Auckland Street,
  London SE11 5AB
Stein, Mr S, *RIBA ARB* Unit 115, 300 Kensal Road, London W10 5BE
Stephens, Mr R c/o His Honour Judge Lloyd, 1 Atkin Building, Grays Inn,
  London WC1R 1AT
Stevens, Miss L Flat A, 2 Hamilton Terrace, London NW8 9UG
Stevens, Mr M J 28 Haldon Road, London SW18 1QG
Stevenson, Dr C Field Cottage, Pudding Lane, Brightwalton,
  Newbury RG20 7BY
Stevenson, Dr J Merrifield, Down St Mary, Crediton, Devon EX17 6ED
Stewart, Mr A B 26 Payne Road, Wootton, Bedford MK43 9PJ
Stewart, Mr R M 13 Smith Close, London SE16 1PB
Stirling, Mr C R, *BSc CEng MBCS* 3 Meadow Road, Ashtead,
  Surrey KT21 1QR
Stone, Ms J S, *BA(Hons) FRSA* 17 Richmond Crescent, London N1 0LZ
Stone, Mr P 82 Myddleton Avenue, London N4 2FH
Storrie, Mr C 129 Balls Pond Road, London N1 4BG
Stott, Mr R The Woolstore, 111 Winchelsea Road, Rye, East Sussex TN31 7EL
Strong, Mr J, *FRICS* 17 Cameron Court, Princes Way, London SW19 6QY
Stubbs, Ms K, *MA* Flat 2, 17 Primrose Gardens, London NW3 4UT
Sullivan, Miss A, *BArch MA* 124b Fortess Road, London NW5 2HP
Sunderland, Mr P, *MA CEng* 31 Malham Drive, Lincoln LN6 0XD
Surtees, Mr R A 75 Shalimar Gardens, London W3 9JG
Sury, Dr M R J 61 Arbuthnot Road, London SE14 5NP
Sutcliffe, Mr R E, *MA FSA* 95 High Street, Hampton Wick, Kingston KT1 4DG
Sutherland, Ms S M 10 Narraburra Close, Mount Colah NSW 2079 Australia
Swarbrick, The Revd J 54 Kingsfield Avenue, Harrow HA2 6AT
Sweetland, Mr D 15 Wasdale Close, Owlsmoor, Sandhurst, Berks GU47 0YQ
Swift, Mr P 50 Forde Avenue, Bromley, Kent BR1 3EX
Swinson, Mr C, *MA FCA* No Ways, Frithsden, Hemel Hempstead HP1 3DD
Sykes, Dr S Glenside, Hindon Lane, Tisbury, Salisbury SP3 6PZ
Symonds, Mr M, *BA MPhil* 14a Cholmeley Lodge, Cholmeley Park,
  London N6 5EN
Talbot, Mr N Grosvenor Prints, 19 Shelton Street, London WC2H 9JN
Tang, Ms M Room 2220 Lai Ming House, Wah Ming Estate, Fanling Hong Kong
Tanner, Mr G C A 107 Camberwell Grove, London SE5 8JH
Tappin, Mr S E, *BSc MIStructE* 133 Foundling Court, Brunswick Centre,
  London WC1N 1QF
Tatham, Dr D, *PhD* 329 Westcott Street, Syracuse NY 13210 USA
Tatton-Brown, Mr T Fisherton Mill House, Mill Road, Salisbury SP2 7RZ
Taylor, Miss A E 30 Almoners' Avenue, Cambridge CB1 8PA

Taylor, Mr A J   4 Laurier Court, Laurier Road, London NW5 1SE
Taylor, Mr A M, *BA*   22 Fawnbrake Avenue, Herne Hill, London SE24 0BY
Taylor, Mr D F   142 Western Road, Haywards Heath, West Sussex RH16 3LQ
Taylor, Ms D I   41 Fullerton Road, London SW18 1BU
Taylor, Mr J   20 Thurnall Close, Baldock, Herts SG7 6DR
Taylor, Miss J M, *MA*   13e Philbeach Gardens, London SW5 9DY
Taylor, Mr K   14 St Margaret's Court, The Barons, Twickenham TW1 2AL
Taylor, Dr P, *PhD FSA FRHistS*   40 Prince of Wales Road, London NW5 3LN
Teh, Ms Y-Y   8 Hatton Place, London EC1N 8RY
Tennant, Mrs A, *MA BA DipAD*   120 Northcote Road, London E17 7EB
Terroni, Mr J H   51 Brookdale, New Southgate, London N11 1BS
Terry, Mr P M, *BA(Hons) ARCM PGCE*   2 Avenue Gardens, London SW14 8BP
Thick, Mr M F, *BSSc*   2 Brookside, Harwell, Oxon OX11 0HG
Thomas, Mrs A M   22 Manor Gardens, Hampton TW12 2TW
Thomas, Mr L H   13 Hurstwood Drive, Bickley, Kent BR1 2JE
Thomas, Mr R G   1 Metropole Court, The Leas, Folkestone, Kent CT20 2LT
Thompson, Mr E J, *CB*   120 Melrose Avenue, London NW2 4JX
Thompson, Mr G A   41 Honley Road, London SE6 2HY
Thompson, Dr M W, *PhD FSA*   2 Offa Lea, Newton, Cambridge CB2 5PW
Thompson, Mr P J, *CEng MSc*   Larks Edge, The Drift, Henley, Ipswich,
    Suffolk IP6 0RS
Thompson, Mr R H, *FSA MCLIP*   102 College Hill Road, Harrow HA3 7DA
Thomson, Mr N H, *BSc DipLib*   29 Emlyn Road, London W12 9TF
Thorp, Mr A   144 Northchurch Road, London N1 3PA
Thurley, Dr S J, *CBE*   Clifton House, 17 Queen Street, King's Lynn, Norfolk
    PE30 1HT
Tickell, Ms S   8 Koh-I-Noor Avenue, Bushey, Herts WD23 3EJ
Tindall, Ms G   27 Leighton Road, London NW5 2QG
Tiner, Mr R C   24 Thornton Hill, Exeter EX4 4NS
Tompkins, Mr P D G, *MA*   The Clock Tower, 5.01 St Pancras Chambers,
    Euston Road, London NW1 2QR
Torrible, Mr C   Ground Floor Flat, 12 Pepys Road, London SE14 5SB
Towey, Mr P J   4 Channel Heights, Bleadon Hill, Weston-super-Mare,
    Somerset BS24 9LX
Townsend, Mr M J   Oak Lodge, 55 Hunstanton Road, Dersingham, King's
    Lynn, Norfolk PE31 6ND
Traynor, Mr R A   60 Mendip Drive, Frome, Somerset BA11 2HU
Trenerry, Mr M J B   Newhaven, 1 Northfield Drive, Truro TR1 2BS
Trent, Mr T E, *RVM*   Flat 1, 22 Kidbrooke Gardens, London SE3 0PD
Trevette, Mr B S   1 Cherry Tree Walk, Chesham, Bucks HP5 3JN
Tritton, Mr J A, *BSc*   7 Mace Walk, Chelmsford CM1 2GE
Trueblood, Mr S P   74 Brim Hill, London N2 0HQ
Tsushima, Mrs J   Malmaison, Church Street, Great Bedwyn, Wilts SN8 3PE
Tubbs, Mr J R, *BA DipArch RIBA*   66 Marryat Road, London SW19 5BY
Tuckey, Mr J L   246 Kilburn Lane, London W10 4BA
Tuley, Mrs I   35 Dane Heights, Dane Close, Seaford, East Sussex BN25 1EA
Turbett, Ms C   87 Brookdale, London N11 1BS
Turner, Mrs P D H, *MA*   40 Stanlake Road, London W12 7HL
Turner, Mr S J, *MA*   Belziger str. 28, 10823 Berlin Germany

Turnor, Mrs A   12 Church Lane Avenue, Hooley, Coulsdon, Surrey CR5 3RT
Twist, Mr P J, *LLB*   113 Paramount Court, University Street, London WC1E 6JW
Twort, Mr A, *MA LLB*   35 Frankfurt Road, London SE24 9NX
Tyack, Dr G C, *MA PhD FSA*   50 Wytham Street, Oxford OX1 4TS
Tye, Mr R G   112 Pirbright Road, London SW18 5NA
Tyers, Mr N S, *BSc CEng MICE*   6 Aintree Close, Horton Heath, Eastleigh
   SO50 7PU
Underhill, Sir Nicholas E, *QC*   3 Smith Square, London SW1P 3HS
Usher, Mr S   35 Seymour Avenue, Epsom, Surrey KT17 2RS
van Reenen, Miss M   4 Ufton Grove, London N1 4HG
Vander Meulen, Professor D L   Dept of English, University of Virginia, PO
   Box 400121, Charlottesville VA 22904-4121 USA
Vaughan, Mrs J M   5 Bishops Court, 180 St Marychurch Road, Torquay TQ1 3JT
Vaughan, Professor W H T, *BA PhD*   Lower Cockhill Farm, Castle Cary BA7 7NZ
Vereker, Mrs J   5 Grantham Court, Eleanor Close, London SE16 6PT
Vince, Mr M, *MA*   107 Grove Park, London SE5 8LE
Vine, Mr D W   19 Gordon Road, London E11 2RA
Vine, Ms L, *MA*   61 Buckingham Road, London N1 4JG
Wakeham, Ms P   119 Caledon Road, London E6 2HA
Walduck, Mr A G   10 Grove Avenue, London W7 3EP
Walker, Miss R   11 Thornton Grove, Hatch End, Pinner, Middlesex HA5 4HG
Walkling, Dr A R   28 Davis Street, Binghamton NY 13905 USA
Wall, Mr R, *BArch BSc*   4 Laburnum Walk, Abergavenny,
   Monmouthshire NP7 5JX
Walton, Miss J   5 Plas Penwern, Johnstown, Carmarthen SA31 3PN
Ward, Mr A C   125 Carmelite Road, Harrow HA3 5LU
Ward, Mr C, *BSc(Hons)*   21 Tintagel Way, Oriental Road, Woking,
   Surrey GU22 7DF
Ward, Mr M J   27 Greenglades, West Hunsbury, Northampton NN4 9YW
Warden, Mr C D   Moor Cottage, Higher Chillington, Ilminster TA19 0PT
Warner, Ms C, *MA MBA*   27 Chepstow Place, London W2 4TT
Warren, Mr M J   74 Lancaster Drive, Hornchurch RM12 5ST
Wartnaby, Mr S   211 Grange Road, London SE1 3AA
Waters, Mr J, *MA*   40 Maze Hill, London SE10 8XG
Watkins, Mr P D   Basement Flat, 127 Camberwell Road, London SE5 0HB
Watson, Mr C H   1 Sadlers Close, Merrow, Guildford, Surrey GU4 7DA
Watson, Ms I   29 Stepney Green, London E1 3JX
Watson, Ms M   20 Elmsdale Road, London E17 6PW
Watson, Mr R L, *MA AFIMA*   92 College Hill Road, Harrow HA3 7DA
Watson, Mr R O, *ACMA*   3 Willow Fields, Whittle-le-Woods, Chorley,
   Lancs PR6 7JQ
Watts, Miss C   15 Dodbroke Road, London SE27 0PF
Watts, Dr R A, *MA DM*   Bury Hill House, Woodbridge, Suffolk IP12 1JD
Webb, Mr D F   Kestenen, 48d Bath Road, Atworth, Melksham SN12 8JX
Webb, Mr D R, *MA FCLIP Member of Council*   21 Meads Lane, Ilford IG3 8QJ
Webb-Ingall, Ms C   7 Norlington Road, London E11 4BE
Webster, Dr P V, *DLitt FSA*   8 Cefn Coed Avenue, Cyncoed, Cardiff CF2 6HE
Weeden, Mr M, *BSc*   21 Avenue Pasteur, L2311 Luxembourg
Weinstein, Mrs R *Member of Council* 21 Willes Road, London NW5 3DX

Welch, Mr J J   22 The Park Pale, Tutbury, Burton-on-Trent, Staffs DE13 9LB

Wells, Mr C, *MSc CertEd ALCM*   4 Reynards Close, Winnersh, Wokingham,
    Berks RG41 5NT

Wells, Dr E M P   24 Tree Lane, Iffley Village, Oxford OX4 4EY

Wells, Mr R H S, *CBE MA*   7 Tollgate Drive, London SE21 7LS

West, Mr M J   52 Trinity Road, Ware, Herts SG12 7DD

Wetters, Mr B D P   Uplands Lodge, Sheringham Road, West Beckham, Holt,
    Norfolk NR25 6PF

Whaley, Mr I   46 Brights Avenue, Rainham RM13 9NW

Wheatley, Mr M R, *MA*   12 Dangan Road, London E11 2RF

Whetman, Mr P   38 Burwood Avenue, Pinner, Middlesex HA5 2RZ

Whipp, Mr D   4 Gayhurst Road, London E8 3EH

Whipp, Mr G   26 Thorpewood Avenue, London SE26 4BX

White, Mr J   Killock Cottage, Woodcote Road, Leamington Spa,
    Warwickshire CV32 6QB

White, Mr R   AxiCom Court, 67 Barnes High Street, London SW13 9LE

White, Mr R M   7 Westcote Road, London SW16 6BN

Whitehead, Mr J   28 Birchwood Avenue, London N10 3BE

Whitehorn, Mrs A M   4 Woodview, 4 South Hill Road, Bromley, Kent BR2 0RA

Whitehouse, Mr L E   44 Rookery Close, Great Chesterford,
    Saffron Walden CB10 1QA

Whiting, Mr J   Ground Floor, 117 Old Roar Road, St Leonards on Sea, East
    Sussex TN37 7HD

Whittaker, Mr A C, *DipTP*   19 Leith Park Road, Windmill Hill, Gravesend,
    Kent DA12 1LN

Whitting, Mr I J   7c Park Hill, Bickley, Bromley, Kent BR1 2JH

Whytehead, Mr R L   27c Colvestone Crescent, London E8 2LG

Wibberley, The Revd A N, *BSc AKC*   13 Missleton Court, Cambridge CB1 8BL

Wicking, Mr D   Field Cottage, Straight Road, Battisford, Stowmarket,
    Suffolk IP14 2HP

Wicksteed, Mr M R *Honorary Secretary*   103 Harestone Valley Road,
    Caterham, Surrey CR3 6HR

Wiesendanger, Herr I   Romerstrasse 48, Winterthur CH-8400 Switzerland

Wilbraham, Mr D L, *BSc CEng MICE*   21 Tennyson Rise, East Grinstead,
    West Sussex RH19 1SQ

Wilks, Mr K   180 Seren Park Gardens, London SE3 7RS

Williams, Mr A R   78 Fenwick Road, London SE15 4HN

Williams, Mr J C, *BA*   21 Grovelands Road, London N13 4RJ

Williams, Mr J R   2 Cranbourne Road, London E15 2DB

Williamson, Mr R D S   13 Ashburn Gardens, London SW7 4DG

Willingale, Mr M   Willingale Associates, 2nd Floor, 56 Clerkenwell Road,
    London EC1M 5PX

Willis, Ms C L, *MA CQSW*   35 Windsor View, Hebden Bridge HX7 8LE

Willmott, Mr E D   7 Newlyn Way, Parkstone, Dorset BH12 4EA

Willoughby, Mr D   20 Cavendish Road, Barnet EN5 4DZ

Willoughby, Mr J   109 The Causeway, Steventon, Abingdon, Oxon OX13 6SJ

Willsdon, Professor C A P, *MA PhD FRS*   6 Cefn Coed Avenue, Cycoed,
    Cardiff CF2 6HE

Wilsher, Mr R C   26 Arnold Road, Gravesend, Kent DA12 5PU

Wilshire, Mr L J   Studio 4F, Mother Studios, 9 Queens Yard, White Post Lane, London E9 5EN

Wilson, Mr A   1 Isambard Place, London SE16 7DA

Wilson, Mrs A   22 Crescent Grove, London SW4 7AH

Wilson, Mr D   3 Riverdale Road, East Twickenham TW1 2BT

Wilson, Dr K G, *BA PhD*   Dept of English, University of Ottawa, 70 Laurier Avenue East, Ottawa, Ontario K1N 6N5 Canada

Wilson, Mr M   19 Horseley Heath, Tipton, West Midlands DY4 7PA

Wilson, Mr R A   4 Roots Lane, Wickham Bishops, Witham, Essex CM8 3LS

Windas, Mr G R H   58 Scarcroft Road, York YO23 1NF

Wing, Mr D B   PO Box 420, Marion MA 02738 USA

Winkler, Dr K T   4 Impasse des Jardins, F-67220 Dieffenbach-au-Vel   France

Winser, Miss A J   6 Berkeley Row, Lewes, East Sussex BN7 1EU

Wisdom, Mr J J, *MA MCLIP*   15 Sutton Square, London E9 6EQ

Wislocki, Mr A P, *BSc MIMM*   Starehe, Glanteifon, Poppit Road, St Dogmaels, Pembrokeshire SA43 3LF

Wood, Mr P V   Fletcher's Corner, Levens, Kendal, Cumbria LA8 8NL

Woodman, Mr J   Elford Farmhouse, Elford, Seahouses NE68 7UT

Woods, Mr B   31 Woodfield Way, London N11 2NR

Woolf, Mr J P L, *MA*   86 High Street, Eton, Windsor, Berks SL4 6AF

Woolfenden, Mr A P   18 Beresford Road, Cheam, Surrey SM2 6EP

Woollacott, Mr R J, *MBE*   185 Gordon Road, London SE15 3RT

Woollard, Mr R A R, *MA DipArch RIBA*   42 Pearman Street, London SE1 7RE

Woolley, Mr J D   107 East Wayne Avenue, Easton PA 18042 USA

Woolstenholmes, Miss M   76 The Mount, Guildford, Surrey GU2 4JB

Woolstenholmes, Mr P   The Old School House, 71 Mill Lane, Trimley St Martin, Felixstowe, Suffolk IP11 0RP

Woolven, Dr R, *BSc MA PhD*   Top House, Camden Lane, Willersey, Broadway, Worcs WR12 7PG

Worms, Mr L J *Member of Council*   Ash Rare Books, 43 Huron Road, London SW17 8RE

Worrow, Mr A S   Flat C, 34 Brookfield Road, London E9 5AH

Wright, Mr D H   Chance Wood, Carlton Road, Manby, Louth, Lincs LN11 8HH

Wright, Mr D R, *BSc*   8 Spurgeon Avenue, London SE19 3UQ

Wright, Mr W J, *MA MRICS*   The Thatched Cottage, Green Street, Little Hadham, Ware, Herts SG11 2EE

Wyber, Mrs J   7 Mornington Close, Woodford Green, Essex IG8 0TT

Wyber, Mr N G   17 Vines Avenue, London N3 2QD

Yager, Mrs D C   49 Glenmore Road, London NW3 4DA

Yorke, Mr J A, *BA*   64 Peterborough Road, London SW6 3EB

Young, Mr G W   12 Swinburne Court, Basingdon Way, London SE5 8EP

Zenz, Dr S C   24 Sunbury Lane, Walton-on-Thames, Surrey KT12 2HU

Zierau, Ms M   62 Bromley Road, London E17 4PS

Zierler, Mr G D L   14 Regency Lawn, Croftdown Road, London NW5 1HE

Zucker, Mr K   60 Gurney Drive, London N2 0DE

The appearance of a name in this list does not warrant that the individual is a paid-up member for 2015.

INSTITUTIONAL MEMBERS

Altea Antique Maps   35 Saint George Street, London W1S 2FN

Architectural Association Library   36 Bedford Square, London WC1B 3ES

The Athenaeum   107 Pall Mall, London SW1Y 5ER

Birmingham, University of, Main Library   PO Box 363, Edgbaston, Birmingham B15 2TT

Bishopsgate Institute, Library   230 Bishopsgate, London EC2M 4QH

British Library, Serials Acquisitions Unit, HSS   Boston Spa, Wetherby LS23 7BQ

California, University of, YRL Serials Department   11020 Kinross, Box 957230, Los Angeles CA 90095-7230 USA

Camden History Society   Garden Flat, 62 Fellows Road, London NW3 3LJ

Camden, London Borough of, Holborn Library Local Studies   32 Theobalds Road, London WC1X 8PA

Canadian Centre for Architecture Library   1920 Rue Baile, Montréal, Québec H3H 2S6 Canada

Chicago, University of, Library   1100 East 57th Street, Chicago IL 60637-1502 USA

Concordia University Libraries, Sir George Williams Campus   PO Box 2650, Montréal, Québec H3G 2P7 Canada

Covent Garden Area Trust   13 New Row, London WC2N 4LF

Drapers' Company   Throgmorton Avenue, London EC2N 2DQ

Folger Shakespeare Library   201 East Capitol Street, Washington DC 20003 USA

Goldsmiths' Company, Goldsmiths' Hall   Foster Lane, London EC2V 6BN

Guildhall Library   Aldermanbury, London EC2P 2EJ

Hackney Archives, CLR James Library   Dalston Square, London E8 3BQ

Hampton Court Palace   East Molesey, Surrey KT8 9AU

Harvard College Library   Cambridge MA 02138 USA

Henry E. Huntington Library Acquisitions   1151 Oxford Road, San Marino CA 91108 USA

Historic England   The Engine House, Fire Fly Avenue, Swindon SN2 2EH

Illinois, University of, at Urbana   1408 W Gregory Drive, Urbana IL 61801-3607 USA

Institute of Historical Research   Senate House, Malet Street, London WC1E 7HU

Inner Temple Library   Temple, London EC4Y 7DA

Institution of Structural Engineers   47–58 Bastwick Street, London EC1V 3PS

Iowa, University of, Libraries   Iowa City, Iowa 52242 USA

Lambeth Archives   52 Knatchbull Road, London SE5 9QY

The London Library   14 St James's Square, London SW1Y 4LG

London Metropolitan Archives   40 Northampton Road, London EC1R 0HB

Michigan State University Library   366 W Circle Drive, East Lansing MI 48824-1048 USA

Michigan University Library, Hatcher Library   11586655, Ann Arbor MI 48109 USA

Mills & Whipp   Finsbury Business Centre, 40 Bowling Green Lane, London EC1R 0NE

Missouri, University of   52 Ellis Library, Columbia MO 65201-5149 USA

Museum of London Library   150 London Wall, London EC2Y 5HN

National Archives, Library   Ruskin Avenue, Kew, Richmond TW9 4DU

National Art Library   Victoria & Albert Museum, London sw7 2rl
New York Public Library, Map Division   11 West 40th Street, New York ny
   10018 USA
Newberry Library   60 West Walton Street, Chicago il 60610-7324 USA
Pre-Construct Archaeology Unit   54 Brockley Cross Business Centre, 96
   Endwell Road, London se4 2pd
Reform Club Library   104 Pall Mall, London sw1y 5ew
Royal Geographical Society Library   Kensington Gore, London sw7 2ar
Royal Historical Society   University College London, Gower Street,
   London wc1e 6bt
Royal Library   Windsor Castle, Windsor sl4 1nj
Senate House Library   Malet Street, London wc1e 7hu
Society of Antiquaries Library   Burlington House, Piccadilly, London w1j 0be
Society of Genealogists Library   14 Charterhouse Buildings, London ec1m 7ba
Survey of London   1 Waterhouse Square, London ec1n 2st
United Oxford & Cambridge University Club Library   71 Pall Mall,
   London sw1y 5hd
University College London Library   Gower Street, London wc1e 6bt
Victoria, State Library of   328 Swanston Street, Melbourne, Victoria 3000,
   Australia
Victoria Studies Centre, Saffron Walden Library   2 King Street, Saffron
   Walden, Essex cb10 1es
Washington, University of   Box 352900, Seattle wa 98195 USA
Watermen & Lightermen, Company of   Watermen's Hall, 18 St Mary-at-Hill,
   London ec3r 8ef
Westminster City Archives   10 St Ann's Street, London sw1p 2de

The appearance of a name in this list does not warrant that the institution is a
   paid-up member for 2015.

INDEX

References are to pages; *italics* denote illustrations.